Schoenberg and the God-Idea
The Opera *Moses und Aron*

Studies in Musicology, No. 83

George Buelow, Series Editor

Professor of Music
Indiana University

Other Titles in This Series

Schoenberg and the God-Idea
The Opera *Moses und Aron*

by
Pamela C. White

UMI RESEARCH PRESS
Ann Arbor, Michigan

Produced and distributed by
UMI Research Press
an imprint of
University Microfilms International
A Xerox Information Resources Company
Ann Arbor, Michigan 48106

Library of Congress Cataloging in Publication Data

White, Pamela C. (Pamela Cynthia), 1955-
Schoenberg and the God-idea.

(Studies in musicology ; no. 83)
Revision of author's thesis (doctoral—
Harvard University, 1983).
Bibliography: p.
Includes index.
1. Schoenberg, Arnold, 1874-1951.   Moses und Aron.
I. Title.   II. Title: Moses und Aron.   III. Series.
ML410.S283W45   1985   782.1'092'4   85-1033
ISBN 0-8357-1647-3 (alk. paper)

To Arnold Schoenberg

Contents

Figures

Acknowledgments

I am grateful to the many people who have generously given their time and energy to help me with my research. Thanks go first to my three readers: to Christoph Wolff, for his excellent scholarly and editorial advice throughout the entire research process; to Leonard Stein, whose vast knowledge of Schoenberg has been a great resource, and who has thoughtfully read drafts and advised on matters of both history and musical analysis; and to Anne Dhu Shapiro, whose meticulous editorial readings—combined with her wide-ranging scholarly knowledge, common sense, friendship, and humor—have been of tremendous help to me. Special thanks go to Tim Clarke, who spent hours giving me valuable advice on twelve-tone analysis during the first year of this project, and who has posed intriguing questions about Schoenberg's music which continue to inform my analytical thought.

Thanks are also due to all the staff of the Arnold Schoenberg Institute in Los Angeles, to Jerry McBride, and especially to Clara Steuermann who gave me much assistance at the Institute Archive during the first two years of the project, and whose memory is dear. I would also like to thank Lawrence Schoenberg for permission to examine and reproduce facsimiles of the many materials in the Schoenberg *Nachlass*, and the letters in the Library of Congress; Belmont Music Publishers, Los Angeles, California, for permission to reproduce all musical examples from published scores; and the librarians of the Pierpont Morgan Library, the Library of Congress, the Oesterreichisches Nationalbibliothek, and the Staatsbibliothek Preussischer Kulturbesitz, for assistance with examining documents in their care. I am grateful to Elliot Forbes and David Hughes, and the trustees of the Wesley Weyman fund for the three grants which made my research travel possible. Thanks go to the staff of the Eda Kuhn Loeb Music Library at Harvard University, especially to Larry Mowers and David Schwarzkopf, who have often anticipated my needs in ordering books and microfilms. To David Schwarzkopf I am also grateful for hours spent assisting me with transcriptions of Schoenberg's Gothic handwriting, and for numerous impromptu consultations on translations of German passages. Thanks go to Reinhold Brinkmann, John Crawford, Jan Maegaard, Paul Pisk, and Christian Schmidt for information they have provided in conversation and correspondence.

Finally, thanks go to those who provided support in the initial preparation of the manuscript: Cathie Papes, Steve Kett, Steve Ledbetter, and Ross McElwee.

Special thanks go to my parents and to Ross McElwee for their intelligent listening, faith, and encouragement.

Introduction

*I should like to tell the people who have faith, about the holy
fire, and if this will make them salute me in friendship and
sympathy, then I want to accept this not as a person, but bestow
it upon a cause. I want to be seen as above personalities—as the
object I am striving to accomplish: to be the expression in
sound of the human soul and its desire for God.*[1]

Schoenberg's religious and philosophical thinking was an important element
in his creative work. This is exhibited in his frequent use of religious and
philosophical texts, his published letters and other writings, and biographical
data recorded by such authors as Willi Reich[2] and Hans Heinz
Stuckenschmidt.[3] Surely there is a deep psychological bond (as authors such
as Hans Keller,[4] Karl H. Wörner,[5] and Oliver W. Neighbour,[6] have already
observed) between the formation of Schoenberg's religious ideas and his self-
image as a pioneer and a prophet in a new world of musical composition: he
saw himself as a Moses leading an uncomprehending people into a promised
land, with the search more meaningful than its fulfillment. He heeded the call
of an Idea, which he saw as divine, commanding him to compose.[7] As the first
major musical work of his self-avowed Jewish period to have a specifically
Jewish text, *Moses und Aron*—perhaps more than any other of Schoenberg's
works—is the product of his knowingly futile effort to express "the holy fire,"
or, in Schopenhauer's terms, to give Representation to the Idea of the holy.
This book is a chronicle of that effort.

The book is divided into four main chapters, each dealing with a separate
aspect of the genesis of *Moses und Aron*. First, to set the work in its immediate
context, chapter 1 contains a source chronology and an overview of the
compositional process from the original concept, through the 1932 Barcelona
Particell of Acts II and III, to the failed attempts at completing the third act.[8]

In chapter 2, documentary research is presented concerning both
Schoenberg's religious development up to the period of composition of *Moses*

und Aron, and the various religious, philosophical, and literary influences which were important to the formation of his thought through the 1920s. The chapter begins with early biographical data, including Schoenberg's conversion to Lutheranism in 1896. These findings are then related to works of the same years. Little documentary data is known from this period beyond the information contained in Stuckenschmidt's biography.[9] Alexander Ringer has offered some speculations on the meaning and motives behind this conversion.[10] The second part of chapter 2 is a further investigation of this developmental milestone in Schoenberg's life.

From about 1898 on, the period of Schoenberg's earliest compositions, it becomes useful to investigate an almost completely untapped documentary source: Schoenberg's personal library. Partial listings appear in a few secondary sources, particularly based on Schoenberg's own 1918 catalogue of his library up to that time,[11] but almost no research has yet been done in this area. The library sheds important light on sources of intellectual influence throughout the periods under consideration in this study. A few studies on Schoenberg's early use of individual authors such as Dehmel and George,[12] as well as numerous studies on the historical context—influences and currents—of the early and expressionist periods,[13] have also been useful in exploring the early and expressionist periods (ca. 1899–1907 and 1980–21).

In addition to evidence of the direct influence of the expressionist circle around Kandinsky and the *Blaue Reiter* group, documentation is presented which demonstrates the primary importance of Schopenhauer to Schoenberg's philosophical thought in the years ca. 1911–22. While there are already some references in the secondary literature to Schoenberg's thoughts concerning the philosophical concepts of Idea and Representation in relation to Schopenhauer,[14] Schoenberg's library itself proves to be the most important source in pointing the way to the significance of this relationship. A similar examination is then offered of the intellectual relationship between Schoenberg and the Viennese literary figure Karl Kraus, who is mentioned in a few secondary sources[15] but not analyzed in detail to date in the secondary literature.

The section of chapter 2 entitled "The 1920s: Schoenberg and Judaism," enters a field of inquiry which is crowded with general studies on Judaism and German culture.[16] Important groundwork in the study of Schoenberg's Judaism, both its personal and political aspects, has been laid by Alexander Ringer in his numerous essays on the subject,[17] and also an article by Dika Newlin.[18] Leonard Stein's recent list of source materials at the Schoenberg Institute specifically relating to Schoenberg's Judaism is also very useful.[19] It is not the purpose of this book to provide an overview of Jewish life and times in the 1920s in Germany, but rather to clarify background information which is specifically relevant to the genesis of *Moses und Aron*, and to begin to specify those elements in Schoenberg's own personal Judaism which appear constantly both in works leading toward the opera and in *Moses und Aron* itself.

Once the background of Schoenberg's philosophical thought is examined, the opera itself will be discussed. Chapter 3 is an examination of the text of the opera, with a close comparison of the draft oratorio version of 1928 with the published opera version. Almost nothing in the way of analysis of the differences in either content or structure of these two versions has been published to date. This chapter presents a deeper understanding of the shift from an oratorio to an opera conception of the work.

An examination of Schoenberg's religious and philosophical development and an analysis of the genesis of the text of the opera provide background for approaching the music itself, particularly with view toward understanding how the music expresses the text. Chapter 4 contains an analysis of the musical elements of text expression of the opera, including a detailed analysis of the opera's *Leitmotiv* construction. Before focusing on text expressive techniques, however, it is necessary to analyze the music of the opera to discover what abstract principles and techniques Schoenberg employed, and to lay the groundwork for understanding the use of the opera's single twelve-tone row, the means of formal coherence, and the motivic structure of the work apart from its textual significance. This is necessary because, while purely literary and religious studies of the libretto are of interest, they do not penetrate into the composer's own mind to learn more about the inner musical logic of the piece—questions of compositional process and musical structure which are integral to a complete understanding of the meaning of the opera as Schoenberg conceived it.

Several brief precedents for formal analysis of *Moses und Aron* exist. Primary among these are articles by Milton Babbitt,[20] David Lewin,[21] as well as brief identifications of the row form of the opera without further extensive analysis in a few general works on the opera.[22] In Karl H. Wörner's monograph *Gotteswort und Magie: die Oper 'Moses und Aron,'*[23] the author correctly identifies the row of the opera, discusses the largest formal divisions, but does not present further detailed structural analysis. These secondary sources are examined carefully in the course of the present analysis.

In the area of musical text expression, the bulk of the currently available studies of Schoenberg's philosophy in connection with techniques of musical text expression are concerned with works of the expressionist period and before the late 1920s. An example of such a study, which does provide important information on precedents for text expression in later works, is Alan Lessem's *Music and Text in the Works of Arnold Schoenberg: The Critical Years 1908–22.*[24] An older dissertation, by John Crawford, also treats this subject for the dates 1908–24.[25] A dissertation on *Die Jakobsleiter*, a work fairly close in time to *Moses und Aron* and related to its conception, was written by Jean Marie Christensen,[26] but, again, does not extend to the period under consideration in this study. In addition to these extensive works, analyses have been published of individual earlier texted works which include remarks on text expression. These are helpful as precedents for studying text expression in the period of *Moses und Aron*, but do not extend beyond the early 1920s.[27] Studies of later compositions, even studies of text expression in later works, are either preliminary in nature or focus on issues other than Schoenberg's choices of texts or personal religious history, such as on the abstract analytical aspects of the works, particularly the row structure in the twelve-tone works.

Works specifically about the opera *Moses und Aron* are mostly limited in another way. For example, a recent doctoral dissertation on aspects of dualism in the text of the opera,[28] while including some investigations of the religious content of the libretto, does not involve any new research on the religious development of the composer. It is mainly a literary study, albeit of a religious text. Since the author specifically does not focus on the use of twelve-tone analysis in his study, his interpretation of text expression in the music is quite limited. Wörner's monograph is similarly limited in that its discussion of the twelve-tone aspects of the opera are very brief (as noted above) and the religious aspects of the text are not set in any historical or biographical context.[29] Wörner's book is mainly a discussion of the libretto and of some aspects of musical text expression, but it is a preliminary guide rather than a thorough analysis.

The most recent monograph, Odil Hannes Steck's *Moses und Aron*,[30] is an excellent, concise discussion of the biblical and theological content of the opera, condensing much that has been stated previously about the opera and Schoenberg's religious views into a thoughtful, brief analysis. However his work also covers neither the sources for the opera, nor any musical analysis.

Excluding the many brief précis, some quite good, which have appeared before the major performances throughout the 1960s and 1970s primarily as guides to theatergoers,[31] most of the numerous shorter articles on the opera are mainly discussions of various aspects of the opera's plot, its use of symbolism, theology, etc. These also have tended to appear in connection with major performances. The two earliest important works, Hans Keller's first major article on the opera for *The Score* (1957)[32] and Wörner's book (1959), appeared in connection with the first staged performance in the Zurich Stadttheater in June of 1957 and the second performance in Berlin at the Städtische Oper in October of 1959, respectively.

A recent collection mainly of theological studies on the opera[33] includes analyses of biblical and theological aspects of the opera libretto by theologians Hans-Joachim Kraus,[34] Eugen Biser,[35] H.G. Adler,[36] and Helmut Thielicke.[37]

There is a single theory dissertation on the subject of *Moses und Aron* by Michael Cherlin, in which the author does incorporate aspects of the published libretto into his analytical discussions. These focus primarily on structural aspects of the opera and on Schoenberg's treatment of divisions of the row.[38]

However, there has been no previous work which combines both an understanding of the musical techniques of the opera—including motivic and twelve-tone analysis—and an analysis of the text and the factors in Schoenberg's philosophical development which generated the text and the initial concept. This has been the intent of the present study: to provide a synthetic view of all these aspects of the opera—the text, the ideas which inspired it, and the musical techniques which expressed it—as a first step in drawing together the thought, beliefs, and musical technique of the composer. The knowledge gained is then applied to the interpretation of a single major work.

Through historical, textual, and musical analysis, it has therefore been possible to begin to address the questions of how and why this opera was so centrally important to Schoenberg in his own output, and how this is reflected in its music. In the process, a deeper understanding of Schoenberg's religious thought and creative process around the period of composition of *Moses und Aron* (ca. 1926–32) has emerged. Finally, this study offers a methodological approach for more synthetic interpretations of Schoenberg's works incorporating concept, text, and music; and demonstrates further avenues of research into the intimate relationship of Schoenberg's music to his life and beliefs.

1

The Genesis of *Moses und Aron*

To make sketches is a humble and unpretentious approach toward perfection.[1]

Moses und Aron was to the composer, in both text and music, one of the most profoundly personal creative statements of his life. The genesis of the work began with the initial drafting of the deeply thought-out religious text. This came at a time when Schoenberg was examining his own Jewish identity (which led toward his formal re-entry into the Jewish community in 1933); and continued through the musical composition, with its awesome technical task of constructing an opera from a single twelve-tone row. The opera, then, (despite its incomplete third act) constitutes a centrally important stage in Schoenberg's compositional career, both philosophically and musically. The purpose of this chapter is to establish a chronology for the known extant sources of both text and music of the opera. An examination of these sources provides new insight into Schoenberg's compositional procedure.

The sources include a complete score of the first two acts, several text drafts and fragments, three small music sketchbooks and two fairly large groupings of loose sketches, as well as smaller sketch fragments, and the beginning of a piano reduction score. Up to the present time, only partial chronological lists of sources of both text and music have been published. These are the Rufer catalogue,[2] and in Jan Maegaard's *Studien zur Entwicklung des dodekaphonischen Satzes bei Arnold Schönberg*.[3] These lists include the complete score and important text drafts, but do not provide complete detailed lists of sources from all stages of work. The full score in the *Arnold Schöenberg Sämtliche Werke*,[4] edited by Christian M. Schmidt, and one of its two accompanying volumes of critical commentary, have been published to date. The first volume of the critical report contains a complete descriptive list of known extant musical sources with transcriptions of many of the sketches. The projected second volume, which is to contain descriptions and transcriptions of the text sources and Schmidt's chronology of both text and musical sources, remains as yet unpublished.

Chronology of the Sources: An Annotated Summary

Table 1 represents all known extant sources for *Moses und Aron* arranged in chronological order. Since several of these documents were written concurrently over a fairly long span of time, there are several columns to indicate parallel periods of sketching and drafting of both text and music.

Many of the sources of *Moses und Aron* bear dates, which provide a good general picture of the chronology of the work. These sources prove valuable in placing undated documents within the same chronological framework. First, it is useful to examine the dated sources of both text and music in more detail in order to draw a picture of the direct evidence available for establishing a chronology of composition.

A letter to Webern, dated "29.3.26" contains the earliest mention of "Moses am brennenden Dornbusch" as a concept for a new work:[5]

> Jetzt habe ich wieder die Absicht, den 1. Theil der Jakobsleiter zunächst fertig zu machen. Hoffentlich geht das. Dann womöglich die Suite. An dem Text zu der neuen Kantate: 'Moses am brennenden Dornbusch' habe ich jetzt lange nicht weiter gearbeitet.

The earliest dated actual source (seventeen pages) is labeled by Schoenberg "DICH[tung] 17."[6] The opening notation suggests a dating of this early text source not later than the latest dated typescript for *Der Biblische Weg*, which is dated "12.VII.1927."[7] A page of Bible verses labeled "Notizen" is inserted at the end of this source, and appears to belong with the earliest conception of the text. The appearance of a notation "Moses am brenn. Dornbusch" in a source to *Der Biblische Weg*[8] also confirms the interconnectedness of the two works. Both date from 1926, or earlier, as claimed by Schoenberg in the letter to Berg 16 October 1933:[9]

> As you have doubtless realised, my return to the Jewish religion took place long ago, and is indeed demonstrated in some of my published work ("Thou shalt not . . . Thou shalt") and in "Moses and Aaron," of which you have known since 1928, but which dates from at least five years earlier; but especially in my drama "Der Biblische Weg" which was also conceived in 1922 or '23 at the latest, though finished only in '26–'27.

A dating as early as "five years earlier" (1923) cannot be found in any of the sources for *Moses und Aron*. Other datings from 1926 have been described in the current secondary literature, but cannot presently be identified in the extant sources.[10]

The next source (nineteen pages), dated several times throughout, contains the first complete version of the text, entitled "Moses und Aron: ein Oratorium,"[11] and also some handwritten annotations and revisions over the first layer of handwritten text. This manuscript is the last dated document for

Moses und Aron for a period of almost two years. During the period from late 1928 to 1930, Schoenberg apparently put *Moses und Aron* aside, as he became occupied with work on several other pieces[12]—the opera *Von Heute auf Morgen*, op. 32, for which the earliest sketch dates just five days after the completion of the *Moses und Aron* oratorio manuscript; the op. 33a *Klavierstück* from December, 1928; an edition of folksongs for Peters of Leipzig in January, 1927; *Sechs Stücke für Männerchor*, op. 35 containing texts by Schoenberg with religious themes similar to *Der Biblische Weg* and *Moses und Aron*, composed between April 1929 and March 1930; *Begleitungsmusik zu einer Lichtspielszene*, op. 34 with a fair copy dating from October, 1929 to February, 1930; and the unfinished *Stück für Violine und Klavier*, D-Dur, dating from July to September of 1930. Schoenberg's suspension of the work between October 1928 and May 1930 is attested not only by the absence of sources for *Moses und Aron* during this time, but also by the letter he wrote to Berg on 10 April 1930, in which he indicated that he was just beginning to consider composing the opera.[13]

About one month after this letter, on 7 May 1930, follows the first musical source: a single folio, folio 6 of a larger grouping of loose sketches labeled Source Ab by Schmidt.[14] Folio 1 of the other main collection of loose sketches, Source Aa,[15] is dated one day later, and contains a draft for the opening of the opera. In addition, while paper types in the sources to *Moses und Aron* are often too varied to provide useful information, and are mostly undatable, lacking any watermark or printer's stamp, the proximity in time of these two early folios is further suggested by the fact that they are of the same paper type, a paper used throughout Source Aa, with a few sheets of the same paper used in Source Ab.[16] The remainder of Ab folio 6 is also part of the early layer of composition. Begun two months later on 16 July 1930, it is a unity, containing a rough table of themes projected to appear later in Act II in the Golden Calf scene.

The 196-page complete fair score, Source B,[17] is extremely important for documenting Schoenberg's compositional progress. It bears dates not only at the beginning and the end, but also dates and places of composition of new scenes and acts and of interruptions in the work. As shown in the chronological table above, these dates provide the backbone of the source chronology for the period of musical composition.

A few more dated sources remain, though from a much later period. These are text drafts for the third act (from 1934 and 1938)[18] and a small sketchbook, Source Ae—labeled with the Brentwood Park, California address and simply dated "1937"—which contains fragmentary last musical sketches for the third act.[19] It probably represents a brief return to work on the music of *Moses und Aron* around 18 January 1937 when Schoenberg added at the end of a clean typescript of the last opera text,[20]

Table 1. Schoenberg's *Moses und Aron*: A Source Chronology

DATE	TEXT DOCUMENTS	RELEVANT SCHOENBERG LETTERS
I. EARLY TEXT SOURCES: ORATORIO VERSION (c. 1927-1928)		
Mar. 29, 1926		to Webern, Mar. 29, 1926: [a] "An dem Text zu der neuen Kantate: 'Moses am brennen-den Dornbusch' habe ich jetzt lange nicht weiter gearbeitet."
before 1927?		to Berg, Oct. 16, 1933: [b] "'Moses and Aaron', of which you have known since 1928, but which dates from at least five years earlier..."
c. 1927	"Text Fragments, Acts II and III"	
by Dec. 1927- Oct. 1, 1928	"DICH tung 17" with Bible verses: "Ältestes Blatt der Zeit des: Bib-lisher Weg" (=not later than "12.VII.1927"); "Ende September 1928"; "1.X.1928"	
Oct. 3, 1928- Oct. 16, 1928	"Text Manuscript": "Moses und Aron: ein Oratorium" p. 1: "3.X.1928"; p. 9: "8/X/1928"; p. 10: "9/X.1928"; p. 17: "10.X.1928"; p. 19: "16.X.1928"	
c. Oct. 16, 1928	"DICH tung 20" typescript: "Moses und Aron: Oratorium:	
II. SOURCES FROM THE PERIOD OF MUSICAL COMPOSITION, ACTS I & II (1930-1932)		
April 10, 1930		to Berg, April 10, 1930: [c] "But what I'm going to write now, I don't know. What I'd like best is an opera...perhaps I shall do 'Moses and Aaron.'"
May 7, 1930	Handwritten additions to "DICH 20"	
July 16, 1930		

MUSICAL SOURCES

Source Ab, 6^1
"Berlin 7.V.30"
(1st sketch, opening)

Ab, 6^2 "Arbeit
angefangen am
16.VII.30/Reihe
entworfen und I.
Skizze 7.V.30";
page references to
"DICH 20" and
Source Ac.

Sources Ad^{1r},
Af, Ag
(row charts)

Ac^{1-10}
(sketchbook)

DATE	TEXT DOCUMENTS	RELEVANT SCHOENBERG LETTERS
July 17, 1930	"Kompositionsvorlage": "Moses und Aron/Ein Oratorium'von/Arnold Schönberg", "Oratorium" crossed out and "Oper" added below	
Aug. 5, 1930		to Berg, Aug. 5, 1930: [d] "I have already finished the first page, have sketched out a lot and hope soon to be getting up speed. I hope I'll soon be able to produce a decent definitive libretto."
Aug. 22, 1930		
Sept. 9, 1930		
c. Oct. 1, 1930		
Jan. 15, 1931		
May 15, 1931		
June 6, 1931		to Rufer, June 6, 1931: [e] 250 mm. written, including complete instrumentation... "und weil ich ausserdem den Text fast ganz neu mache. Von der ersten Fassung ist kaum mehr viel überhaupt noch geblieben."
July 14, 1931		
July 20, 1931		
July 25, 1931		

MUSICAL SOURCES

Source B (complete score):	Source Aa, 1^1ff	Source Ac, 11 ff
p. 1: "Lugano 17.VII.1930/	"Lugano 17.VII.1930"	(sketchbook)
17 July Schönberg"		

p. 23 (end of Act I, Sc. 2):
"22.VIII.1930"

p. 29 (Act I, Sc. 3, m. 331):
"hier 9 Tage/unterbrochen./
am 9.IX/fortgesetzt"

p. 41 (Act I, Sc. 4, m. 473):
"am 30.IX.1930/hier abge-
brochen: die nächsten/10
Takte/in den ersten Oktober-
tagen/1930 in Meran./Dann/
Pause/bis Berlin!"

p. 42 (Act I, Sc. 4, m. 483):
"in Berlin hier fortge-/
setzt Januar (15) 1931; aber
ohne Erfolg! Störungen/in
Territet fortgesetzt 15/V.31."

p. 85 (End of Act I):
"Territet/14.VII/1931"

p. 87 (Beginning of Zwischenspiel):   Source Ad^{1v-2}
"Territet 20/VII.1931"

p. 91 (End of Zwischenspiel):
"25/VII.1931"

DATE	TEXT DOCUMENTS	RELEVANT SCHOENBERG LETTERS

July 26, 1931   "Kompositionsvorlage"
                 (continued)

Aug. 8, 1931

to Berg, Aug. 8, 1931: [f]
250 mm. of Act II, completed,
enjoying a brief pause.
"The text takes on its final
form while I am composing
it." Work slower than in the
beginning, when composing
ave. 20 mm./day

"Box A," "Box B," "Text
Fragments," "Typescript
pp. 30-34"

"Vorarbeit"

Sept. 12, 1931   "Kompositionsvorlage"
                 (continued)

to Webern, Sept. 12, 1931: [g]
About 800 mm. completed, 300
more sketched. Anticipates
Act II will have 500 more.
"I expected too much, for,
after all, I am writing a
full score and really completing the text only now,
too!...I hardly dare estimate
the duration of the 3rd act
(which, up till now, I had
thought would be 20 mm. long
at most...It was a very great
deal of work getting the scene
'Dance Round the Golden Calf'
worked out properly."

End of Sept. 1931

Mid-October 1931

Dec. 2, 1931-
Jan. 2, 1932

Jan. 20, 1932

to Berg, Jan. 20, 1932: [h]
"...the fact is, after you
had read the 2nd act, I worked
it over again several times
and I'm sure you'd be astonished
to see how extensive the changes
are (though certainly in the
spirit of the thing)."

MUSICAL SOURCES

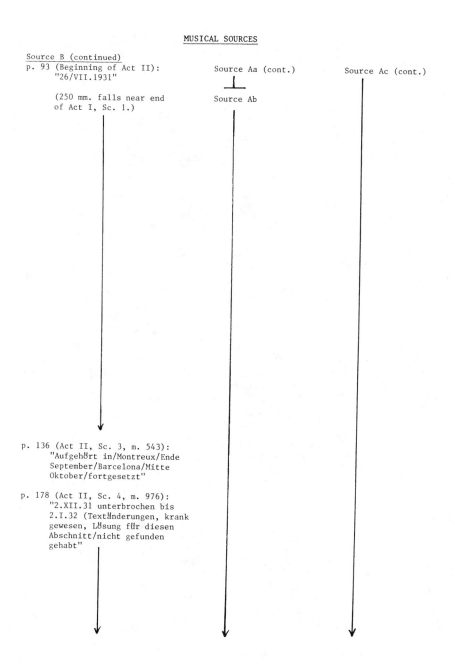

Source B (continued)
p. 93 (Beginning of Act II):
     "26/VII.1931"

     (250 mm. falls near end
     of Act I, Sc. 1.)

Source Aa (cont.)

Source Ab

Source Ac (cont.)

p. 136 (Act II, Sc. 3, m. 543):
     "Aufgehört in/Montreux/Ende
     September/Barcelona/Mitte
     Oktober/fortgesetzt"

p. 178 (Act II, Sc. 4, m. 976):
     "2.XII.31 unterbrochen bis
     2.I.32 (Textänderungen, krank
     gewesen, Lösung für diesen
     Abschnitt/nicht gefunden
     gehabt"

DATE	TEXT DOCUMENTS	RELEVANT SCHOENBERG LETTERS
Mar. 10, 1932	Clean typescript, "DICH tung 21," "DICH tung 22"	

III. SOURCES FOR ACT III ONLY (1933-1951)

DATE	TEXT DOCUMENTS	RELEVANT SCHOENBERG LETTERS
Mar. 15, 1933		to Eidlitz, Mar. 15, 1933:[i] "My third act, which I am working over again, not to say re-writing for at least the fourth time, is for the present still called: Aaron's Death. Here I have so far encountered great difficulties because of some almost incomprehensible contradictions in the Bible..."
June 22, 1934– June 23, 1943	Text sketches for Act III: "22.VI.34," "23.VI.34"	
1934	"Ein Notizenbuch mit Ideen, auch Musikalischen"	
May 5, 1935	Single text draft for Act III: "5/V.1935"	
Jan. 18, 1937	Handwritten addition to "DICH 22: "Das ist Seite 39 (das ist 3 x 13) wo ich 1932 in Barcelona zu komponieren aufhörte in der Hoffnung, den 3ten Akt in ein bis zwei Monaten zu beenden. Seitdem sind fünf Jahre vergangen und ich habe das Werk noch nicht vollendet. Los Angeles 18 Januar 1937."	
Jan. 22, 1945		to H.A. Moe, Jan. 22, 1945[j] (Guggenheim Foundation): "...I feel, as long as I am living I must try to complete at least some of the works which for a number of years wait for that. I feel: my life task would be

(cont. next page)

Source B (continued)
p. 196 (end of Act II; end of MS):
    "Barcelona/10/III.1932/
    Arnold Schönberg"

                B' (rejected sheet of B)

                C (beginning of piano reduction, n.d.)

III. MUSICAL SOURCES FOR ACT III ONLY

                Source Ae, small sketchbook, dated "1937"
                (last musical source)

fulfilled only fragmentarily
if I failed to complete at
least those two largest of
my musical...works. The two
musical works are: (a) MOSES
AND AARON...(b) DIE JAKOBS-
LEITER...The completion of
the opera might occupy me for
about 6-9 months..."

Nov. 5, 1948

to Leibowitz, Nov. 5, 1948: [k]
"If I can work I should
really like best to finish
'Die Jakobsleiter' and
'Moses and Aaron'..."

1949

to ?, 1949: [l]
"But I have already conceived
to a great extent the music
for the third act, and believe
that I would be able to write
it in only a few months..."

1950

to ?, 1950: [m]
"...but since then I have
found neither the time nor
mood for composing of the
third act...In fact the
third act consists of a
single scene...All of that
depends upon my nervous eye
affliction."

1950

to ?, 1950: [n]
"It is not entirely impossible
that I should finish the third
act within a year."

Nov. 27, 1950

to Francesco Siciliani, [o]
Nov. 27, 1950:
"It is with greatest joy
that I hear of your intention
to give a performance of my
opera 'Moses und Aron' during
the Maggio Musicale Fiorentino.
However, only the first and
second acts have been composed,
the third existing only as
a libretto..."

June 29, 1951

to Hermann Scherchen, [p]
June 29, 1951:
"...if you look at the poem
you will see that the second
act can be performed alone--
perhaps introduced by a few
words from the first act--
and this is really the only
act which I want to be performed. If one performs the
third act without music, as
an extra piece or just reads
out the text, this reproduces
the main content of the work."

a   *Arnold Schönberg Gedenkausstellung 1974,* ed. E. Hilmar, (Vienna: UE, 1974), p. 46.

b   Erwin Stein, ed., *Arnold Schoenberg Letters,* p. 184. (N.B. For Schoenberg's own—numerological?—reasons, the spelling "Aaron" should not be used, as in this translation.)

c   Ibid., pp. 138–39. (Also cited in Maegaard, *Studien,* p. 128.)

d   Ibid., pp. 142–3.

e   Cited in Maegaard, *Studien,* p. 129; original in the Library of Congress.

f   Cited in Rufer, *The Works of Arnold Schoenberg,* p. 87.

g   Ibid., pp. 87–88; partially cited in *Arnold Schoenberg Letters,* pp. 152–3.

h   Cited in Maegaard, *Studien,* p. 129; in *Arnold Schoenberg Letters,* pp. 157–8.

i   Cited in *Arnold Schoenberg Letters,* p. 172; in Rufer, *The Works of Arnold Schoenberg,* p. 88; in Maegaard, *Studien,* p. 129.

j   *Arnold Schoenberg Letters,* pp. 231–2.

k   *Arnold Schoenberg Letters,* p. 256.

l   Gertrud Schoenberg, Preface to Act III in Arnold Schoenberg, *Moses und Aron,* (Mainz: Schott's Söhne, 1958), Studien-Partitur, Edition Schott no. 4590.

m   Ibid.

n   Ibid.

o   *Arnold Schoenberg Letters,* p. 285.

p   Cited in H.H. Stuckenschmidt, Arnold Schoenberg, trans. H. Searle, (New York: Schirmer, 1977; German ed. 1974), p. 519.

Das ist Seite 39 (das ist 3 × 13) wo ich 1932 in Barcelona zu komponieren aufhörte in der Hoffnung, den 3ten Akt in ein bis zwei Monaten zu beenden. Seitdem sind fast fünf Jahre vergangen und ich habe das Werk noch nicht vollendet.

Los Angeles 18 Januar 1937

(That is page 39 (that is 3 × 13) where I left off composing in 1932 in Barcelona in the hope of finishing the third act within two months. Since then well nigh five years have gone by and I still have not finished the work.)

In addition to datings in source materials, Schoenberg also documented the progress of his work on *Moses und Aron* in several letters throughout the period of composition. Relevant excerpts have been included in Table 1. Perhaps the most illuminating of these is a letter from Schoenberg to Berg on 20 January 1932 which further describes the interruption in work on the musical composition due to "Textänderungen" and illness, already noted in the full score between 2 December and 2 January 1932:[21]

I should have liked to show you two stages of the work: the fact is, after you had read the second act, I worked it over again several times and I'm sure you'd be astonished to see how extensive the changes are (though certainly in the spirit of the thing). But in order to do that I'd have to copy a fairly large part of it, and I'm afraid I didn't do so: and now it's too late, because the intermediate versions have all been cancelled out by continual changes.

From the foregoing documentation alone, a good general picture of the stages of work on the opera is provided. Schoenberg first conceived of the idea of a work around Moses and Aaron by ca. 1926–27, during his work on *Der Biblische Weg*. A complete draft of a text version was completed by 16 October 1928. The work was suspended while Schoenberg worked on other pieces until he drafted the row and began the first musical sketching on 7 May 1930. Two months later, early sketches for Act I, Scene 1 and an outline of musical themes planned to appear later in the opera were written, dating from 16 and 17 July 1931. The major compositional work then proceeded, starting on 17 July. Most important, notations in the full score establish that, with the exception of the early outline of Act II themes, Schoenberg composed the opera consecutively, from the beginning to the end of the second act (the end of Schoenberg's main compositional effort), rather than planning certain scenes throughout the opera and then filling in material or following other possible plans for composition.

Using this established time frame as a reference, it is possible to proceed to the next step of placing undated sources within the chronology. The first major undated text source is a twenty-seven-page typescript, labeled by Schoenberg "DICH[tung] 20" and entitled "Moses und Aron: Oratorium." Handwritten corrections, and laid in and tipped in additions are numerous. While there is no date on the document, the first typed layer is exactly the same as the nineteen-page text manuscript bearing the dates from 3 to 16 October 1928. This layer, then, represents the typing up of that manuscript, probably accomplished just following the completion of the handwritten draft on 16 October and before the first sketches for *Von Heute auf Morgen* on 21 October. The additions may have been begun in the early period, but more likely date from the earliest period of musical composition (around 7 May 1930), since page references still appear on folio 6 of musical Source Ab corresponding to the page numbers in the typescript itself. This indicates that this typescript was still in use as Schoenberg's first reference text when he began to compose the music. A further indication that the added layers in the typescript belong to the time of musical composition is one handwritten addition to the typescript itself, a marginal notation "SkIV," which is a reference to the music sketchbook, Source Ac. The idea for changing the piece from an oratorio to an opera must have occurred to Schoenberg some time before this, by the time he wrote to Berg, "But what I'm going to write now, I don't know. What I'd like best is an opera... perhaps I shall do Moses und Aron."

Addresses stamped on the cover of "DICH 20" support these conclusions. The earliest address is Charlottenburg in Berlin, where Schoenberg lived from 1 June 1928 until November 1930. Later addresses from the period of musical composition, Nürnberger Platz in Berlin, and Territet, Switzerland, are also stamped on the cover.

The next most important working draft of the text, with a cover labeled by Schoenberg "Kompositionsvorlage," and a title page reading "Moses und Aron/ein Oratorium/von/Arnold Schöenberg" with the word "Oratorium" crossed out and "Oper" added below in ink, is a large, undated typescript with numerous handwritten revisions and up to ten layers of revisions on separate scraps of paper, laid in, tipped in and even sewn in in some sections. It has been assumed, because of its title, that it preceded all musical sketches.[22] However, since the "DICH 20" text was used during the earliest phase of musical composition, the *Kompositionsvorlage* (and thus the major reworking from an oratorio to an operatic version of the work) must have followed the handwritten additions to "DICH 20." This probably occurred during the early period of musical composition when the earlier typescript—with its many layers—became too cumbersome to be used as a reference for composing. It appears to be contemporaneous with the complete fair score, and most likely was used as a companion working draft of the text beginning around 17 July 1930. In addition, the *Kompositionsvorlage* bears firm evidence for dating its earliest layer not later than November 1930: as with the "DICH 20" source, it is stamped on the front cover with the Charlottenburg address. This document also bears Schoenberg's successive addresses, the Nürnberger Platz, Territet, and Barcelona, and appears to have been used throughout the period of composition. This corresponds well with the consecutive process of composing documented in the full score, since many of the layers of reworking appear in Act II where Schoenberg wrote in the score of difficulties and interruptions due to extensive text changes. It is to this multilayered libretto source that Schoenberg must have been referring when he wrote to Berg in January 1932 that "the intermediate versions have all been cancelled out by continual changes."[23]

A clean typescript original and two copies labeled "DICH 21" and "DICH 22" are also preserved in the *Nachlass.*[24] These correspond to the final version of Acts I and II in the full score, and a one-scene text of Act III which was used by Gertrud Schoenberg as the Act III text for the study score published by Schott after the composer's death.[25] The typescript dates from before the emigration from Berlin—it is also stamped with the Nürnberger Platz address—and was most likely typed around the time of the completion of the full score in March 1932. It is at the end of the original of this typescript that Schoenberg added the note in January 1937, "Das ist Seite 39 . . . wo ich 1932 in Barcelona zu komponieren aufhörte. . . . "

A fragment containing notes such as instructions for the orchestra, remarks to a (presumably future) copyist concerning style for writing *Sprechstimme* parts, and stage directions for various scenes[26] is also stamped with the Charlottenburg address. These therefore must belong to the early period of musical composition, sometime between May and November of 1930. A later set of schema sheets giving timings and formal breakdowns for all of Act I bears the Nürnberger Platz address, and must date from around the completion of Act I in July 1931.[27]

One additional source, a pocket notebook labeled "Ein Notizenbuch mit Ideen, auch Musikalischen," which contains miscellaneous personal and teaching notes, contains three undated bound-in pages plus one inserted page of notes for ACT III of *Moses und Aron,* one page of which is labelled "III. Akt Moses und Aron."[28] It is stamped with Schoenberg's first California address in Canyon Cove, Hollywood. Several pages in the book are dated from 1934; and it also contains a handwritten note of the Rockingham Avenue address indicating a 1934 date for these Act III notes, probably some time around the move from Hollywood to Brentwood.

Only a few text sources (which are undated and mainly fragmentary in nature) remain somewhat difficult to date with certainty. An examination of paper types does not yield any consistent evidence for dating since the sources in question are mainly small fragments of several different paper types. Handwriting and writing materials also give no clue in and of themselves, since these sources are written in black ink with colored pencil corrections, a consistent practice of Schoenberg from well before the composition of *Moses und Aron*[29] which he continued throughout the early 1930s. Nor does the

Gothic handwriting appearing in these sources aid in dating, since this writing style was not abandoned by Schoenberg until the time of his emigration from Germany in 1933. It is therefore necessary to turn to internal evidence for the dating of the remaining sources.

One short text fragment, on four large loose sheets,[30] provides a sketchy dramatic plan with Moses encountering the burning bush in Act II, Scene 1, and dialogue between Moses and Aron in Act III, Scene 1. None of these sketches corresponds to any draft version, and must be a part of the earliest conception of the work from 1927 or earlier.

Three groupings of handwritten text fragments, labeled in the Archive "Box A," "Box B," and "Text Fragments,"[31] all contain text sketches for Act II with corrections in colored pencil and black ink. They have the appearance of a small unified outline with accompanying notes, presently unbound but in notebook form, of the order of appearance of characters in Act II, Scene 3 (the Golden Calf scene), and closely resemble the final version of the opera in the number and ordering of events. In addition, "Box A" and "Text Fragments" contain occasional musical jottings of the young girl's theme, as heard in the final version of Act I, Scene 3, m. 255: "Ich hab ihn geseh'n . . . " and also of the man at m. 279: "Ich rief ihn. . . . " These musical jottings are not only rough outlines or counters, which might have suggested an early origin, comparable to the rougher theme tables, but present exactly the same notes and rhythmic values as in the final version as illustrated by the two "Box A" sketches in figures 1-1 and 1-2.

It may also be seen that the musical annotations in figures 1-1 and 1-2 are marked by Schoenberg, as if to remind himself, "(I. Akt)." These Act II outline notes therefore must date from the period of musical composition of Act II, Scene 3, when Schoenberg was at the point (mm. 759ff in the final version) in which the thematic material of the young girl and the man were to be recapitulated from Act I, Scene 3. An additional fragment of typescript[32] which contains text from Act II and is numbered pages "30–34" (corresponding to page numbers of Act II in the *Kompositionsvorlage*), and also corrected with black ink and colored pencils, is likely, on the basis of its content, to belong to the same period of composition as well.

These Act II fragments all are likely to date from around the time of musical composition of Act II with the attendant text revisions: either at the beginning of the compositional process for Act II, Scene 3 (some time shortly after 8 August 1931 when Schoenberg wrote to Berg of having completed 250 measures of Act II[33]), or as late as 2 December 1931 to 2 January 1932, during the text changes documented in the letter to Berg quoted above and the notation of the same interruption in work in the complete fair score.

A very advanced outline of Act II, Scene 3 representing the sequence of events in the Golden Calf scene as it now occurs in the opera appears in an

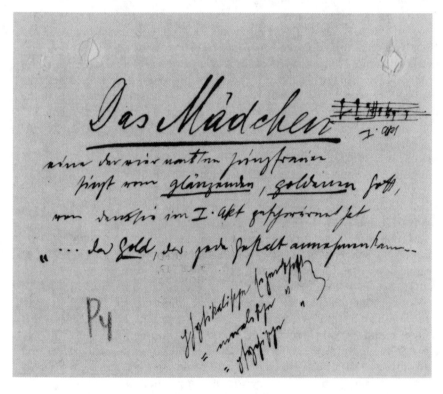

Figure 1-1.   Box A—"Das Mädchen" (facsimile)

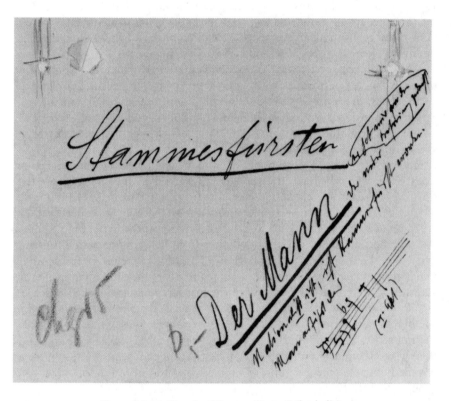

Figure 1-2.   Box A—"Stammesfürsten" (facsimile)

undated, untitled text source written on ten pages of music manuscript paper.
It is labeled "Vorarbeit" in the Schoenberg Institute archive, has notes about
the music to accompany the actions, and appears to be a verbal musical
sketch.[34] Because this sketch contains such an advanced state of the outline of
the scene, it cannot belong to the earlier layer of theme tables and text drafts
for Act II. Rather, it must date from slightly later than the "Box A," "Box B,"
and "Text Fragments" sources, probably immediately preceding the
composition of Act II, Scene 3 in the full score (sometime before September
1931). Also, since it represents a slightly more advanced state of the text than
the three groups of fragments just described above, it is likely to date shortly
after them, reinforcing an August 1931 dating for them and making the later
dating of December 1931 to January 1932 less likely.

The balance of musical sources presents a fairly clear chronological
picture when taken together with firmly dated source materials. As with the
text sources, those musical sketches which do not bear dates or addresses—
Sources Ac, Ad, Af, Ag, and undated portions of Aa and Ab—may be placed
within the chronological framework by internal evidence. It has already been
shown that once Schoenberg began writing the complete fair score, he
composed the opera consecutively from its beginning to the end of Act II.
Source Aa, which begins with the date "13.VII.1930," four days before the
opening of the full score, contains sketches for material from Act I and a little
of Act II. These are in small sections almost entirely in order as they
correspond with the full score. A large percentage of the material in Source
Aa, whether in sketchy or fairly complete form, is the same as the finished
version in the full score.[35] The relationship of this source to the full score is
made more evident by the abundant appearances of measure numbers in the
sketches which correspond exactly to the measure numbers in the full score.

Based on these observations, it seems most likely that the loose sketches
of Source Aa represent the working-out of certain sections of music alongside
the full score. Schoenberg first sketched on the loose sheets and folios, and
then wrote the music out with full orchestration, giving the whole source a
terminal date of some time not long after Act II was begun in the full score,
around 26 July 1931.

In Source Ab, Schoenberg began with a new outline of various themes for
Act II, and then resumed sketching shortly after the place in Act II where
Source Aa left off. There is no overlap of material between Source Aa and Ab.
Source Ab also contains sketches in sectional presentation, with measure
numbers corresponding to the full score. Therefore, Source Ab appears to be
the continuation of Source Aa as companion working sketches for the
progress on the full score. Unlike Source Aa, however, it is not arranged
neatly section by section in order of appearance in the final version. There are
also many more versions of some of the same sections in various places in the

source. This less orderly state of these undated Act II materials fits well with the increasing difficulty Schoenberg had with the composition of Act II, as documented in the letter to Berg and in the full score. The main body of Source Ab, then, must date from shortly after the beginning of Act II in the full score (26 July 1931) to around the time of its completion on 3 March 1932.

The folio bearing the early dates "7.V.30" and "16.VII.30," mentioned above, appears to be inserted into Source Ab from an earlier period of composition. Because sides 2–4 of the folio contain an early concept of Act II themes, his insertion is easy to explain. The sketch on the first side was for Act I, Scene 1, and was probably the first musical sketch for the opera. The paper type of the folio also conforms to many sheets of the same type in Source Aa, including the early-dated first folio of Source Aa.[36] Therefore, it is likely that this folio in Source Ab was part of the earliest layer of Source Aa. When Schoenberg reached Act II in the full score, he wrote a new theme table (the first folio of Source Ab), with material for the Golden Calf scene. At that point he referred back to the older theme table, which contained his initial conception of Act II. This explains how the folio with the earliest date of any source was inserted into Source Ab, which otherwise appears to be contemporaneous with the writing of Act II material in the full score.

Source Ac,[37] a small sketchbook with "Moses und Aron" printed on the cover in black crayon, appears to divide into two main layers of compositional activity. The first consists of the first ten pages and some related scattered sketches on later pages. These represent contrapuntal exercises and jottings for motivic ideas accompanying choruses in Act I, Scenes 3 and 4. There are also three pages (6–8) of choral melodies which are referenced in both theme tables presently contained in Source Ab (folios 1 and 6), and in early pages of Source Aa (sheets 2 and 4). The sketches on these three pages bear a good deal of resemblance to the earlier thematic sketches in Source Ab of the choruses "Ist Aron der Knecht dieses Moses..." (mm. 689ff in the final version) and "Bringt ihr Erhörung..." (mm. 443ff in the final version). The precise relationship of this layer of the sketchbook to the theme tables is not clear. The sketchbook uses the same text as in the score, and is musically fairly close to the final version. However, the earlier theme table of Source Ab, folio 6 refers to the "DICH 20" oratorio text, and is not as close musically to the final version. Although closer dating is not possible, the relationship of these pages of the sketchbook with the earliest layers of Sources Aa and Ab indicate that they probably belong to the earliest period of musical composition, ca. 16 July 1931.

The remaining sketches, from pages [11]ff, (archive #3030ff), are less fragmentary and contain more complete indications for orchestral accompaniment of choral and solo vocal parts. This latter portion of the sketchbook contains final versions of mm. 523–50 and 642–46 of Act I, as well as three fragments corresponding to the full score for Act II. The sketchbook only contains six fragments from Act II in all, most of which appear on inserted folios. On an inserted folio, numbered "22a–h" by Schoenberg—the last written pages in the book except for unrelated musical jottings near the end of the book—he indicated a measure number corresponding to the full score as he often did in Sources Aa and Ab. The pages following 22a and 22b, which contain more material for Act I, Scene 4, contain fragments from Act II, Scene 1 (mm. 49–52) corresponding to the full score, and an early motivic exercise for mm. 129–30, as well as a fragmentary sketch for Act III labeled "drt. Akt" on page 22f. The scattered sketches of the second half of the book appear to be jottings at random stages during the compositional process. Sometimes these are in an earlier state than Source Aa or Ab, and sometimes they represent the sketch just prior to the full score, but the sketchbook appears to have been used only sporadically, especially compared to Sources Aa and Ab.

Sketches for choruses in Act I, Scene 4 are particularly prominent in the sketchbook, especially the chorus "Bleib uns fern . . . " (I,4, mm. 563–81) which appears in sketch version six times throughout the book. These sketches possibly are associated with the difficulties Schoenberg noted in the full score during the work on that scene, which stretched from September 1930 until July 1931 with a long interruption from January to May 1931.

The sketchbook, then, appears to have been used especially for the working out of choral scenes in Act I. Perhaps Schoenberg began with the jotting down of a few choral sketches in the very earliest period of composition and then used the book again for later work on the same passages sometime between the fall of 1930 and summer of 1931. He subsequently used the book for only a few small sketches for Act II, probably close in time to the writing of the full score of Act II in the first three months of 1932.

Remaining musical sources do not greatly affect the overall chronological picture presented by the evidence above. Source Ad[38] is a brief three-page source containing a complete row chart and then a working out of the *Zwischenspiel*. The sketches for the *Zwischenspiel* most likely date from the period of time noted in the full score between the beginning of the *Zwischenspiel*, "20/VII.1931" and the beginning of Act II six days later.

Sources Af and Ag constitute a small sketchbook and two loose sheets which were inserts in the back of the book. They contain systematic listing of row forms which are arranged as a little reference book. The first twelve openings are numbered consecutively; and each opening contains a prime row form on one side of the binding, beginning with "T_a" (that is, "Thema" or "Tonika"[39] beginning on the pitch A) on the first opening, and its semicombinatorially related inversion form, beginning with "U + 6" ("Umkehrung," beginning a major sixth above the pitch A), on the other side of the binding. Following these twelve openings is one more opening in the book with three pairs of "T" and "U" forms, and the two sheets of Source Ag contain more paired row forms in similar format.

It is likely, given its neat and systematic ordering and well-worn appearance, that this sketchbook was a reference source for composing, and that it was written up on or near the date "Reihe entworfen und I.Skizze 7.V.1930." There is no firm evidence for dating this source, however. The larger single-page row chart on the first side of Source Ad may also be an earlier layer than the *Zwischenspiel* sketches on the rest of its pages, possibly also as early as the summer of 1930.

With the chronology of the sources established, it becomes possible to investigate the genesis of *Moses und Aron* by analyzing the contents of the sources. First, what is the background and context for the concept of the libretto? And, second, what conclusions may be made concerning Schoenberg's musical compositional methods for this work?

Chronology of the Concept: A Brief Critical Review

Moses und Aron is the first large-scale musical work for which Schoenberg wrote a text with specifically Jewish subject matter. Although the opera remains unfinished, it nevertheless embodies all of the major philosophical components of the Jewish faith held by Schoenberg in the middle 1920s. The original formation of the libretto as an oratorio took place long before the period of musical composition; and, according to Schoenberg's own comments concerning his initial conception of the text, the idea for the work occurred to him much earlier than even the first dated text sources. The work's immediate predecessor, both chronological and philosophical is the play *Der Biblische Weg*, first conceived ca. June 1926 and written in the spring and summer of 1927.[40] The composition of *Moses und Aron* spans the years 1927 through 1932, years just prior to Schoenberg's formal re-entry into the Jewish community in Paris in October 1933, and at the end of a decade-long effort to come to grips with his own Judaism in the face of increasing anti-Semitism in his environment.

Schoenberg's increasing concern with religion had begun by the early 1920s, as documented in the now-famous letter to Kandinsky in which Schoenberg refers back to the period of creating *Die Jakobsleiter*:[41]

> When one's been used, where one's own work was concerned, to clearing away all obstacles often by means of one immense intellectual effort and in those eight years found oneself constantly faced with new obstacles against which all thinking, all power of invention, all energy, all ideas, proved helpless, for a man for whom ideas have been everything it means nothing less than the total collapse of things, unless he has come to find support, in ever increasing measure, in belief in something higher, beyond. You would, I think, see what I

mean best from my libretto "Jakob's Ladder" (an oratorio): what I mean is—even without any organisational fetters—religion. This was my one and only support during those years—here let it be said for the first time (20 July 1922).

It was in December of the same year that Schoenberg wrote to Marya Freund, "I have never at any time in my life been anti-religious, indeed, have never really been un-religious either."[42]

While neither of these statements as yet reflects any specifically Jewish religious consciousness, Schoenberg himself also dated the growth of his personal Jewish identity to around 1922 or 1923 at the latest. This is seen in the letter to Berg dated 16 October 1933, shortly after his celebrated re-entry into the Jewish community in Paris.[43]

These ideas expressed in the 1920s represent the background for the increasingly religious subject matter of Schoenberg's prose texts leading from *Die Jakobsleiter*—with its mystical Swedenborgian images—to the specifically Jewish content of *Der Biblische Weg*, and culminating in *Moses und Aron*. While documentation does not exist for any written work on the play or the opera earlier than 1926, Schoenberg clearly believed both works to have had a long and interconnected period of mental gestation. Schoenberg's notation on the early *Moses und Aron* source DICH[tung] 17, "Ältestes Blatt aus der Zeit des: biblischer Weg," and the references to Moses within the play itself as jotted in the early *Biblische Weg* source DICH[tung] 33 directly confirm the chronological link between these two works. In Act I, Scene 10 of the play is the first appearance of the important, incantationlike words "Einziger, ewiger, unsichtbarer und unvorstellbarer Gott" which resonate in the opening of the opera; and already, in both the play and the oratorio version of *Moses und Aron*, appear all the themes which would be used in the final opera text. For example, there are several pages of dialogue about Moses between the prophetic character Asseino and the Zionist activist/statesman Max Aruns, in Act II, Scene 3, such as: "God gave the Idea to Moses but Moses' power of speech failed him; Aaron could not understand this Idea, but he was able to repeat it and inspire the masses..."[44]

The content of this earliest dated source, DICH[tung] 17, does not begin with Moses's calling, as in subsequent oratorio drafts and in the opera, but rather with Moses on the mountain and the beginning of the orgy. The small volume is entitled "Das Goldene Kalb," showing that this most dramatic scene was among Schoenberg's earliest ideas for the work, along with the images of Moses before the burning bush and Moses drawing water from the rock (which already interested Schoenberg in writing *Der Biblische Weg*). Much later, Schoenberg's earliest musical jottings after writing the opening of the first scene included an early outline of Act II themes—the Golden Calf scene was obviously always centrally important to Schoenberg's concept of the opera.

The source chronology shows that the completed libretto draft, DICH[tung] 20, and the early typescript layer of the *Kompositionsvorlage,* were separated from the period of musical composition by approximately nineteen months while Schoenberg turned to work on other projects; and that the shift from an oratorio to an operatic conception probably occurred to Schoenberg just prior to the earliest period of musical composition. The actual differences between the oratorio and opera conceptions of the work are mainly in the lengthening and shortening of certain sections, especially Aron's speeches and the large choral hymns. Some changes in the text also include changes from prose to metrical poetry. The orgy scene in particular—and other scenes as well—are made more dramatic and somewhat less polemical in style. In general, however, none of the changes greatly affects the central philosophical content or God-concept from the first conception. Schoenberg himself stated that the changes were "certainly in the spirit of the thing." Major plot changes appear only in different versions of the third act, for which no definitive text was ever established.

The relationship between the re-formation of the text during the process of musical composition and the composing of the music itself is less complex than might be expected, given Schoenberg's comments in letters concerning the many text revisions during the process of composition. In fact, except for the very earliest theme table for Act II in Source Ab which makes specific reference to the text source "DICH 20," and a very few scattered exceptions, the musical sketches bear the same text as the final version. It appears that, while Schoenberg found the need for revising the text as he proceeded through the composition section by section, he accomplished the text changes (in however many layers he found necessary) in the *Kompositionsvorlage* before proceeding to the musical sketches. A cursory glance at the sectional and, at times, very broad conception of the music in the sketches seems to indicate that much of the detailed work for the piece took place mentally rather than on paper. Perhaps in this mental process of composing the music the need for text changes was brought to mind again and again.

Stages of Musical Composition

The answer to the question of what conclusions may be made concerning Schoenberg's musical compositional methods—involves a close examination of the contents of the musical sources. Schoenberg did not write about his own methods of composing the opera beyond the following general comments in his essay "Composition with Twelve Tones":[45]

> In the first works in which I employed this method, I was not yet convinced that the exclusive use of one set would not result in monotony. Would it allow the creation of a sufficient number of characteristically differentiated themes, phrases, motives, sentences,

and other forms? At this time, I used complicated devices to assure variety. But soon I discovered that my fear was unfounded; I could even base a whole opera, *Moses und Aron,* solely on one set; and I found that, on the contrary, the more familiar I became with this set the more easily I could draw themes from it. Thus, the truth of my first prediction had received splendid proof. One has to follow the basic set; but, nevertheless, one composes as freely as before.

This comment is consistent with the working methods revealed by a study of the sources. A table of sources to *Moses und Aron* broken down by sketch types is provided for reference in Appendix 1.

First, Schoenberg worked with entire discrete sections of the music in mind, as has been seen in the source descriptions. This is in keeping with the sectional design of the opera as is evident from analysis of the completed score. Schoenberg's broad conception of the work is seen in the haste and scope of these sectional sketches. The fluidity of his writing, in addition to the presence of the early theme table for Act II in Source Ab, confirms that two of Schoenberg's own statements about his general methods of composing apply also to *Moses und Aron*:[46]

I personally belong to those who generally write very fast, whether it is "cerebral" counterpoint or "spontaneous" melody.

I cannot help but think logically.... This comes about because in my case the productive process has its own way; what I sense is not a melody, a motive, a bar, but merely a whole work. Its sections: the movements; their sections: the themes; their sections: the motives and bars—all that is detail, arrived at as the work is progressively realized. The fact that the details are realized with the strictest, most conscientious care, that everything is logical, purposeful and organically deft, without the visionary images, thereby losing fullness, number, clarity, beauty, originality, or pregnancy—that is merely a question of intellectual energy, which may only be taken amiss by those who themselves possess it and believe themselves entitled to despise it.

Schoenberg also worked out the smaller details of the music section by section, usually beginning a new sketch at the measure corresponding to the beginning of a new section in the full score. He often, as noted above, marked the corresponding measure numbers from the full score in the sketch. The sketches, whether fully worked out with orchestral details or only presented in skeletal form, most often present complete small sections as they appear in the score. For example, on sheet 12[r] of Source Aa,[47] Schoenberg drafted the choral fugue now beginning at Act I, m. 335 in the final version. After nine measures, he crossed it out and began the whole section again on sheet 12[v], writing out the choral fugue as it now appears in mm. 335–46, ending the section with fermatas. Sheet 13 contains more cancelled fragments of choral counterpoint for the section in mm. 335–46, probably written in conjunction with the sketches on 12[r] and 12[v], but ultimately discarded. He then went on to the next section of music, up to m. 350, continuing with mm. 351–66 on 14ʳ, and ending with the first beat of m. 366, which is the end of a complete section of music in the final version.

A second major characteristic is that long sketches are often written hastily with solo vocal or choral parts only, leaving out accompaniment (about one-third of all the sketches, and over one-third of all texted sketches). Sometimes only partial accompaniment is included; and sometimes only a few motivic gestures are indicated at the opening of such a passage (about one-fourth of all sketches, and a little less than one-third of all texted sketches). Roughly three-fourths of all the sketches for the opera are for texted music, and appear either to be drafts of solo melodic themes, with or without suggestions of accompaniment or contrapuntal working-out of choral parts. In addition to melodic material and accompaniment where included, row forms are usually marked beside the first staff of a new section. The example from Source Aa described above is presented with choral parts only until sheet 14, where orchestration is also included.

Many of Aron's solos are written out with vocal melodic line only—for example, Aron's speech "Volk Israels...," in Act I, mm. 173–99, is presented in Source Ab, 9ʳ, as a long stretch of melody only, as shown in figure 1-3. This shows that the beautiful lyrical and virtuosic melodies, especially in Aron's part, did not generate from a struggle with piecing together small row components to make a complete textural unity. Rather, the melody was constructed first, and the filling-out of the rest of the texture was often a relatively perfunctory task which was sometimes suggested by a jotting of a motivic idea under a few bars of melody, and completed in the act of writing out the complete fair score.

In this case, the melody in the sketch was again revised before it was committed to the final version. However, the initial concept for the melodic line was not changed: the first six notes and much of the contour of the first line are the same as the final version. In addition, this sketch is of particular interest because it is one of the rare sketches where the text is not identical with that of the final libretto. The text of the sketch[48] is quite similar to the final version, and quite different from the much earlier "DICH 20" oratorio version of the same dramatic moment.[49] Hence, the sketch represents one of the few instances of documentation for a composed melody's being revised after, and probably because of, the extensive "Textänderungen" noted by Schoenberg and reinforced by the thick layering of the *Kompositionsvorlage* text.

Similarly, choral sections were most often conceived first by working out the contrapuntal relationships of singing parts without accompaniment. As an example, Source Ab, 24ʳ, contains a sketch for Act II, Scene 2, mm. 151–65, the beginning of the choral section "Die Götter haben ihn getötet," shown in figure 1-4. The measure numbers over some of the measures correspond to measures in the full score.

Figure 1-3. Ab, 9ʳ (2988) Aron: "Volk Israels..." (facsimile)

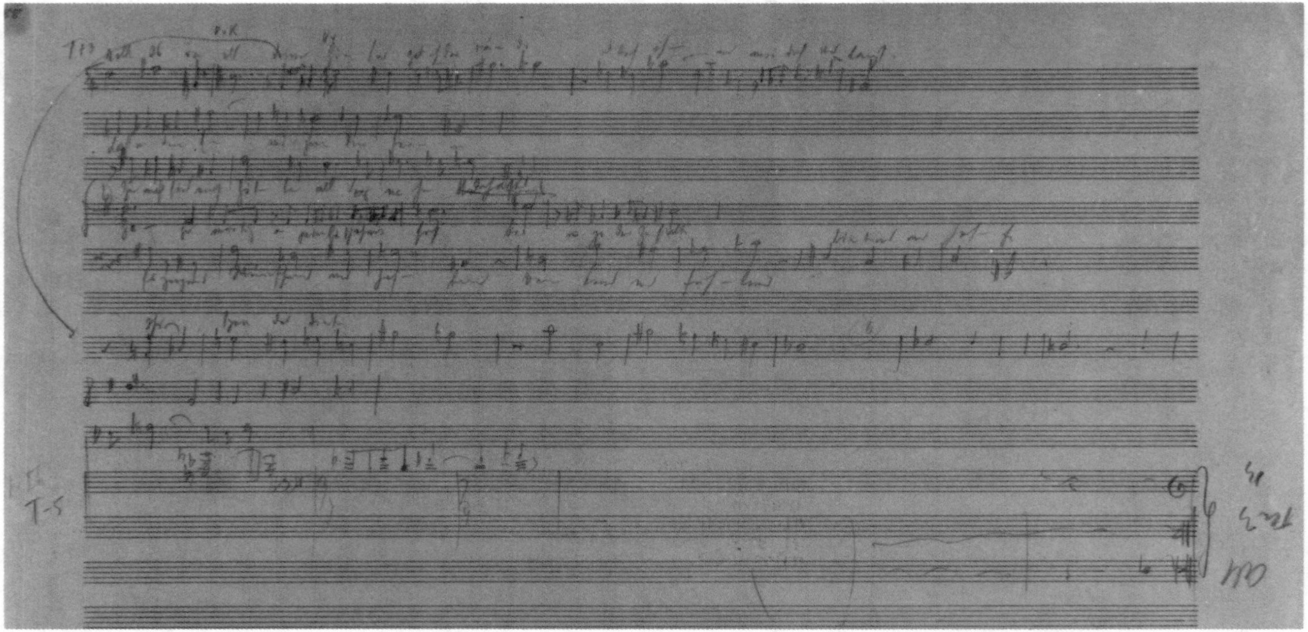

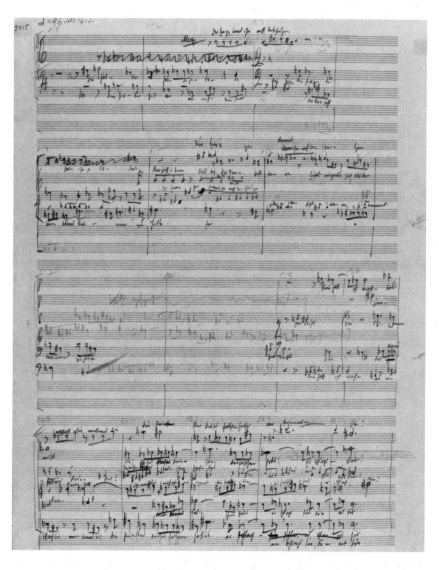

Figure 1-4.   Ab, 24ʳ (3015) "Die Götter haben ihn getötet" (facsimile)

The procedure of formulating a main melody as the main task of drafting a section of music was not restricted to vocal music. Of the sketches for purely instrumental passages in the opera, which altogether make up only about one-fourth of all the sketches, slightly more than half are incomplete renderings. These have either a main melody (whether designated as a *Hauptstimme* or not) and sketchy supporting material, or a working-out of a particular motivic idea into a lengthier passage. Most of these untexted sketches are for Act II, Scene 3, the Golden Calf scene. In many of these, the filling-in of music to be supplied later, presumably directly in the writing of the full score, is suggested by the jotting of stems without noteheads to indicate accompanying rhythms without pitches. A good example appears in Source Ab, 10^2, a draft of Act II, Scene 3, mm. 881–902 in the final version, shown in figure 1-5.

As with many of the sketches for vocal music, the fluidity of thought and the haste of drafting are striking. The clean writing-out of the full score directly following these sketches (with no apparent intermediate steps) shows that the music not actually notated in the sketches was nevertheless probably already quite clear to Schoenberg in his conception of a given passage. Again, rather than laboring over the manipulation of row material to produce a given melodic line or motivic figuration, Schoenberg first conceived of each section by its melody, which tends to suggest underlying harmonies, and may invite certain accompanimental figurations as well.

A few examples of the broadest possible kind of drafting also exist in the sketches. In this category, besides the two theme tables discussed at length above, are three verbal sketches, two appearing in Source Ab for the opening of the *Zwischenspiel* and for Act I, Scene 4, and one in Source Ad for the continuation of the *Zwischenspiel.* The verbal sketch for mm. 1094ff of Act I, Scene 4 in Source Ab, 23^v, which reads:[50] "Orchester/vorn/Canon/erklingt und hinter der Scene/Orchester schweigt/12–15 Takte/4taktiges Motiv/ verkleinert/enggeführt/Aron verschwindet/mit der Musik."

The small text source labeled "Vorarbeit," described above, also contains material which could be considered to be verbal musical sketches, mainly in the form of jottings of projected lengths of sections of music.

In addition to the predominantly sectional drafts of main melodies or melodies with partial accompaniment, about one-fourth of all the sketches to the opera are completed drafts of sections; and in all but a few cases, these complete sectional sketches directly correspond to the final version.

Some smaller row-related motivic manipulations occur only occasionally in the sketches, usually in fragmentary form. As mentioned above, many sketches contain marginal notations of the row form which governs the particular section being drafted. In many cases this was enough to serve as a guide to the later writing-out in full of an accompaniment to a main melody. In a few cases, slightly more detail concerning the actual row material appears

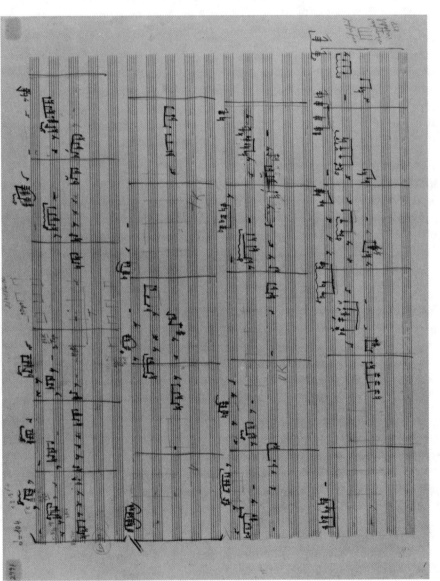

Figure 1-5. Ab, 10² (2991) Stems without Noteheads (facsimile)

in the sketches, particularly concerning the precise division of row material (i.e., hexachordal, trichordal, tetrachordal, etc.) to be used.

It may be seen by surveying the row charts in the sources described above that there are no sketches of the actual drafting of the row itself. No earlier version of the row or any part of the row appears in any extant source. It has already been seen that the earliest sketch in Source Ab, 6[1], was composed on the same day as the row was drafted according to Schoenberg's own annotation. It is impossible to determine whether the content of the sketch (the first few bars of the opera, with its use of trichordal divisions of row material and emphasis on the semicombinatorial relationship of two row forms) or the drafting of the row itself actually came first. It seems clear from the context of this earliest sketch that the creation of the row and the creation of the earliest music were inseparable. This is in keeping with Schoenberg's comment in "Composition with Twelve Tones":[51] "The basic set functions in the manner of a motive. This explains why such a basic set has to be invented anew for every piece. It has to be the first creative thought." Completed row charts, such as the little row notebook, Source Af, thus functioned as references for composing, following this process. The clearest manuscript chart of the row on a single page, Source Ad, 1[r], is reproduced in figure 1-6. Figure 1-7 shows the working row sketchbook, Source Af, with semicombinatorially related T and U forms laid out on facing pages of the sketchbook.

Sketches of specific row manipulations are rare. In two cases in Source Aa, combinatorially related hexachords were drawn at the bottom of a sketch page in red and blue pencil as guides to the melodic material to be manipulated. These occur on folio 3, and sheet 9[v]. A more intricate example of row manipulation occurs in Source Ab, 2[v], shown in figure 1-8, where Schoenberg experimented with 2 + 4 and 4 + 2 divisions of hexachordal material, matching groupings of four among several semicombinatorially related row forms in which resulting tetrachords all have the notes B, C, C♯, and D in common.

This sketch is very likely a preliminary exercise for the section in Act II, Scene 2 in which the elders press Aron into action: "Aron, hilf uns, gib nach!" This section is built from precisely the same row forms, utilizing the shared tetrachordal materials highlighted in the sketch on 2[v] as shown in musical example 1-1.[52]

The relationship of the row sketch to this passage is reinforced in a subsequent sketch on 4[r], in which he hastily drafted the passage, writing down *only* the tetrachords in question for mm. 166–68, as shown in figure 1-9.[53] A close dating of these two sketches, which would support a conscious connection between them on Schoenberg's part, is suggested by the fact that they share a positively identifiable paper type.[54] This paper was used only for

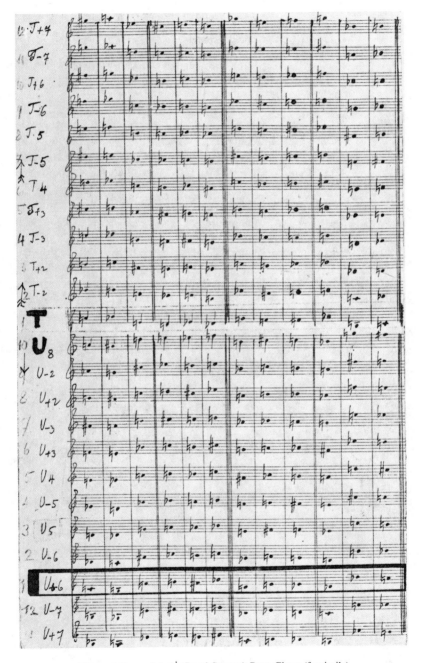

Figure 1-6.   Ad, 1[1] (Basel Source) Row Chart (facsimile)

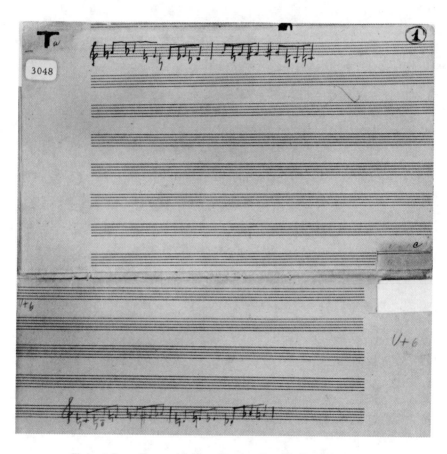

Figure 1-7.   Source Af, First Opening Showing T and U + 6
Row Forms (facsimile)

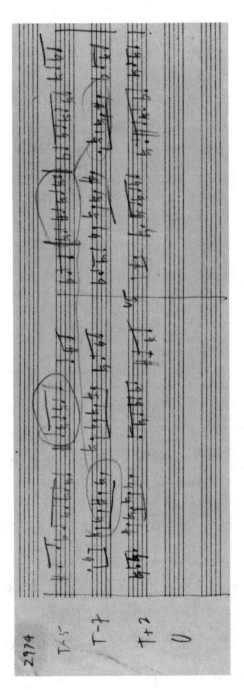

Figure 1-8. Ab. 2ᵛ (2974) Row Sketch (facsimile)

Musical Example 1-1

Musical Example 1-1 (continued)

Figure 1-9.   Ab, 4^r (2977) mm. 166–68ff (facsimile)

folio 1 containing the Act II theme table, and for sheets 2–5 and 24, which all contain sketches for roughly the same dramatic action of Scene 2, from mm. 143ff, except for sheet 5 which contains later material from Scene 3.

A more involved use of the same 2 + 4 divisions of the same row forms was used again by Schoenberg in the Dance of the Butchers, mm. 397–428. This section is heard as a set piece between two similar passages of ostinati built on trichords of open-string fifths (mm. 371–96 and 435–52). It uses the contrasting sonorities of the 2 + 4 and 4 + 2 row divisions to set the section apart; and in this lengthier passage, it uses the groupings of four notes and dyads held in common between row forms to modulate from one row form to another.[55]

The section begins in Schoenberg's row "T + 2," using trichordal row divisions, then quickly introduces a new row, "T–7," with trichords A–F–E and B♭–G♭–E♭, similar in sound to the trichords just heard in the previous measure belonging to "T + 2": D♯(E♭)–B–F♯(G♭) and (linearly) C–F–E. A long section follows using "T–7" together with its semicombinatorially related inversion form "U + 7," where the B–C♯–C–D and F♯–E–E♭–F tetrachords found internally in "T–7" are juxtaposed with the C♯–B–D–C and F♯–E–F–E♭ tetrachords of retrograde "U + 7." The section ends with a transition back through "T–5" and related "U–3," exploiting the shared C♯–B–C–D tetrachord to move from the second hexachord of retrograde "T–7" (B–C♯–C–D–G–G♯) to the second hexachord of "T–5" (C♯–B–C–D–F–F♯). A final section moves by similar means into the row area "T + 7."

This sketch in figure 1-8 is unusual in the sources to *Moses und Aron,* for this attention to details of row manipulation. The opera itself, however, abounds with such manipulations of row divisions, often utilizing shared material between row forms, in effect, to modulate from row to row.[56] This fits in with the sectional nature of the piece, which, in turn, generates an overall structure for the opera where large blocks of material "in" one row area or another articulate the form (much as key areas articulate the form of a tonal opera). While the orchestral texture and formal structure of the piece largely depend on such minute manipulations of row material and on relationships set up by the semicombinatorial nature of the row, most of the working-out of the piece involving such manipulations occurred directly as Schoenberg wrote out the full score. He presumably worked out the details in his head as he went along; and it was the larger-scale planning of vocal melodies and the interweaving of choral parts which required sketching prior to committing them to the final version.

Schoenberg wrote in a letter to Rudolf Kolisch, 27 July 1932:[57]

You have rightly worked out the series in my string quartet. . . . You must have gone to a great deal of trouble, and I don't think I'd have the patience to do it. But do you think one's any better off for knowing it? I can't quite see it that way. My firm belief is that for a composer who doesn't yet quite know his way about with the use of series it may give some idea of how to set about it—a purely technical indication of the possibility of getting something out of the series. But this isn't where the aesthetic qualities reveal themselves, or, if so, only incidentally. I can't utter too many warnings against overrating these analyses, since after all they only lead to what I have always been dead set against: seeing how it is done; whereas I have always helped people to see: what it is!... I can't say it often enough: my works are twelve-note *compositions,* not *twelve-note* compositions....

In letters and essays on earlier composers, Schoenberg often portrayed himself not only as a revolutionary figure in the history of musical composition, but also as a composer owing a great debt to the heritage of western European music in general, and to the German/Austrian heritage of Bach, Beethoven, Wagner, and in particular Brahms.[58] The development of Schoenberg's style from a late nineteenth-century romantic idiom to free atonality and the subsequent "discovery" of the twelve-tone method may be seen as an evolutionary process rather than as a series of unprepared breaks with tradition. So, too, it is demonstrated in these sketches that Schoenberg's working procedures in the creation of a twelve-tone piece did not turn away from traditional methods of drafting sections of large works—often first shaping a main melodic line, vocal melody, or choral part, or sketching larger sections hastily to capture first the overall design with only incomplete notation of accompanying motivic ideas. The presence of so many drafts of only a single melodic line or a melody with only scant notations of accompaniment does not differ substantially from monolinear drafts found in sketchbooks of nineteenth-century composers such as Beethoven, Mendelssohn, and Schumann (for whom extensive source studies have been published), or even further back in the German/Austrian compositional tradition to Mozart and Haydn.

Schoenberg's twelve-tone vocabulary and structural "laws" did not necessitate a fundamental change in working procedure—the twelve-tone system, as Schoenberg claimed, truly did function as an architectural substitute for the system of tonality.[59] This finding in the sketches supports what the music itself has to reveal about its design: that the opera is given an overall sectional form where large sections are governed by certain row forms, aggregates, or families of related row forms, just as nineteenth-century operas most often had an overall tonal plan. On a more local level, this structure is related to the opera's motivic design, where certain musical motives bearing strong textual connotations also have strong associations with certain row areas. This also occurs in Wagner's operas, where the *Leitmotive* have strong associations with certain keys. For example, the opening of *Moses und Aron* contains two main motives. The first is a chordal motive comprised of the first and last trichords of the primary row form "T", and its semicombinatorially related partner "U + 6." The second motive is an arpeggio comprised of the

Musical Example 1-2

I. Akt

two inner trichords, or inner hexachord, of the same rows, as shown in musical example 1-2. These motives are strongly associated with the primary row aggregate ("T" and "U + 6"), the sonority of which is set up throughout the first scene as a referential point of return. The motives also carry a strong textual association with the presence of God and God's commandment as portrayed in the libretto. This association is carried consistently throughout the opera and may be considered comparable to a Wagnerian *Leitmotiv*.

The music of the opera itself, then, is built upon an intertwining structure of motivic transformation and pitch relationships—a structure in theory no different from any tonal composition. But it is clearly audible in the opera that Schoenberg's manner of approaching the composition of the work differs from nineteenth-century tonal music in the vocabulary and grammatical rules of its language, but not in either compositional procedure or in resulting overall musical and dramatic design.

2

Deeper into the Background:
The Development of Schoenberg's
Religious Thought

Introduction to Documentary Evidence: Schoenberg's Library

In one of Schoenberg's Bibles,[1] at Deuteronomy ("V Mose"), Chapter 22, there is an editorial subtitle which Schoenberg underlined in red: "Vermischte Vorschriften, besonders der Menschenliebe und des Mitleidens mit Tieren Gesetze wegen Sünden und Unkeuschheit" (Various prescriptions, especially of love and compassion, with law against vice and unchasteness). On the next page, which begins with Deuteronomy 22:6 and ends with 23:26, a manila paper marker is tipped in at the top of the page. On it is written in red pencil, "Siehe Schopenhauer!" The passage meant is indicated by a red pencil in the margin at Deuteronomy 22:6:

> Wenn du auf dem Weg findest ein Vogelnest auf einem Baum oder auf der Erde, mit Jungen oder mit Eiern, und dass die Mutter auf den Jungen oder auf den Eiern sitzt, so sollst du nicht die Mutter mit den Jungen nehmen....

> (If on your way you find a bird's nest in a tree or on the ground, with young ones or with eggs, and the mother sitting on the young or on the eggs, you shall not take the mother with the young ones....)

This bit of marginalia which makes the connection between the Bible passage and Schopenhauer's concept of *Mitleid* (pity), belongs to a whole series of marginal inscriptions, underlinings, and inserted notes in several Bibles in Schoenberg's library. These inscriptions occur at various passages which concerned Schoenberg at different times, as related in his letters or his vocal texts or essays. For example, the passsage from Deuteronomy just cited probably was part of Schoenberg's reading in preparation for *Moses und Aron*, since it is part of a section of law traditionally attributed to Mosaic revelation. A piece of paper laid in at an Exodus passage with *Versöhnungstag*

(Yom Kippur or Day of Atonement) written on it probably has to do with Schoenberg's concern about the annulment of vows on Yom Kippur and his re-entry into the Jewish community, nullifying his earlier Christian conversion. Markers and annotations in the Psalms and some of the Prophets are more generally applicable—they were important to his thought late in life, but they are also reflected earlier in the blessing passages of *Moses und Aron*, *Die Jakobsleiter*, and *Der Biblische Weg*.

Another useful indicator of when certain marginalia were written is Schoenberg's handwriting. The "Siehe Schopenhauer" note not only pertains to Mosaic law, which may suggest a possible connection with *Moses und Aron*, but it is written in Gothic script, which Schoenberg abandoned after leaving Germany. Thus, a date not later than the period of writing *Moses und Aron* is indicated.

All the Bibles in Schoenberg's personal library (as it is now preserved) are already listed in Schoenberg's own library catalogue[2] with an entry date of January 1913, proving a date of acquisition of these books well before the first sketches of *Moses und Aron* were begun. When books do appear in Schoenberg's own catalogue, then, it is possible to come close to the period of time in which Schoenberg was concerned with them. (There is the obvious caution that one may read a book well before buying a copy of one's own, and also one may buy a book and never read it.) This sort of evidence can only be useful in conjunction with other clues.

The Bibles are only a small portion of the entire personal library preserved in the Schoenberg *Nachlass*. Hundreds of volumes rich in annotations, underlinings, and inserted notes and markers are kept at the Arnold Schoenberg Institute. These various annotations provide clues to when Schoenberg was reading a particular book, and what he was thinking about at the time.[3]

Much is already known in a general way about Schoenberg's philosophical and literary interests and preferences. This information is drawn partly from the authors whose texts he chose to set: Dehmel, Balzac, etc., and partly from the company he kept and their recollections: comments by contemporaries reveal a shared interest in Karl Kraus, Arthur Schopenhauer, Friedrich Nietzsche, and others.[4] The Schoenberg library, however, provides an excellent primary resource for more specific inquiries into this subject, which until now has been largely untapped.

This library will be used throughout the present study of Schoenberg's religious and philosophical development, both as a source of new information, and as documentary evidence to confirm certain beliefs about the influences and crosscurrents in the development of Schoenberg's thought. This information becomes increasingly relevant as the study proceeds out of Schoenberg's childhood experiences into the first period of adult questioning and seeking, from about 1896 onward. It is also of particular importance in the study of early literary and philosophical influences on Schoenberg's choices of texts, as in the first period of composition, ca. 1898–1908, and in the examination of the influence of Schopenhauer's thought on Schoenberg's later philosophical development, especially in the years ca. 1911–22.

Schoenberg's Religious Development: Early Years

Little is actually known about Schoenberg's earliest religious experiences. No recent biographer has pointed to any documentary evidence besides what is contained in Stuckenschmidt's biography about Schoenberg's religious upbringing.[5] Through Stuckenschmidt, it is now well known that Schoenberg's mother, Pauline Nachod, was a devout Jew whose old Prague family included several cantors at the "Altneuschul," the chief synagogue in the family's home city. His father was, in the words of Schoenberg's maternal uncle, Fritz Nachod, "an idealistic freethinker."[6] In 1952, Hans Nachod (1883–1966) described the dichotomy between Schoenberg's mother's and father's influences: "If his musical gifts came from the Nachod family, I am sure that his genius was inherited from his father; his father was a dreamer and a thinker and a kind of anarchistic idealist."[7]

Documentation of Schoenberg's introduction into the Jewish community of Vienna managed to survive the devastations of World War II. Stuckenschmidt records that Schoenberg's birth was listed (as number 8023, 13 September 1874) in the register of the Viennese Jewish religious community, and his circumcision took place, properly according to Jewish law, one week later.[8]

Nothing further of Schoenberg's religious growth before 1898 is given in primary or secondary accounts, except for a letter written in May of 1891 by Schoenberg to his cousin Malwina, for whom Schoenberg experienced his first romantic infatuation. He wrote to her:[9]

> You go on to say that you have only disputed the amount of nonsense that is in the Bible; now I must oppose you, as an unbeliever myself, by saying that nowhere in the Bible is there any nonsense. For in it all the most difficult questions concerning Morals, Lawmaking, Industry and Medical Science are resolved in the most simple way, often treated from a contemporary point of view; in general the Bible really gives us the foundation of all our state institutions (except the telephone and the railway).

The letter demonstrates the point which Schoenberg had reached in his philosophical thinking at the age of sixteen: he considered himself "an unbeliever;" but, in spite of that, he defended the Bible as worthy of respect.

What were the steps during Schoenberg's adolescence which brought him to this point? Whose influence was important in his self-profession as an "unbeliever," which at the age of sixteen seems more a declaration of freedom from orthodoxy than any sort of matured conviction? The combination of skepticism with respect for the Bible no doubt reflects an assimilation of his father's "free-thinking" with his mother's piety and devout practice of Judaism in the home.

The very environment of his youth—Vienna—is probably of significance also. Vienna was Schoenberg's home until 1901. It was, then, the environment in which his intellectual life was first stimulated and nourished, and in which it continued to grow for most of the first fifty-two years of his life—most of the entire period up to the composition of *Moses und Aron*.

These early years of Schoenberg's life were precisely in the period of Viennese culture's last gasp, the last flourishing of the coffeehouse lifestyle which nurtured generations of intellectuals. Vienna in the roughly twenty-five years on either side of the turn of the century was a fantastic mixture of intellectual movements, submovements, and countermovements. As such, it has recently been the focus of numerous history books,[10] whose authors try from various perspectives to perceive patterns in this fascinating, chaotic period. The explosion of intellectual ideas from ca. 1870-1930 took place under the shadow of death, in a hysterical, suicide-prone culture reflecting its own imminent decay and death (perhaps most spectacularly manifested in the suicide of the young Crown Prince Rudolf of Austria in 1889).[11] It is therefore little wonder that Schoenberg at the age of sixteen could declare himself an "unbeliever" in an intellectual environment where it was most fashionable to do so—a statement of freedom by the young Schoenberg which only really began a period of questing which ultimately confirmed and strengthened the mature faith at which he arrived in the 1920s.

Recent studies of developmental psychology as applied to the formation of faith in stages throughout the life cycle provide a useful way of thinking about this adolescent stage in Schoenberg's religious growth. Developmental theory identifies the compelling nature of environmental influences during adolescence and often continuing into young adult years, and the consuming search for identity via affiliation.[12] Although adult patterns of thought emerge in early adolescence, psychological research has yielded much data to suggest that the adolescent person is only about midway in his or her progress through stages of development of moral reasoning and faith toward a fully realized or mature faith posture.[13] Schoenberg's status as a "free-thinker" may be viewed in this light as naturally dependent upon the influences of his father and his environment in general, and not as an independently formed judgment based on a mature set of internal principles. His world view was at that time still ripe for change and further development, and was highly dependent upon external influences.

Schoenberg's much-discussed conversion to Protestantism in 1898 can also be examined in this light. The conversion has been logically attributed to the influence of Walter Pieau, an opera singer who sang songs of Zemlinsky and Schoenberg and later participated in the *Ansorgeverein* concerts of 1907.[14] Pieau is listed in the Evangelische Dorotheerkirche's records as Schoenberg's godfather at the latter's baptism on 25 March 1898, and his first name was adopted by Schoenberg as a new Christian name: "Arnold Franz Walter Schoenberg."[15] In a separate act, Schoenberg formally left the Viennese Jewish community four days earlier, and his birth records were transferred to the church.

The question most often asked is how much this conversion was due to actual religious motivation and how much it was simply to follow a trend and belong to what must have been perceived by many Jewish composers to be a more receptive community in which to find musical jobs. And why, in predominantly Catholic Vienna, the conversion to Lutheranism? The records of the Evangelische Dorotheerkirche attest that although a large proportion of the Viennese population was Catholic, many Jewish Viennese converted to Lutheranism,[16] perhaps feeling that in some way it was a lesser degree of betrayal than converting to Catholicism. Alexander Ringer also draws a connection between the worker movement, with which Schoenberg was identified through his workers' chorus, and their "deeply rooted animosity" to the Roman Catholic Church.[17] Another possible reason for Schoenberg's attraction to Lutheranism is that the *Augsburger Konfession* embraced Luther's insistence on scripture as the sole authority for Christian believers *("sola scriptura")* in opposition to the Catholic church's twin authorities of scripture and church dogmatics. Even in converting to Christianity, this much is consistent with Schoenberg's lifelong attachment to and reverence for the Bible. His Luther Bible stayed with him all his life.

Although these considerations are interesting, the psychological dimension of Schoenberg's earlier posture as a "free thinker" perhaps suggests a more relevant way to regard the conversion. Schoenberg's shift in orientation from "free-thinking" to Lutheranism may be viewed as a much less dramatic change if one considers the underlying psychological dimensions of both orientations. While the conversion to Protestantism was a radical change in the content of professed belief, it did not probably represent a radical change in psychological orientation toward religious questions at all. Both faith postures were dependent upon external influence within a wholly normal young adult stage of faith development. In making his conversion to Christianity Schoenberg was transferring the object of his affiliation, but the essential underlying need for affiliation itself did not change. In addition to the natural movement from attachment to the home to attachment to an outside circle of friends during the time from adolescence young adulthood, Schoenberg's shift in perspective would have been further affected by his father's death in 1891, which logically hastened his turning to trusted figures outside the home for a locus of affiliation and identification.

Thus, the apparent mystery of Schoenberg's conversion may be explained as a change in loyalties from an earlier adolescent affiliation with values in the home—his "free-thinking" father—to a young adult's affiliation with peers. It was not a radical step—whether viewed positively or negatively—into a new phase or stage of faith development. The intellectual and philosophical content of Schoenberg's religious thinking underwent change, but the mode of thought and the underlying process of locating truth in external influences remained essentially undisturbed.

Apparently Schoenberg's relationship with the Dorotheerkirche lasted as long as he remained in Vienna, roughly three and a half years, until his move to Berlin in 1902. The continued association with the church is attested by his marriage there to Mathilde Zemlinksy on 18 October 1901, recorded in the church's *Trauungsbuch.*[18] The church records also show that the couple were already married in a civil ceremony in Pressburg on 7 October. No personal friends are listed as witnesses, the witnesses being a Heinrich Kleinfeldt and a Ferdinand Plotiwinsky who lived in and presumably were employees of the church. The follow-up of a civil ceremony with a specifically Christian wedding would seem to indicate that Schoenberg's relationship with the church still had at least formal significance for him by 1901.

The church records indicate no further contact with the church after the Schoenbergs moved to Berlin in 1902. Schoenberg's Christianity appears to have been more formal than deeply convicted: his involvement with Dehmel and the expressionistic group shortly after this time and through the 1920s led him easily through various stages of existentialism, German rational philosophy, theosophy, mysticism, and other diverse modes of religious and philosophical thought. This further transformation in Schoenberg's religious thought may be viewed as another shift within the psychological context of affiliation and identification, again, mitigating the view that Schoenberg was making a series of radical religious moves during these years.

That Christianity had some small, lasting influence is, however, perhaps demonstrated in a quotation from the New Testament: "Knock, and the door will be opened to you" (Matthew 7:7) in the text for *Die Jakobsleiter*, drafted 1915–17; in the Christlike sacrificial death of Max Aruns (the hero of his play *Der Biblische Weg*, 1926–27; and in one of the last texts of his life, one of the *Modern Psalms*, which treats the subject of Jesus with great honor. The degree to which Schoenberg identified Jesus in this Psalm with his own personal creed (i.e., the abandonment of personal will to the one, eternal, all-powerful God) reflects a synthesis of his own later theological language, which, as will be seen, Schoenberg formulated by the 1920s, with a profound respect for the biblical Jesus, as shown in the excerpts below:[19]

> Es ist tragisch, dass die jüdische Geschichtsschreibung es unterlassen hat, die Geschichte Jesu's zu berichten ...
> Jesus war zweifellos das reinste, unschuldigste, selbstloseste, idealistischeste Wesen, das je auf dieser Erde gewandelt hat. Sein Wille, sein ganzes Denken und Streben, war darauf gerichtet, die Menschen zu erlösen, indem er sie zu dem wahren Glauben an den Einzigen, Ewigen, Allmächtigen führte ...
> Es lässt sich kaum beweisen, dass Jesus beabsichtigt habe, die jüdische Nation zu spalten. Keines seiner Worte, keine seiner Handlungen steht im Widerspruch zur mosaischen Auffassung Gottes. Er wollte, im Gegenteil, die Religion in ihrer reinsten Form wiederherstellen und in deren weitgehendsten Konsequenzen. ...

Fin-de-Siècle Literary Influences

There is an unbreakable relationship between Schoenberg's musical compositions themselves and the personal, literary, and philosophical influences which contributed to their genesis. Thus, from the period of about 1898 onward, it is perhaps most fruitful to survey the development of Schoenberg's thought in the context of his works and the stylistic periods associated with them.

The growth of certain religious and philosophical ideas occurred in stages which correspond roughly in time to the stylistic divisions commonly made within Schoenberg's œuvre. These stages are not, of course, cleanly demarcated in time. However, they serve adequately as general guides to phases within an ongoing, connected process of evolution: the early tonal period (of ca. 1898 and before to the Second Quartet completed in 1908), which corresponds with a period of still youthful philosophical exploration involving both the conversion to Christianity and an opposite bent toward agnosticism or even existentialism, all strongly influenced by his environment of peers; the "expressionistic" period (from about 1908 or even earlier through ca. 1921), which is intertwined with his relationship to Dehmel and the artists of the *Blaue Reiter* and their wide scope of interests including occult, oriental, and theosophical writers and which includes a work toward the end of this period, *Die Jakobsleiter*, based on a theosophical vision in Balzac's novel *Seraphita*; the first serial period (beginning ca. 1922), which corresponds with the emerging reaffirmation of faith in God and in the Jewish religious tradition—exemplified by an inscription "mit Gott" on the cover of a new sketchbook begun "31/V 1922"[20]—culminating in the work on *Moses und Aron* through ca. 1934; and the later, somewhat less strict serial period (from ca. 1934 and the emigration to America), works which are for the most part devoted to expressing Schoenberg's vision of Jewish destiny and faith.

In the earliest tonal period, from ca. 1896 to 1900,[21] Schoenberg's choices of text show a wide diversity, and draw heavily upon writers whose texts were already set quite frequently by other composers. Richard Dehmel was clearly the most important in this period. His *Verklärte Nacht* is the program for Op. 4 in 1899, and Schoenberg also set seven poems as songs—three without opus number, three in Op. 2 (1899) and one in Op. 3 (1899), as well as a fragment "Gethsemane" (1899). Also chosen often before 1900 were poems of Ludwig Pfau, in nine songs without opus number plus a fragment for male chorus in 1897. Other writers chosen included Paul Heyse (two), Karl von Levetzow (two), Nicolaus Lenau, Hugo von Hofmannsthal, and Robert Reinick. Schoenberg did not write texts of his own until after ca. 1908 (beginning with *Die Glückliche Hand*). A complete list of writers whose works Schoenberg used as texts in completed works as well as in large fragments is given in Table 2, divided into the style periods under consideration.

It may be seen from this table that the diversity of texts used before 1900 continued into the period 1900–1907. Texts popular in the late nineteenth century head the list. These include three poems of Stefan George, which were used in Op. 14 (1907), two of Dehmel used in Op. 3 (1903) and Op. 6 (1905), and three songs from *Des Knaben Wunderhorn*, a choice obviously influenced by Mahler, used in Op. 8 (1903–4). Three poems of Petrarch (trans. Förster) are used in Op. 8 (1904), Maeterlinck's *Pelléas et Mélisande* served as the basis for Schoenberg's symphonic poem of the same title in German, Op. 5 (1902–3), suggested to him by Strauss, and Nietzsche's poem "Der Wanderer" is used by Schoenberg in Op. 6 (1905). Texts which served for settings left unfinished again included poems by Dehmel, which served as the basis for a programmatic orchestral piece, *Ein Stelldichein* (1905). While the choices of texts in this early period are generally unremarkable, this early use of texts, especially those by Dehmel, George, Nietzsche, and Maeterlinck, provides a preview of Schoenberg's later literary interests.

Schoenberg's library holdings published before 1908 correspond in many cases to the texts he set in the same period. (Although the date of acquisition of the books does not necessarily depend on the date of publication, it seems reasonable to assume—because of the close correspondence of the datings of text settings to publication dates of most of the books—that he purchased the books reasonably close to their publication dates.) Authors represented in the library in volumes published by 1908 include: R. F. Arnold, *Europäische Lyrik*, 2nd ed. (1906), a later edition of a book which served as a source ca. 1900 for *Gurrelieder* and a song "Hochzeitslied"; Otto Bierbaum, *Lobetanz. Ein Singspiel* (1895), whose author provided a text for one of Schoenberg's cabaret songs; Dehmel, *Gesammelte Werke*, 3rd ed., 10 vols. (1906) which contains the numerous Dehmel texts used by Schoenberg before 1908; five separate volumes of Stefan George (1901, 1901, 1905, 1905, and 1907) used for three songs in Op. 14 (1907) and the fifteen songs of *Das Buch der hängenden Gärten*, Op. 15 (1908–9); a *Briefwechsel zwischen Goethe und Schiller* (1905), Gerhardt Hauptmann, *Gesammelte Werke*, 6 vols., (1906) used for *Und Pippa Tanzt* (1906–7); Jens Peter Jacobsen, *Novellen, Briefe, Gedichte* (1903), a battered volume showing much use, the main source for the monumental *Gurrelieder* (1901–3) and "Hochzeitslied," a song in Op. 3 (1900); K. F. von Levetzow, *Hohenlieder: Gedichte und Aphorismen* (1898) which provided texts for two songs in Op. 1 (1898); fifteen separate volumes of Maeterlinck in translation published between 1902 and 1907, including *Pelleas und Melisande*, used for the symphonic poem, Op. 5 (1902–3) and *Herzgewächse*, Op. 20 (1911); Conrad Ferdinand Meyer, *Gedichte* (1892) which provided *Friede auf Erden*, Op. 13 (1907); *Das Neue Testament* (1901), likely acquired in connection with Schoenberg's conversion to Lutheranism three years before; four volumes of Nietzsche (1901, 1903, 1904, and 1906), including *Also Sprach Zarathustra* (1906); and *Dichtungen* (1904), the source of "Der Wanderer," Op. 6 (1905); two volumes of Rilke, *Neue Gedichte* (1907), including "Am Strande" (set by Schoenberg in 1908–9) and the three song texts of Op. 22 (1914–16), and *Zwei Präger Geschichte* (1899); two volumes of Strindberg (1903, 1904) who is mainly represented in Schoenberg's library with publication dates after 1908 and whose thought also became more important to the composer later. The works of Lenau, represented in Schoenberg's œuvre by one song before 1900, also belong to the collection in an undated volume published in Leipzig, probably also acquired in this period. Schoenberg's library contains only a few remaining literary works published in this period which the composer did not set to music. These are textbooks dealing with music, history, and the English language.

While some of the texts set in this early period are not represented in the library (for example, Förster's translations of Petrarch, or poetry of Heyse, Hofmannsthal, and a few others), it becomes clear that there are very few volumes in the library from this period which are unrelated to musical compositions. This demonstrates that Schoenberg's knowledge of literature of nineteenth-century Germany—as well as his understanding of some other European literature of the same period—was connected in his intellectual life with his thinking as a composer of music. It was not a highly developed separate interest.

In summary, the literary aspect of texted works before 1908 may be seen as consistent with typical fin-de-siècle subject matter of interest to generally educated people, as in texts to songs of Mahler, Strauss, and Zemlinsky. While in this early period no particular strong tendencies emerge, the early presence of Dehmel and Nietzsche among authors represented in the library shows a continuity between this period and Schoenberg's later literary interests.

Table 2.   Texts Used by Arnold Schoenberg*

Before 1900

Ada Christen (1839–1901)—1 song (n.o.)
Richard Dehmel (1863–1920)—*Verklärte Nacht,* Op. 4 (1899); 3 songs (n.o., n.d.); 3 songs in Op. 2 (1899); 1 song in Op. 3 (1899)
Franz Emmanuel Geibel (1815–84)—1 song (n.o., 1896)
A. Gold—1 song (1893)
Martin Greif (1839–1911)—1 song (n.o., n.d.)
Klaus Groth (1819–99)—"Ei die Lutte," choral (n.o., n.d.)
Paul Heyse (1830–1914)—1 song (n.o., n.d.)
Hugo von Hofmannsthal (1874–1929)—1 song (n.o., 1899)
Nicolaus Lenau (1802–50)—1 song (n.o., n.d.)
Ludwig Pfau (1821–94)—9 songs (n.o., n.d.)
Robert Reinick (1805–52)—1 song (n.o., n.d.)
Johannes Schlaf (1862–1941)—1 song in Op. 2 (1899)
Karl von Levetzow (1871–1945)—2 songs in Op. 1 (1898)
Oscar von Redwitz (1823–91)—1 song (n.o., n.d.)
Joseph Christian von Zedlitz (1790–1862)—1 song (n.o., 1896)
W. . .—1 song (n.o., n.d.)
Wilhelm Wackernagel (1806–69)—1 song (n.o., n.d.)

(Fragments: Dehmel—*Gethsemane* (1899), G. Falcke (see below)—basis for programmatic orchestral piece *Toter Winkel* (before 1917); Pfau—male chorus (1897)

Schoenberg wrote no texts which he set to music in this period.

1900–1907

H. Amman—ballad in Op. 8 (1907)
K[urt] Aram—1 song (n.o., 1905)
Heinrich Conradi (1862–90)—1 song (n.o., 1903)
Dehmel—2 songs, in Op. 3 (1903) and Op. 6 (1905)
G. Falcke [Gustav? 1853–1916]—1 song (n.o., 1901)
Stefan George (1868–1933)—3 songs in Op. 14 (1907)
Joh. Wolfgang von Goethe (1749–1832)—1 song (n.o., 1903)
Heinrich Hart (1855–1906)—1 song in Op. 8 (1903–4)
Julius Hart (1859–1930)—1 song in Op. 6 (1903)
Jacob Peter Jacobsen (1869–1918)/trans. R.F. Arnold—*Gurrelieder* (1901–3; 1910–12) and 1 song in Op. 3 (1900)
Gottfried Keller (1819–90)—2 songs (n.o., 1903)
Victor Klemperer (1881–1960)—ballad in Op. 8 (1907)
Des Knaben Wunderhorn (1806–8)—3 songs in Op. 8 (1903–4)
Hermann Lingg (1820–1905)—1 song (n.o., 1900)
John Henry Mackay (1864–1933)—1 song in Op. 6 (1905)
Maurice Maeterlinck (1862–1949)—basis for symphonic poem *Pelleas und Melisande,* Op. 5 (1902–3)
Conrad Ferdinand Meyer (1825–98)—*Friede auf Erden,* Op. 13 (1907)
Friedrich Nietzsche (1844–1900)—1 song in Op. 6 (1905)

---

*   Based on list of works in O.W. Neighbour, "Schoenberg, Arnold," *New Grove,* XVI, 719–23. The abbreviation "n.o." stands for "no opus number." Birth and death dates are listed wherever known.

Francesco Petrarch (1304–74)/trans. Förster—3 in Op. 8 (1904)
Paul Remer (1867–?)—1 song in Op. 6 (1905)

(Cabaret Songs: O. Bierbaum, Colly, G. Falcke, G. Hochstetter, H. Salus (2), Schikaneder, Wedekind)

(Canons: Goethe (2 completed, 3 uncompleted))

(Fragments: Dehmel—basis for programmatic orchestral piece *Ein Stelldichein* (1907); Goethe—2 songs (1908); G. Hauptmann—*Und Pippa Tanzt* (1906–7); Lenau—basis for a symphonic poem *Frühlings Tod;* H. Lons—ballad intended for Op. 12 (1907))

Schoenberg wrote no texts which he set to music in this period.

1908–1921

Ernest Dowson (1867–1900)/trans. George—"Seraphita" (after Balzac), in Op. 22 (1913)
George—15 songs in *Das Buch der hängenden Gärten*, Op. 15 (1808–9)
Albert Giraud (1860–1929)/trans. O.E. Hartleben—21 in *Pierrot Lunaire*, Op. 21 (1912)
Karl Henckell (1864–1924)—1 song in Op. 14 (1908)
H. Hovesch—chorale arrangement (n.o., 1918–25)
Ottokar Kernstock (1848–1928)—*Der Deutsche Michel*, choral piece (n.o., 1914 or 1915)
Maeterlinck/trans. K.L. Ammer & F. von Oppeln-Bronikowski—*Herzgewächse*, Op. 20 (1911)
Marie Pappenheim—*Erwartung*, Op. 17 (1909)
Petrarch/trans. Förster—mvt. iv in Serenade, Op. 24 (1920–23)
Rainer Maria Rilke (1875–1926)—[?] *Am Strande* (1908 or 1909) and 3 orchestral songs in Op. 22 (1914, 1914–15, 1916)

(Fragment: George)

Schoenberg set 2 of his own texts to music in this period: *Die Glückliche Hand*, Op. 18 (1910–13); and *Die Jakobsleiter* (incomplete), (1917–22; 1944).

1922–1933

Folksong settings—3 choral (n.o., 1929–30), 4 solo vocal (n.o., 1929–30)
J. Haringer—3 songs in Op. 48 (1933)
Hung-So-Fan/trans. Bethge—1 song in Op. 27 (1925)
Gertrud Schoenberg (under pen name M. Blonda)—opera libretto for *Von Heute auf Morgen*, Op. 32 (1928–9)
Tschan-Jo-Su/trans. Bethge—1 song in Op. 27 (1925)

Schoenberg set twelve of his own texts in this period: primarily the opera *Moses und Aron* (ca. 1926–32) and 11 songs and choral pieces: 3 Satires in Op. 25 (1925); "Unentrinnbar" and "Du Sollst Nicht, Du Musst" in Op. 27 (1925); 6 pieces for male chorus in Op. 35 (1929–30); plus 8 canon texts. The play *Der Biblische Weg* also falls in this period.

1934–1951

Biblical texts—Psalm 103 *De Profundis*, Op. 50b (1950), and the Book of Genesis, basis for wordless Choral Prelude, Op. 44 (1945)
George Gordon, Lord Byron (1788–1824)—*Ode to Napoleon*, Op. 41 (1942)
Folksong settings—3 (n.o., 1929)
Kol Nidre (Jewish liturgy for Yom Kippur)—Op. 39 (1938)
Dagobert David Runes (1902–)—*Dreimal tausend Jahre*, Op. 50a (1949)

Schoenberg set 3 of his own texts to music in this period: *A Survivor from Warsaw*, Op. 46 (1947); *Israel Exists Again* (incomplete, 1949); *Modern Psalm*, No. 1, Op. 50c (1950); plus 5 canon texts. Seventeen more "Modern Psalms" were written in this period, not set to music.

Expressionism and Mysticism

Two pieces of 1907–8 were important in inaugurating the style Schoenberg described as "emancipation of the dissonance."[22] These are String Quartet No. 2, Op. 10 (1907–8) and the fifteen songs of *Das Buch der hängenden Gärten*, Op. 15 (1908). These pieces are generally known as the first in the new expressionist "atonal" period of composition. The evolutionary aspects of the musical language from late nineteenth century chromaticism are clear, as described by Schoenberg himself:[23]

> Most critics of this new style failed to investigate how far the ancient "eternal" laws of musical aesthetics were observed, spurned, or merely adjusted to changed circumstances. Such superficiality brought about accusations of anarchy and revolution, whereas, on the contrary, this music was distinctly a product of evolution, and no more revolutionary than any other development in the history of music.

Both Op. 10 and Op. 15 also employ texts by Stefan George, whose cooler, more mystical and symbolic tone contrast with the lush, romantic language of Richard Dehmel which appealed to Schoenberg near the turn of the century. A recent dissertation by Albrecht Dümling describes "George als Antipode Dehmels" in detail, relating the shift in choice of texts to the change in musical style ca. 1908.[24]

The expressionist period, particularly from the years of Schoenberg's friendship with the painter Kandinsky which began around 1911,[25] was one of intense involvement with the aesthetic of the *Blaue Reiter* group. Schoenberg's opera *Die Glückliche Hand*, Op. 18, 1910–13,[26] is an excellent representative of the works of this period and has particularly strong associations with the *Blaue Reiter* and Kandinsky.[27] In spite of its brevity, it incorporates several large, Wagnerian-style themes of love, redemption, and creativity with expressionist themes of existential despair, loss, and perpetual unfulfilled seeking. As such, it stands as an important precedent in Schoenberg's operatic composition for *Moses und Aron*.

Schoenberg began *Die Glückliche Hand* in 1910.[28] The text and scenario were completed and published by Universal Edition in 1910. He began the music 9 September 1910, and then stopped, distracted by a move from Vienna to Berlin. This move was made because of increasing disappointment with the lack of response to his music in Vienna, and because of his frustration with not receiving a post as a professor at the Vienna Academy, where he was teaching as a *Privatdozent*. Work on *Die Glückliche Hand* was further delayed by work on several other pieces, and by conducting engagements all over Europe to introduce *Pierrot Lunaire* in 1912 and to conduct *Pelleas und Melisande*. He returned to work on *Die Glückliche Hand* only in 1913, for a projected performance in Dresden which never actually materialized.[29]

The work belongs to a whole group of contemporary stage works with expressionist themes by artists of the same movement. These plays represented a particular aesthetic world of their own. Walter Sokel has described key "modernist" elements of expressionist drama as "the musicalization" [i.e., direct artistic communication, unmediated by formal logic, as in Schopenhauer's theories of music], and "functionalization" of art, the abandonment of external frameworks, and the creation of a self-contained universe.[30] The expressionist artist Kokoschka had just written two one-act plays in 1907, *Mörder, Hoffnung der Frauen* (later set as an opera by Hindemith), and *Sphinx und Strohmann*, which were premiered in Vienna in 1908 and 1909, respectively.[31] It was Kokoschka whom Schoenberg designated in his letter to Emil Hertzka as his first choice as scene designer for a contemplated film of *Die Glückliche Hand*.[32] His second and third choices were Kandinsky and Roller, respectively.

While *Erwartung* presents an intensely personal story, rich with narrative details which unfold slowly by implication and in symbolic imagery from the depths of the character's unconscious, *Die Glückliche Hand* intensifies these by universalizing them and attaching to them only the vaguest, most dreamlike narrative plot. Of the three main characters, the Man represents both a kind of Everyman and also the concept of the artist/composer who has within him a spark of the divine by virtue of his creativity. The Woman represents the worldly object of desire, a kind of aloof and capricious version of Wagner's *"ewig Weibliche."* The third character, the Gentleman, represents the social world of elegance and surface charm which lures the eternal feminine way. All three of these characters are essences, not personalities or even types. There is no psychological development—especially in comparison to *Erwartung*, which is nothing but psychological development.

The action of the opera is best understood as a continuous symbolic rendering of various psychological states and the feeling of *having experienced* desire, loss, power, etc. It unfolds like a dream or a free association, where the essence of a feeling is all that remains of a former historical experience, and is expressed through symbolic figures and images. John Crawford has suggested such an historical experience in Schoenberg's own life behind the essences of feelings in the opera: the painful triangle between him, his wife Mathilde, and the Austrian painter Richard Gerstl.[33] The opposition received by the Man to his artistic creation has obvious parallels to the struggles Schoenberg endured in Vienna in attempting to have his music performed and understood.

As in many expressionist dramas, the characters in *Die Glückliche Hand* function as bizarre archetypes. They are not simple allegorical figures or symbols, but are vividly unique expressions of inner existential states. They may be compared to characters in other expressionist drama, and bear striking resemblance to characters in Strindberg's play *Nach Damascus* (1898), which Schoenberg knew well: the Unknown Man, the Lady, and her husband the Doctor. Walter Sokel's description of these Strindberg characters could have been written about *Die Glückliche Hand*:[34]

> The drama is a composition of the hero's essential existence, and each character plays the role of a musical leitmotiv expressing an aspect or a possibility of the hero, who is called the Unknown Man. The Lady embodies the Unknown Man's link with life. She is nameless, like the hero himself, because she is not the portrait of a particular lady, but that amalgamation of the sexual and the sublime, the infernal and the celestial through which existence provokes, harasses, torments, and inspires the man. She possesses many concrete characteristics based on Strindberg's memories of his first and second wives.... But these specific biographical features are used in a highly abstract way. They are not intended to illuminate the Lady's personality, but to define her function in the Unknown Man's existence....

In this way, both *Nach Damascus* and *Die Glückliche Hand* share the characteristics of expressionist "Ich-Drama," comparable to Reinhard Johannes Sorge's early, somewhat prototypical expressionist play *Der Bettler* (1911).[35]

Some expressionist stage works of the same period actually incorporated tone and color in a way similar to *Die Glückliche Hand*. The Mahler-Roller production of Wagner's *Tristan und Isolde* at the Vienna Staatsoper in 1903 also was an experimentation with symbolic uses of colored lighting to reflect the drama, and may have been an influence on Schoenberg's initial conception of *Die Glückliche Hand*.[36] Strindberg's play *Nach Damascus* calls for symbolic use of color and tone as well.

Another expressionist drama with music appeared in 1909: Kandinsky's *Der Gelbe Klang* with music by Thomas Hartmann (1885–1956).[37] This work more than any other shares with Schoenberg's *Die Glückliche Hand* the central association of sound and color to characterize emotional states. The striking similarity between the two works is attributable to a very important common source, also written by Kandinsky, the theoretical treatise *Über das Geistige in der Kunst*.[38] Though published late in 1911, this work contains ideas that must have been discussed in expressionist circles several years earlier, since both stage works closely realize Kandinsky's theories.

That Schoenberg knew the Kandinsky book is demonstrated by a letter he wrote to the artist 14 December 1911:[39]

> Lieber Herr Kandinsky, ich habe Ihr Buch noch nicht ganz gelesen; erst zwei Drittel. Trotzdem muss ich Ihnen aber schon jetzt schreiben, dass es mir ausserordentlich gefällt. Sie haben mit so vielem unbedingt recht. Insbesonderer was Sie über die Farbe sagen im Vergleich mit der musikalischen Farbe. Das stimmt mit meinen eigenen Empfindungen überein....

Both Schoenberg and Kandinsky believed in art as an expression of the artist's "inner need": in *Über das Geistige in der Kunst*, Kandinsky writes, "That is beautiful which is produced by inner need, that which springs from the soul."[40] And Schoenberg wrote in "Problems in Teaching Art," also in 1911, "I believe art is born of *I must*, not of *I can*. . . . For that is how it is in the real work of art: everything gives the impression of having come first, because everything was born at the same moment. Feeling is already form, the idea is already the word."[41] Similar statements may be found also in his *Harmonielehre* (1911), for example:[42]

> The artist's creative activity is instinctive. Consciousness has little influence on it. He feels as if what he does were dictated to him. As if he did it only according to the will of some power or other within him, whose laws he does not know. He is merely the instrument of a will hidden from him, of instinct, of his unconscious. Whether it is new or old, good or bad, beautiful or ugly, he does not know. He feels only the instinctual compulsion, which he must obey. And in this instinct the old may find expression, and the new.

In addition to the use of color associated with Kandinsky's theory, Schoenberg incorporated certain bizarre images from a personal iconography which became characteristic elements in his own expressionist paintings. The disembodied faces of the chorus in the first and last scenes correspond to favorite images of Schoenberg, faces gazing out of a blend of colors, which he called *"Blick"* and *"Vision,"* as in his famous paintings *Rotes Blick* (1910)[43] and *Christ, Vision,*[44] included in the *Blaue Reiter* exhibition 18 December 1911.[45]

Schoenberg's own color sketches for the stage sets of the opera are very similar to these paintings.[46] In an unpublished lecture given at Breslau in 1928 in connection with a performance of the opera, Schoenberg discussed the association of colors, tones, images, and meanings, and specifically described the chorus as appearing like "gazes."[47]

While no other piece that Schoenberg wrote is as direct an application of the aesthetic of expressionist visual art to music, all the pieces in the period 1908–13 share the same lyrical (in the sense of an outpouring of self) raw expression of emotion. *Erwartung*, written in 1909, comes closest to *Die Glückliche Hand* in both dramaturgical and musical style, partly because it was conceived as another expressionist stage work. However, the musical and dramatic structure of *Die Glückliche Hand* is characterized by a very tight motivic construction and clear, symmetrical dramatic form; while *Erwartung*—though still constructed of motivic recurrences—is a freer, more through-composed expression of raw emotion. The year 1909 was very productive in general: in it, Schoenberg wrote the Opus 11 *Klavierstücke*, which are important for later development of serialism because of their rigorous, near-serial use of cellular motives within a moody atonal language;

the Fünf Orchesterstücke, Op. 16, including the first use of *"Klangfarben-melodie"* in No. 3, "Farben;" and *Erwartung.* The year 1910 saw the completion of the orchestration of the much earlier *Gurrelieder,* a monumental chromatic but tonal choral work which, except for a small portion, had already been written and orchestrated in 1901.

In 1911, an important year for Schoenberg's involvement with the *Blaue Reiter,* the first version of his *Harmonielehre* was completed. In the *Harmonielehre,* Schoenberg describes the functions and resolutions of quartal harmonies similar to those used in *Die Glückliche Hand.* Going beyond the transmission of theoretical principles, he uses the book to voice an aesthetic and a philosophy of freedom in composing which is demonstrated in his musical compositions of the period from 1908–17. Sonorities and principles of compositional structure expounded in the *Harmonielehre* are also seen in his serial works and may be found in *Moses und Aron,* demonstrating the evolutionary nature of Schoenberg's serialism.

In 1911, after Schoenberg moved with his family to Berlin, he completed the Six Little Piano Pieces, Op. 19, and the *Herzgewächse,* an atonal work similar in musical style to *Die Glückliche Hand,* but with a symbolist text by Maeterlinck. *Pierrot Lunaire,* Schoenberg's first great popular success in this period, was finished in 1912, and he spent the year conducting it and his *Pelleas und Melisande.* The Maeterlinck texts, *Pelleas und Melisande* and *Herzgewächse,* represent a bridge between the influence of Kandinsky (who highlighted Maeterlinck's language of the spirt, heart, and soul in *Über das Geistige in der Kunst*)[48] and Schoenberg's own growing interest in the theosophical and mystical thought expressed in the writings of Swedenborg, Balzac, and Strindberg. Stuckenschmidt records 1909 as Schoenberg's first documented reference to Strindberg.[49] Stuckenschmidt also notes Schoenberg's correspondence and conversations about Strindberg's "Jacob Wrestling" with many friends, including Berg, Webern, Erwin Stein, Heinrich Jalowetz, and Karl Linke.[50]

Schoenberg owned forty-four volumes of Strindberg in all, published from 1904 to 1930.[51] *Strindbergs Werke,* Vols. 1–6 (1906–8), and especially *Ein Blaubuch: die Synthese meines Lebens* (1908), contain many marginal notes and underlinings. Schoenberg also owned the complete works edition of Balzac, plus ten individual books, published from 1908–12 and 1921. Chapters 3 and 7 of Balzac's *Seraphita* are underlined (at the description of Wilfred[52] and at the assumption scene,[53] respectively). In a second edition of *Seraphita,* translated into German, the same description of Wilfred is again underlined.[54] Schoenberg also owned Swedenborg's *Theologische Schriften,*[55] but did not write in the book.[56]

Schoenberg's interest in theosophy and mysticism seemed to grow more after his move to Berlin in 1911. This interest is particularly evident in his growing attraction to the works of Balzac after this time.[57] Schoenberg completed *Die Glückliche Hand* in 1913, and was already planning an oratorio or opera on Balzac's *Seraphita* at that time. This work was never completed—a text draft and two musical fragments remain from 1912,[58] as well as the orchestral Lied "Seraphita" from the Four Songs for Voice and Orchestra, Op. 22, also dated 1913. These were then followed by the three Rilke settings in Op. 22, which he completed in 1913.

Schoenberg's interest in Balzac, particularly his fascination with the vision of heaven in *Seraphita*, remained to some degree throughout his life. Walther Klein wrote in the special 1924 edition of *Anbruch* for Schoenberg's fiftieth birthday of Schoenberg as "the theosophist";[59] and Schoenberg's interest in Balzac seemed to resurface again, especially in the 1940s. He made reference to the author in four essays during this period.[60] "Art and the Moving Pictures" (1940), "Composition with Twelve Tones" (1941), "Heart and Brain in Music" (1946), and "Criteria for the Evaluation of Music" (1946). He even dreamed of a "realization in sound pictures" (i.e., film) of *Seraphita* or Strindberg's *Nach Damascus*.[61] It was also in this late period that Schoenberg remarked to Leonard Stein what a wonderful scene the ascension in *Seraphita* would make for an opera.[62]

Due to political unrest and the dramatic decline in economic support for the arts during World War I, the period following 1913 was for Schoenberg (as it was for everybody else) a "dry" period. During his own military service, 1915–17, Schoenberg was only able to draft the texts for *Totentanz der Prinzipien* and *Die Jakobsleiter*, which bear to a greater degree than any works preceding or following the influences of theosophy, Swedenborg, Strindberg, and especially of Balzac. The largest work which Schoenberg attempted in connection with the influence of Balzac was, of course, the unfinished oratorio, *Die Jakobsleiter*.[63] Sources for this work can be traced specifically back to the drafts for the earlier versions of *Seraphita* mentioned above. Like Strindberg's "Jacob Wrestling," *Die Jakobsleiter* not only drew on the theosophical sources in Schoenberg's background, but also upon specifically Old Testament images. Schoenberg's fascination with these images seems to have been the central force in precipitating his movement to a new phase of personal religious development, first expressed in this striking religious confession in a letter to Dehmel, dated as early as 13 December 1912:[64]

And here now is your very kind letter, which at last gives me courage to ask you a question that has long been in my mind. It is this. For a long time I have been wanting to write an oratorio on the following subject: modern man, having passed through materialism, socialism, and anarchy, and despite having been an atheist, still having in him some residue of ancient faith (in the form of superstition), wrestles with God (see also Strindberg's "Jacob Wrestling") and finally succeeds in finding God and becoming religious. Learning to pray!

It is *not* through any action, any blows of fate, least of all through any love of woman, that this change of heart is to come about. Or at least these should be no more than hints in the background, giving the initial impulse. And above all: the mode of speech, the mode of thought, the mode of expression, should be that of modern man; the problems treated should be those that harass us. For those who wrestle with God in the Bible also express themselves as men of their own time, speaking of their own affairs, remaining within their own social and intellectual limits. That is why, though they are artistically impressive, they do not offer a subject for a modern composer who fulfills his obligations.

Originally I had intended to write the words myself. But I no longer think myself equal to it. Then I thought of adapting Strindberg's "Jacob Wrestling." Finally I came to the idea of beginning with positive religious belief and intended adapting the final chapter, "The Ascent into Heaven," from Balzac's "Seraphita." But I could never shake off the thought of "Modern Man's Prayer," and I often thought: if only Dehmel...!

It was two years later that Schoenberg wrote the letter to Henri Hinrichsen at C. F. Peters in which he expressed the desire to "be the expression in sound of the human soul and its desire for God."[65]

It is with this religious change, around the year 1912, that a clearly new stage of development in Schoenberg's religious faith may be perceived. This stage has characteristics of being both critically self-authored (rather than relying on external authority) and synthetic of previous philosophical and literary learning and upbringing (e.g., the first rekindling of interest in Judaism via Old Testament images).[66]

The musical style with which Schoenberg experimented at this time also became eclectic, synthetic. When Schoenberg began to compose the music to *Die Jakobsleiter* in 1916, between two periods of military duty, he continued to use the expressionist atonal style of *Die Glückliche Hand* and *Erwartung*, a similarity which he himself noted in a letter as late as 22 May 1950.[67] But he also incorporated some earlier stylistic elements, including some tonal writing in a somewhat retrospective and synthetic manner, mediating between expressionism and his earlier style closer to the turn of the century.

Very little else was composed during this time, and *Die Jakobsleiter* was to be a stylistic anomaly in Schoenberg's œuvre. The period from Schoenberg's military duty to 1923 marks the famous "silence" out of which then came in 1923 a whole new period of composition, with the first twelve-tone serial works, the Five Piano Pieces, Op. 23 (begun in 1920), and the famous Serenade, Op. 24 (begun in 1921) constructed on three tetrachords which combine into a twelve-tone scale, using as text Petrarch's sonnet #217 in German translation.

To sum up, a progression of thought can be seen in the texts chosen, from expressionist ("Ich") texts to those which represent spiritual questing of a mystical sort with a particular fascination for Balzac's "Seraphita" vision. Other influences, however, were also critically important in the formation of Schoenberg's thought prior to the 1920s and thus have direct relevance to the genesis of *Moses und Aron*. Two important intellectual influences, one philosophical and one literary, became prominent in Schoenberg's thinking at this time: Arthur Schopenhauer and Karl Kraus. It is also precisely in this period, just prior to the 1920s, that Schoenberg first began to personally feel the anti-Semitism in his environment, a feeling which was to become strong around 1922. These influences will now be examined.

Schoenberg and Schopenhauer

Feeling is already form, the Idea is already the word.[68]

Documentary Evidence

The philosophy of Arthur Schopenhauer was an important part of Schoenberg's thought in general, and also specifically in relation to Schoenberg's probings for the text of *Moses und Aron*. The marginalia described above demonstrate Schoenberg's interest in the philosopher. What further evidence exists concerning Schopenhauer's influence on Schoenberg, and of which philosophical concepts contributed most to Schoenberg's world view?

Schoenberg owned almost all of the works of Schopenhauer in his private library by the year 1913. Extant in the collection are the *Sämtliche Werke*, all six volumes of the first Reclam edition, 1891, edited by Eduard Grisebach.[69] These are all entered by Schoenberg in his library catalogue with the date 23 January 1913. Marginal annotations appear in four volumes: in volume II, a marginal note, "Jakobsleiter!", appears on p. 264 of *Die Welt als Wille und Vorstellung*; in volume IV, *Parerga und Paralipomena*, in the essay "Von Dam, was Einer Vorstellt" are found marginalia, a small sheet tipped in, and a small sheet of notes inserted in "Baranesen und Marimen;" in volume V, *Über Religion*, many marginal notes plus two large pages tipped in dated "12/XII.1914" and "5/12.1914" are present; and in volume VI, *Farbenlehre*, a brief note and a longer sheet dated "6.4.1922" appear, as does a separate sheet tipped in containing notes on God. In addition, one of the most well-worn books in the library is the *Parerga und Paralipomena: Kleine Philosophische Schriften*, volume 2, a second copy of the Reclam *Werke*. The book is not listed in Schoenberg's own catalogue, and therefore was probably added to the collection after 1918. The copious annotations in the margins of this book cover a wide range of topics, and there is heavy pencil underlining on every page, indicating very close reading.

Additional evidence exists for dating Schoenberg's interest in Schopenhauer to as early as 1911, when Schoenberg made reference to Schopenhauer (*Parerga und Paralipomena*) in the first edition of the *Harmonielehre*.[70] The following year, Schoenberg also referred to Schopenhauer in two essays:[71]

"Gustav Mahler," and "The Relationship to the Text." The two short essays inserted into the Schopenhauer *Werke*, volume V, both bear dates indicating a similar, only slightly later period of interest: "12/XII 1914," and "5/12 1914." In addition, the quotation at the head of this section, from "Problems in Teaching Art" (1911), already contains the words "feeling" and "form," "idea," and "word," the importance of which will be described below.

Schopenhauer continued to be important to Schoenberg throughout the 1920s: an unpublished manuscript in the *Nachlass* entitled "Schopenhauer und Sokrates" is dated "Potsdach, 23.VII.1927."

Oskar Adler was an important personal influence on Schoenberg's philosophy and no doubt also reinforced the latter's interest in Schopenhauer. Schoenberg acknowledged Adler as an important early influence on his philosophical thinking in the essay "My Evolution" (1949):[72]

> Through him [Oskar Adler] I learned of the existence of a theory of music, and he directed my first steps therein. He also *stimulated my interest in poetry and philosophy* and all my acquaintance with classical music derived from playing quartets with him, for even then he was already an excellent first violinist. (Emphasis added.)

Adler's personal influence has also been described by contemporaries of Schoenberg as communicating a specific interest in the philosophy of Schopenhauer. Lona Truding, one of the pianists in the *Verein für musikalische Privataufführungen*, and a student of Schoenberg's at the Schwarzwald school seminar, is recorded as saying, "Oskar Adler, Dr. Adler was a great admirer of Schopenhauer and they were all Kantians. That was the time. Yes, Kantianism hadn't died out yet."[73]

Karl Kraus, who also greatly influenced Schoenberg's philosophical, literary, and political thought,[74] has also been described as deriving his philosophical orientation from Schopenhauer. Janik and Toulmin, authors of *Wittgenstein's Vienna*, have written:[75]

> Kraus himself was no philosopher, still less a scientist. If Kraus' views have a philosophical ancestry, this comes most assuredly from Schopenhauer; for alone among the great philosophers, Schopenhauer was a kindred spirit, a man of philosophical profundity, with a strong talent for polemic and aphorism, a literary as well as philosophical genius. Schopenhauer, indeed, was the only philosopher who at all appealed to Kraus.

Schoenberg's use of his Schopenhauer volumes may be compared to the works of other philosophers represented in his library: of Kant, Schopenhauer's direct intellectual forbear, he owned practically everything: the Reclam *Sämtliche Werke* in eight volumes, plus *Kritik der reinen Verkunft*, *Kritik der Urteilskraft*, and *Prolegomena zu einer jeden Kunftigen*

Metaphysik, die als Wissenschaft wird auftreten können (also undated Reclam editions). Of Hegel, no books at all! Of Nietzsche, who admitted a great debt to Schopenhauer, several works:[76] *Der Face Wagner: Götzen Dämmerung, Nietzsche Contra Wagner, Umwertung aller Werte, Dichtungen* volume VIII (published 1904), *Das Geburt der Tragödie* volume I (published 1903), *Also Sprach Zarathustra* (published 1906), and *Gedichte und Sprüche* (published 1901). Other philosophical writings in his library included one volume of Feuerbach, *Ein Vermächtnis* (1912); several volumes of Henri Bergson; complete *Werke*, two volumes (1910), *Entweder/Oder*, 2 volumes (1911), and *Die Tagebücher*, volume II of two volumes (1923) of Søren Kierkegaard; the *Wörterbuch der Philosophischen Begriffe* by Rudolf Eisler (father of the composer Hanns Eisler), (published in Berlin in 1927 and likely acquired there); as well as Aristotle, *Nikomachische Ethik* (1909); Hippocrates, *Erkenntnisse* (1907); and Plato, eight volumes published in the years 1906–10, including *Platon Staat* (1909), which contains a bookmark and one small annotation and appears well worn.

As for the dating of the period during which Schoenberg's interest in these other philosophers began, Schoenberg's own library catalogue further confirms datings earlier than the 1920s for his reading of other philosophers. Schoenberg entered eleven volumes of Kant in the catalogue on 23 January 1913, with five of Bergson, four of Nietzsche and one of Swedenborg in 1913 as well. Feuerbach is listed with one volume, an undated entry probably made between 1915 and 1918, as deduced from surrounding entries in Schoenberg's library catalogue. (Kierkegaard is not listed, moving the probable date of purchase of the three Kierkegaard volumes in the current library to a date after 1918.) Schoenberg also made references to Nietzsche in essays dated as early as 1911,[77] also in 1922,[78] and as late as 1947.[79]

It may be seen from these data that Schoenberg's interest in Schopenhauer, Kant, and Nietzsche was well developed by 1913 (Schoenberg was then twenty-nine years old), and he had done extensive reading of other philosophers by that time as well.

What is remarkable by its absence is any evidence in Schoenberg's library of the works of Ludwig Wittgenstein (1889–1951) and his circle. While Wittgenstein's writings became available as early as 1914, there is no evidence that Schoenberg ever investigated this line of philosophical thought, although it was being developed virtually in his own backyard. The curious intermingling of philosophers, artists, and critics in Vienna at this time, and the resurgence of interest in Kant, Schopenhauer, and Kierkegaard occurring simultaneously with "modernist" movements in philosophy like logical positivism, are described in more detail in *Wittgenstein's Vienna* by Allan Janik and Stephen Toulmin.[80]

The Influence of Schopenhauer on Schoenberg

The influence of Schopenhauer on Schoenberg's thinking can be seen in several different ways. First, the influence is reflected directly in Schoenberg's own essays and philosophical writings about music and other matters. Schopenhauer's use of the Platonic Idea (*Idee*) becomes extremely important. On the basis of the documentary evidence from Schoenberg's library, it seems that it is primarily through Schopenhauer that Schoenberg became preoccupied with this concept of Idea (*Gedanke*, Platonic *Idee*, or, as in Schopenhauer, *Vorstellung*),[81] and its Representation (*Darstellung*).[82]

These concepts had become a commonplace by 1910 in virtually all fields of Viennese cultural debate,[83] and were an important environmental influence on all creative artists of the time in one way or another. The discussion of these concepts included, for example, works before 1900 by science theorists Gustav Hertz (1887–1973) and Hermann Helmholtz (1821–94), and inspired the linkage of philosophy and aesthetics with criticism of language (*Sprachkritik*) and theory of knowledge in the first decade of the twentieth century by such philosophers as Ernst Mach (1838–1916), Fritz Mauthner (1849–1923), Ernst Cassirer (1874–1945),[84] as well as Wittgenstein. Schoenberg did not own any writings by these authors, however, and there is no documentary evidence that they played a direct role in the formulation of his thoughts about Idea and Representation in the way that Schopenhauer's writings clearly did.

The Platonic Idea and its relationship to art is discussed at length by Schopenhauer:[85]

> The truth which lies at the foundation of all that we have hitherto said about art, is that the object of art, the Representation of which is the aim of the artist, and the knowledge of which must therefore precede his work as its germ and source, is an Idea in Plato's sense, and never anything else; not the particular thing, the object of common apprehension, and not the concept, the object of rational thought and of science.

Schopenhauer even develops a specific view of the purpose of music, from which the connection with Schoenberg is easily drawn:[86]

> The Platonic Ideas are the adequate objectification of will. To excite or suggest the knowledge of these by means of the Representation of particular things (for works of art are themselves always Representations of particular things) is the end of all the other arts, which can only be attained by a corresponding change in the knowing subject. Thus all these arts objectify the will indirectly only by means of the Ideas; and since our world is nothing but the manifestation of the Ideas in multiplicity, through their entrance into the principle of individuality (the form of the knowledge possible for the individual as such), music also, since it passes over the Ideas, is entirely independent of the phenomenal world, ignores it altogether, could to a certain extent exist if there was no world at all, which cannot be said

of the other arts. Music is as direct an objectification and copy of the whole will as the world itself, nay, even as the Ideas, whose multiplied manifestation constitutes the world of individual things. Music is thus by no means like the other arts, the copy of the Ideas, but the copy of the Will itself, whose objectivity the Ideas are. This is why the effect of music is so much more powerful and penetrating than that of the other arts, for they speak only of shadows, but it speaks of the thing itself.

Schoenberg adopted these constructs virtually whole. The most familiar expression of these ideas by Schoenberg in prose is the now famous essay "New Music, Outmoded Music, Style and Idea" (1946), in which the whole issue of the Idea and Representation is thrashed out. The Idea in any true art form is proclaimed as primary, and style the servant which expresses it.[87] In the same year, in "Heart and Brain in Music," Schoenberg also stated that in writing *Verklärte Nacht* he "wanted to express the *idea* behind the poem."[88] Schoenberg's essays entitled "Der musikalische Gedanke, seine Darstellung und Durchführung," and "Der musikalische Gedanke und die Logik, Technik, und Kunst seiner Darstellung," unpublished manuscripts at the Arnold Schoenberg Institute Archive, (dated "6.7.1925" and "21," "22," and "29.6.34" with an earlier outline dated "5.6.34" and a later introduction dated "Ende September 1934"),[89] reflect this artistic preoccupation with Idea and Representation.

Schoenberg dealt directly and not uncritically with Schopenhauer's "demand that the evaluation of works of art can only be based on authority" in "Criteria for the Evaluation of Music" (1946):[90]

Unfortunately he does not say who bestows authority nor how one can acquire it; nor whether it will remain uncontested, and what will happen if such an authority makes mistakes. Mistakes like his own, when he, disregarding Beethoven and Mozart, called Bellini's *Norma* the greatest opera.

Schoenberg criticized Schopenhauer's theory of music much earlier in "The Relationship to the Text" (1912), beginning the essay as follows:[91]

Even Schopenhauer, who at first says something really exhaustive about the essence of music in his wonderful thought, "The composer reveals the inmost essence of the world and utters the most profound wisdom in a language which his reason does not understand, just as a magnetic somnambulist gives disclosures about things which she has no idea of when awake"—even he loses himself later when he tries to translate details of this language *which the reason does not understand* into our terms. It must, however, be clear to him that in this translation into the terms of human language, which is abstraction, reduction to the recognizable, the essential, the language of the world, which ought perhaps to remain incomprehensible and only perceptible, is lost. But even so he is justified in this procedure, since after all it is his aim as a philosopher to represent the essence of the world, its unsurveyable wealth, in terms of concepts whose poverty is all too easily seen through.

He also referred to Schopenhauer's distinction between sorrow and sentimentality in regard to Mahler's music in his essay "Gustav Mahler" (1912;1948).[92]

> What is true feeling? But that is a question of feeling! That can only be answered by feeling! Whose feelings are right? Those of the man who disputes the true feelings of another, or those of the man who gladly grants another his true feelings, so long as he says just what he has to say? Schopenhauer explains the difference between sentimentality and true sorrow. He chooses as an example Petrarch, whom the painters of broad strokes would surely call sentimental, and shows that the difference consists in this: true sorrow elevates itself to resignation, while sentimentality is incapable of that, but always grieves and mourns, so that one has finally lost "earth and heaven together...."

Like the references to Schopenhauer in "The Relationship to the Text," the untitled essay dated "5/12 1914" inserted into volume V, *Über Religion*, of the Schopenhauer *Werke*, also indicates that while Schoenberg took Schopenhauer's writings very seriously, he did not absorb them uncritically.[93] In it, he criticizes Schopenhauer's attitude toward Judaism as careless and reflecting a personal aversion or prejudice. He criticizes very particular statements of Schopenhauer, pointing out that Judaism does not lack a messianic vision of hope, and further criticizing Schopenhauer's uncritical use of the Ahasueras myth, citing the hardships of the chosen people as evidence that Judaism continues to exist against all odds because it adheres to spiritual rather than material rewards. (The shorter inserted essay, "12/XII 1914," is a curious and misogynist excursus—acknowledged by Schoenberg himself as fanciful—expanding on a reference by Schopenhauer to jealousy, stating that male jealousy is needed to prevent women from fornicating with lower life forms and contaminating the human species!)

The 1927 unpublished essay "Schopenhauer und Sokrates" is also a critical one, accusing Schopenhauer of indefensibly dismissing Socrates as a fiction of Plato. Schoenberg argues that Schopenhauer should know that great ideas cannot always be expressed easily, and may be especially difficult to put on paper. Therefore, Socrates very likely did exist but needed Plato for expression—the very issue of Idea and Representation and the core issue of *Moses und Aron* again.

In addition to these direct references, elements of Schopenhauer's thought seem to be echoed in other writings of Schoenberg as well. Schoenberg comes close to quoting Schopenhauer's philosophy of art in a letter (ca. 1913) to Emil Hertzka about the purpose of his opera *Die Glückliche Hand*.[94]

> The whole thing should have the effect (not of a dream) but of chords. Of music. It must never suggest symbols, or meaning, or thoughts, but simply the play of colours and forms.

Just as music never drags a meaning around with it, at least not in the form in which it (music) manifests itself, even though meaning is inherent in its nature, so too this should simply be like sounds for the eye, and so far as I am concerned everyone is free to think or feel something similar to what he thinks or feels while hearing music.

A similar passage occurs in a charming letter of Schoenberg to Walter Koons of NBC, written in English in 1934. Note in addition to the definition of music, the Schopenhauerian attention to the theme of fulfillment of desires:[95]

Music is a simultaneous and a successive-ness of tones and tone combinations, which are so organized that its impression on the ear is agreeable, and its impression on the intelligence is comprehensible, and that these impressions have the power to influence occult parts of our soul and of our sentimental spheres and that this influence makes us live in a dreamland of fulfilled desires, or in a dreamed hell of ... etc., etc., ...

What is water?

H_2O; and we can drink it, and can wash us by it; and it is transparent; and has no Colour; and we can use it to swim in and to ship; and it drives mills ... etc., etc.,

I know a nice and touching story:

A blind man asks his guide: "How looks milk?"

The Guide answered: "Milk looks white."

The Blind Man: "What's that 'white'? Mention a thing which is white!"

The Guide: "A swan. It is perfect white, and it has a long white and bent neck."

The Blind Man: "A bent neck? How is that?"

The Guide, imitating with his arm the form of a swan's neck, lets the blind man feel the form of his arm.

The Blind Man (flowing softly with his hand along the arm of the Guide): "Now I know how looks milk."

The preoccupation with the Idea and its Representation is clearly written into the text of *Moses und Aron*.[96] For example, the first mention of *Gedanke* is made by Moses in connection with God: "Gott meiner Väter, Gott Abrahams, Isaaks und Jakobs, der du ihren Gedanken in mir wiedererweckt hast." ("God of my fathers, God of Abraham, Isaac and Jacob, who has reawakened their Ideas in me.") This passage may be compared to the Biblical passage from which it was drawn, Exodus 3:6: "And he [God] said, 'I am the God of your father, the God of Abraham, the God of Isaac, and the God of Jacob,' " echoed again at Ex. 3:15 and 3:16. The concept of the Idea was Schoenberg's own addition to the original Biblical material.

Schoenberg's *Wort*, or Word, is also akin to the concept of Representation or *Darstellung*. At the end of Act II in the extremely powerful moment which closes the musical portion of the opera as it was left by the composer, Moses addresses God as the Idea itself: "Unvorstellbarer Gott! Unaussprechlicher, vieldeutiger *Gedanke*!" ("Inconceivable God! Inexpressible, ambiguous Idea!") Here the nominalism of Kant and Schopenhauer loudly resonates, equating the ultimate Idea with the *noumena* which can never be directly known. In reaction to the salvation of the people in spite of their apostasy, Moses cries out in despair, "Lässt du diese Auslesung zu? Darf Aron, mein Mund, dieses *Bild* machen?..." ("Will you allow this interpretation? Is Aron, my mouth, permitted to make this Image?") The problem again is of *Gedanke* vs. *Bild*. "So habe *ich* mir ein Bild gemacht, falsch, *wie ein Bild nur sein kann!* So bin ich geschlagen! So war alles Wahnsinn, was ich gedacht habe...." ("So I have created an Image, false, as an Image can only be! So I am defeated! So all was madness that I thought before.")—the ultimate realization, that the *noumena* can never be fully known—"und kann und *darf* nicht gesagt werden! *O Wort, du Wort, das mir fehlt!*" ("and can and dares not be spoken! O Word, thou Word that I lack!")

The words of the opening formula "Einziger, ewiger, allgegenwärtiger, unsichtbarer und unvorstellbarer Gott" appear frequently throughout. Essential components of Schoenberg's personal theology, in *Moses und Aron* they take on an invocational, almost incantational quality. The words also appear periodically by themselves or in pairs, for example, "unvorstellbar-unsichtbar" in Aron's words in Act I, Scene 2, and, as nouns: "Allmächtiger" or "der Allmächtiger." Of all these adjectives, "unvorstellbar" is the best clue to the philosophical genesis of Schoenberg's own *Gottesgedank*. Together with "unsichtbar," "unvorstellbar" directly echoes the language of Schopenhauer, the concept of *Vorstellung* and *Darstellung* and the nominalist principle that nothing can be known in its essence, but only incompletely through the senses. This thought is directly expressed in the dialogue between Moses and Aron in Act I, Scene 2 in the oratorio, when Moses says "Kein Bild kann Dir ein Bild geben vom Unvorstellbaren."

Aron responds with a similar thought: "Nie wird Liebe ermüden sichs vorzubilden." Schoenberg's own religious application of this Schopen-hauerian concept is precisely in connection with the biblical idea of a Chosen People. The people are happy or blessed precisely because they can think about or contemplate and love a God which in essence is invisible and unknowable. This working out of Schopenhauer's thought and terminology through a religious, and specifically Old Testament mode, is perfectly exemplified in the following excerpt from Act I, Scene 2 in the oratorio text:

"Moses: Nur im Menschen kann Gott bekämpft werden. Nur in seiner *Vorstellung. Gott aber übertrifft jede Vorstellung.*

Aron: Gebilde der höchsten Phantasie, wie dankt sie dirs, dass Du sie reizest zu bilden.

Moses: *Kein* Bild kann Dir ein Bild machen vom Unvorstellbaren.

Aron: Nie wird die Liebe ermüden sichs vorzubilden. Glückliches Volk das so seinen Gott liebt. Auserwähltes Volk, einen einzigen Gott, ewig zu lieben mit tausendmal der Liebe mit der alle andern Volker ihre vielen Götter lieben—und sie wechseln.

Moses: Auserwähltes Volk: einen einzigen, ewigen, unvorstellbaren, allgegenwärtigen, unsichtbaren Gott zu denken.

Aron: Unvorstellbar-unsichtbar-Volk, auserwählt den einzigen zu liebe, wirst Du ihn unvorstellbar wollen, wenn schon unsichtbar?

Moses: Wollen? Kann Gott sein, dass wir ihn uns *vorstellen* können? Wenn er sichtbar ist, kann er überblickbar sein? Wenn er überblickbar wäre, also nicht unendlich kann er dann ewig sein—wenn er endlich im Raum?"

This is the central conflict of the opera, the tension between Idea (God) and Representation[97]—the long chain of increasingly inaccurate communication from God as thing-in-itself at the very opening (wordless sound, like Schopenhauer's description of music, communing directly with the *noumena*, or Will), to God speaking out of the burning bush to Moses, through Moses to Aron, and from Aron and the priests to the people.

This was not a new theme to Schoenberg. A development can be seen in Schoenberg's texts from expressionism, the portrayal of feeling, of raw emotion (either as an individual's unconscious, as in *Erwartung*, or as essences of subjective states, as in the "Ich-drama"-style of *Die Glückliche Hand*), to a more universal state—the Idea. Idea is equated in *Jakobsleiter* as well as in *Moses und Aron* with the holy, the universal. *Die Jakobsleiter* is the transitional work, its music stylistically an amalgamation of Schoenberg's pre-twelve-tone compositional techniques, its text rooted in the theosophical and Swedenborgian/Strindbergian influence described in the previous chapter.

Moses und Aron inherits that stream of development—the orgy scene still retains some of the features of the expressionistic works a decade earlier. The concept of Idea is used in this context as similar to the Platonic archetype—the artist draws from another "plane" where archetypal images are eternally pre-existent. This transcends the more lyrical heroic image of the artist in *Die Glückliche Hand*. The dilemma of all art is the unattainability of the archetype—the loss of the archetype to the concrete expression of it. It is impossible to capture the archetype in a moment, on canvas, etc. The artist's product is always something less than the unformed vision. In Schoenberg's terms, Style can hinder the Idea. The best use of style is to come as close as possible to expressing the Idea, the pre-existent reality equated with the Word, even with the Holy. Thus, in *Moses und Aron* the religious level and the level of meaning as an allegory for the creative process are drawn together as the same mystery, with the word as Idea and Holy at once.

The concept of *Gedanke* is also expounded in a similar way in *Der Biblische Weg*, Schoenberg's play about founding a new Jewish state in Israel which just preceded his work on *Moses und Aron*. As in *Moses und Aron*, Schoenberg is concerned with the invisible and inconceivable God. The hero of the play, Max Aruns, is very similar to Moses and represents a kind of Schopenhauerian genius. The ring of Schopenhauer's philosophy is heard in Aruns's and his aid Pinxar's words:[98]

> Aruns: "Our belief in an invisible and inconceivable God offers no material fulfillment...."
>
> Pinxar: "Our religion will never be a very popular one: it is too intellectual for that."
>
> Aruns: "And for this very reason, our entire history is dominated by religious struggles. Everything in this history culminates in an attempt to explain the *pure* concept of God. Everything tries to make *this* concept comprehensible and popular...."

Schoenberg links the concept of the Chosen People with this comprehension—that God *cannot* be known. The lengthy speech which concludes the play is a didactic exposition of this belief, applied to Schoenberg's vision of an ideal Jewish state, a political entity espoused to this philosophical and religious ideal:[99]

> The Jewish people lives for one Idea: the Idea of a single, immortal, eternal, and inconceivable God. Our only desire is to establish the rule of this concept. Perhaps this idea in its purest form will some day rule all the world....
>
> Our destination is that of every ancient people: we must spiritualize ourselves. We must disassociate ourselves from all material things.
>
> But there is one other goal: we must all learn to think the Idea of the one, eternal, invisible, and inconceivable God.
>
> We wish to lead our spiritual life and shall allow no one to hinder us in so doing.
>
> We wish to perfect ourselves spiritually, we wish to be permitted to dream our dream of God like all ancient peoples who have overcome materialism and left it behind them.
>
> End of the Drama

Schoenberg and Karl Kraus

Documentary Evidence

Another very important and long-lasting influence on Schoenberg, again in the period 1908–20, was Karl Kraus, an exact contemporary of Schoenberg living in Vienna.

Schoenberg himself stated in 1913 that Kraus was the primary literary figure in his own life, writing:[100]

> In der Widmung, mit der ich Karl Kraus meine "Harmonielehre" schickte, sagte ich ungefähr: "Ich habe von Ihnen vielleicht mehr gelernt, als man lernen darf, wenn man noch selbständig bleiben will...." Damit ist gewiss nicht der Umfang, wohl aber das Niveau der Schätzung festgestellt, die ich für ihn habe.

(In the dedication with which I sent Karl Kraus my *Harmonielehre* I said essentially, "I have perhaps learned more from you than one dares to learn if one still wants to remain independent...." While this is certainly not the whole of it, yet it testifies to the greatness of the esteem I have for him.)

Schoenberg also made reference to Kraus in the book itself:[101]

The mediocre person fears nothing else so much as he fears being compelled to change his view, his philosophy, of life. And he has also set up an ideal for himself, which expresses this fear: character. The man of character, that's the one (to paraphrase a saying of Karl Kraus) whose hardening of the arteries comes from his view of the world.

A manuscript in Schoenberg's own handwriting of the fourteenth song, "Sprich nicht immer von dem laub," from *The Book of the Hanging Gardens,* Op. 15, was reproduced in Kraus' literary journal *Die Fackel* in April 1910.[102] Willi Reich and H.H. Stuckenschmidt also describe occasions as early as 1909 and 1910 when Schoenberg sent material for possible publication in *Die Fackel,* which Kraus did not publish.[103] These incidents, together with the quotation in 1911 in the *Harmonielehre,* and the dedication in the copy sent to Kraus personally, represent the earliest firm documentation of Schoenberg's serious interest in Kraus, as early as the first years of publication of *Die Fackel.* Schoenberg himself was mentioned many times in the journal throughout the course of its publication: six times in connection with newspaper critics or reviews, in 1909, 1913 (twice), 1914, and as late as 1930 and 1931; four times in connection with events reported, in 1913 (twice), 1917, and 1929; as well as two special references in connection with Paul Pisk's falling out with Kraus and a subsequent letter by Eduard Steuermann.

Schoenberg makes brief references to Kraus in several essays, not only from these early years, in "Problems in Teaching Art" (1911), and "The Relationship to the Text" but also later in his life, in "Krenek's 'Sprung über den Schatten' " (1923), and the second of "Two Speeches on the Jewish Situation (1935).[104]

Schoenberg's library holdings also confirm his avid reading of Kraus. According to Stuckenschmidt, there were twelve volumes of Kraus in 1913 (exceeded only by Maeterlinck with eighteen and Strindberg with twenty-eight. Balzac was also represented with twelve.) By 1918 he had the complete works of Kraus, as well as other writers of the same circle—Peter Altenberg, Kandinsky, Kokoschka, and Otto Weininger.[105] The entry in Schoenberg's library catalogue reads [191]4 for twelve volumes of Kraus, with no additions listed at later dates.[106]

Schoenberg's personal contact with Kraus would actually have been quite limited because of the schedule Kraus kept, sleeping all day and working all night. Kokoschka described Kraus' habits in his autobiography as follows:[107]

Kraus slept during the day and worked at night. He had his dinner at the coffee house, and always followed it with innumerable cups of black coffee. It was a great mark of distinction to be invited to his table, while he went over every letter, every comma and full-stop, in an article for the next issue of *Die Fackel*. In the war years, even the blank spaces were expressive.

Rudolf Kolisch spoke of the relationship with Kraus as follows:[108]

Kolisch: Well, private relationship with Kraus was, you know, a very special and difficult matter. He slept during the day and was awake only at night, and he really didn't see anybody.... We hardly talked. They played music and Karl Kraus was eating his dinner."

Olda Kokoschka: "The circle of Karl Kraus met practically every evening because he started living in the afternoon and then went and had his dinner, and then he worked at night. And that was his circle, really, but Schoenberg of course worked differently....

Interviewer: "How do you explain that you had so much in common—that you were all getting rid of ornament in various ways?"

Oskar Kokoschka: "It was probably because we all were on the edge of society. We didn't belong to society. We were well known, well known—too well known maybe—but on the edge. We didn't belong. So we were like a disease, you know. Don't touch. So of course that makes a bond. We stuck together. Karl Kraus was a frightening figure in Vienna. No one would have dared to talk to him.... They were very frightened by his edition, *The Fackel*.... He was a cruel man, so he was frightening for the Viennese...."

The Influence of Kraus on Schoenberg

The influence of Kraus may be seen in Schoenberg's work in both style and content. Kraus' obsession was the German language. He saw purity of culture in purity of language, and decay of culture in decadence of language. Allying himself with what Adolf Loos was trying to do in architecture, he wrote:[109]

Adolf Loos and I—he literally and I grammatically—have done nothing more than show that there is a distinction between an urn and a chamber pot, and that it is this distinction above all that provides culture with elbow room. The others, those who fail to make this distinction, are divided into those who use the urn as a chamberpot and those who use the chamberpot as an urn.

Kraus' sharpest attacks were directed at the press, particularly *Die Neue Freie Presse* for the pretentiousness of its *feuilleton* writers—including Schnitzler, Stefan Zweig, and another friend of Schoenberg's, Hermann Bahr.[110] Other objects of his attacks were Freud and psychoanalysis, sensationalism in the theater, the operettas of Franz Lehar (like Paul Bekker, he advocated didacticism in theater), women—especially feminists, mysticism, and hypocrisy or pretentiousness of every kind.

A similarity in style was remarked upon by Max Deutsch in an interview in which he linked Schoenberg and Kraus, as well as Peter Altenberg and Adolf Loos, as being the only four thinkers to express themselves, within their respective fields, in the particular literary manner promulgated by Kraus.[111] Kraus' great concern for language was appreciated by Schoenberg, who referred twice to Kraus' phrase, "language, mother of the idea" in "Problems in Teaching Art,"[112] and "The Relationship to the Text."[113]

Kraus wrote extremely long and complicated sentences and paragraphs especially in his longer essays and plays. Like the philosopher in the next generation, Adorno, he believed that difficult thoughts should be expressed in an equally complicated manner to convey their seriousness. But Kraus equally loved to write pithy aphorisms. For example,[114]

"My son is not doing well. He is a mystic."

"Education is what most receive, many pass on and a few possess."

"I saw a terrible apparition: an encyclopedia walked toward a polyhistor and looked him up."

"Much knowledge has room in an empty head."

Both styles may be found in Schoenberg's writing. Schoenberg even wrote a series of aphorisms for publication in *Die Fackel*, but these were among the submissions which Kraus did not publish.[115] The stiff, didactic language of Kraus' play *Die Letzten Tage der Menschheit* (The Last Days of Humanity) is echoed in Schoenberg's play *Der Biblische Weg*. In both plays, ideologies are exposed and debated in a very unconversational style. Political and philosophical truths, according to the authors, are spoken by the characters in long, formal speeches even within dialogues.

The word play which Kraus loved is reflected in the letter of Schoenberg to Koons, cited above in connection with Schopenhauer. Here Schoenberg uses the Krausian trick of metamorphosizing language in order to illuminate an idea more fully.

In *Moses und Aron* and *Der Biblische Weg,* as in Kraus' *Letzten Tage,* the dialogue is in a very formal style, using the characters as mouthpiece for ideologies. Moses' words to Aron, for example, are always didactic.

The concept of purification which occurs throughout *Moses und Aron* and *Der Biblische Weg* also reflects Kraus' sense of prophetic mission. A Jew by birth, Kraus had an intense love-hate relationship with Judaism: he hated the Jewish intellectuals like Stefan Zweig the most because he considered them most dangerous, but loved the prophetic and ethical side of the Jewish tradition. Like Schoenberg, he formally left Judaism in 1899. He later even converted to Catholicism in 1911, until 1922 when he left the church in protest over its involvement with the Salzburg Festival.[116] But the particular mark of Judaism on Kraus is well worth noting, since it is very similar to the highly personal brand of Jewish faith which Schoenberg developed by the 1920s:[117]

> The accusation of anti-Semitism has often been leveled against Kraus. With equal justice the prophets of the Old Testament could have been so accused for castigating the Israelites who worshipped the Golden Calf. Born into a Jewish family, Kraus was highly sensitive to the moral conduct of Jews, particularly journalists. He considered Jewish journalists more talented, and therefore more dangerous, than their gentile colleagues—an accurate observation in the Vienna of his time. He actually berated them for being better at nourishing anti-Semitism than combatting it. Yet Kraus affirms, speaking of himself, that "in reverence" to ravished life and befouled language he is gratefully aware of the vital strength of an uncompromisable Judaism he deeply loves. He sees it as resting in itself, between troglodytes and profiteers.
>
> Despite his eagerness to assimilate to German culture, despite his hatred of the forces of materialism with which so many Jewish intellectuals associated themselves—forces hostile to esthetic and spiritual values—Kraus in many ways remained intensely Jewish. His vision of language was the specifically Jewish concept of the revelation of the will of God through the word, the word that brings to pass what it says. Kraus's relationship to language was of a magical and religious character. He firmly believed in preestablished harmony of word and world. He had the gift of letting the spirit of language, as it were, think for him, and would then follow it into the labyrinth like a somnambulist. "I have drawn out of language many a thought I did not have or could not put into words." Language for him was the divining rod that locates the springs of thought, the key to bringing order out of chaos.

This almost religious concern for language resembles the concepts of Idea and Representation, and has a strong parallel in *Moses und Aron* in Schoenberg's conception of the Word. In *Moses und Aron*, Aron and the Volk represent a tendency toward embellishment and spectacle similar to that of the Viennese society—in the original Bible story it is God who performs the miracles, to convince Moses and the people (Ex. 4:1–9). In Schoenberg's opera, it is Aron who tears the rod away from Moses to give the people the miracles they want. In *Der Biblische Weg* the same problem is expounded more explicitly:[118]

> Just point out a miracle to people of your kind, and they immediately doubt it and demand to see it. But as soon as you show it to them, it's no longer a miracle—or, at most, it's a technical one. "And Moses struck upon the rock twice with his staff." It's much easier for you to believe that water began to flow when Moses struck the stones, than it would be if he had only *spoken to them*.

Schoenberg was still preoccupied with this precise thought—the contradiction between the two versions of the miracle of water from the rock in Exodus 17:6 and in Numbers 20:8 in a letter dated 15 March 1933 to Walter Eidlitz, author of *Der Berg in der Wüste*.[119]

My third act, which I am working over again, not to say rewriting, for at least the fourth time, is for the present still called: "Aaron's Death." Here I have so far encountered great difficulties because of some almost incomprehensible contradictions in the Bible. For even if there are comparatively few points on which I adhere strictly to the Bible, still, it is precisely here that it is difficult to get over the divergence between: "and thou shalt smite the rock" and: "speak ye unto the rock"! You have worked on this material for so long: can you perhaps tell me where I could look up something on this question? Up to now I have been trying to find a solution for myself. As for my drama itself, I can manage even without solving this problem. Still, it does go on haunting me!

The Golden Calf scene similarly represents the gaudy materialism of the age, as much as it also represents Schopenhauer's concept of concrete objectification of the Will. So, Schoenberg also had a contemporary didactic message incorporated into the text for *Moses und Aron*, expressed in a lecturing manner through the mouths of his characters. The very central conflict of the drama, the faulty communication between God, the ultimate Idea, and the medium of Representation (in Schopenhauerian terms), is very close to Kraus' concern with the pollution of language reflecting the decay of culture and society. For both Kraus and Schoenberg, the concepts of Idea and Representation are closely related to the formation of a cultural ethic, where art is exalted, as the truest medium of the Idea, rather than a decadent objectification of style for its own sake. Where the Word is no longer heard or understood, it can no longer be lived.

The 1920s: Schoenberg and Judaism

It was only on the 1st October that my going to America became definite enough for me to believe it myself. What was in the newspapers before than and since is fantasy, just like the alleged ceremonies and the presence of "tout Paris" on the occasion of what is called my return to the Jewish religion. (*Tout Paris* consisted, apart from the rabbi and myself, of: my wife and a certain Dr. Marianoff, presumably the source of all these sensational stories.) As you have doubtless realised, *my return to the Jewish religion took place long ago and is indeed demonstrated in some of my published work* ("Thou shalt not . . . Thou shalt") and in "Moses and Aaron", of which you have known since 1928, but which dates from at least five years earlier; but especially in my drama "Der biblische Weg" which was also conceived in 1922 or '23 at the latest, though finished only in '26–'27. (Emphasis added)

This letter to Berg of 16 October 1933 was Schoenberg's comment on an event which sealed a long period of religious development, which had begun at least as early as the 1920s: his formal re-entry into the Jewish community and his public reaffirmation of his identity as a Jew. Why did this change occur in the early 1920s?

Certain specific events ca. 1922–23, as well as the increasing anti-Semitic climate in Germany and Austria in general in this period, certainly raised Schoenberg's awareness of his own Jewish heritage. Alexander Ringer has already described in detail the growth of anti-Semitism in Schoenberg's environment, and the specific historical events through the 1920s which could not have escaped Schoenberg's attention. These included the formation (as early as 1907) under the leadership of Karl Lueger of an anti-Semitic Christian Socialist caucus in Vienna; the Waidhofen Manifesto (1912) barring Jewish students from German and Austrian student organizations; and the *Judenzählung* in the Army begun October 1916, just before Schoenberg's second period of military service.[120]

More important, Ringer also describes key specific events which forced Schoenberg to confront the issue of anti-Semitism directly and personally— probably the initial shock came in relation to an unpleasant scene in the Salzburg resort Mattsee, when Schoenberg and his family were "given to understand that Jews were not welcome."[121] It affected him so, that he wrote to Kandinsky on 4 May 1923:[122]

> Must not Kandinsky have an inkling of what really happened when I had to break off my first working summer for five years, leave the place I had sought out peace to work in, and afterwards couldn't regain the peace of mind to work at all?

In a letter about two weeks earlier, Schoenberg also refused Kandinsky's offer to join him in Weimar at the Bauhaus, where he heard from Alma Mahler that there were incidents of bigotry, and he attacked Kandinsky as an anti-Semite as well. He wrote:[123]

> For I have learnt the lesson that has been forced upon me this year, and I shall not ever forget it. It is that I am not a German, not a European, indeed perhaps scarcely even a human being (at least, the Europeans prefer the worst of their race to me), but I am a Jew.
>   I am content that it should be so!...

In these two letters Schoenberg argued forcefully against the anti-Jewish prejudice which he observed spreading through Germany and Austria. In the second letter he also accurately predicted that anti-Semitic actions would not stop with the restrictions on social and civil liberties:[124]

> What is antisemitism to lead to if not acts of violence? Is it so difficult to imagine that? You are perhaps satisfied with depriving Jews of their civil rights. Then certainly Einstein, Mahler, I, and many others, will have to be got rid of. But one thing is certain: they will not be able to exterminate those much tougher elements thanks to whose endurance Jewry has maintained itself unaided against the whole of mankind for twenty centuries. For these are evidently so constituted that they can accomplish the task their God has imposed on them: to service in exile, uncorrupted and unbroken, until the hour of salvation comes!

Although Schoenberg's formal re-entry into the Jewish community did not occur until 1933, precipitated by Hitler's rise to power and Schoenberg's subsequent dismissal from the Academy in Berlin and emigration from

Germany, by ca. 1922 Schoenberg's wide-ranging quest in both musical and philosophical realms had ended with a sense of arrival and a sense of matured fulfillment of personal destiny. No doubt prompted by personal confrontation with prejudice and rejection as both an artist and a person, his faith had acquired a critical, independent, and more self-authored stance, representing a further developmental shift to a high level of moral reasoning and a more dialectical and complex world view.[125]

It is probably no coincidence that the most often remarked-upon change in Schopenhauer's musical style, the emergence of twelve-tone serialism ca. 1922 out of a period of very limited compositional activity, took place roughly at the same time as this open reaffirmation of Jewish faith. It has been seen that neither arrival—musical or religious—was precipitous or unprepared. The experimentation with cellular construction in such pieces as the Op. 11 Piano Pieces and the tight motivic construction of *Die Glückliche Hand*, were important in leading to the twelve-tone system—itself a system of manipulating larger motivic segments and deriving themes from the tightly organized serial context. So did Schoenberg's choices of texts progress from an early concern with the dichotomy between the material and the spiritual, as in the George text of the Second String Quartet, *Herzgewächse*, *Die Glückliche Hand*, through the openly religious search in *Die Jakobsleiter*, and finally to the outright statement of Jewish faith identity, stimulated all the more by an increasing awareness of anti-Semitism in his environment, in the play *Der Biblische Weg* and the opera *Moses und Aron*.

This quality of sureness, once achieved ca. 1922, was retained in both Schoenberg's music and his religious thinking throughout the rest of his life. Rather than seeking further for newer and newer ways to say what he found was his belief, both in music and in religion, he devoted his energies to expressing more and more fully the truths at which he had finally arrived. And in both realms, he followed his own vision with the sureness and zeal of a lawgiver and prophet, certain that the quest was over and the promised land was in sight.

In the twelve-tone compositions from Op. 23 onward certain consistent compositional techniques may be observed and catalogued in a quite systematic way—as Leibowitz and others have demonstrated.[126] So, too, can certain consistent elements in Schoenberg's own personal brand of Judaism be identified as having reached full flower in the 1920s, and be seen in his texts, literary writings, and letters thereafter.

To reiterate from chapter 1, 1922 was the year of Schoenberg's letter to Kandinsky, in which he refers back to the period of *Die Jakobsleiter*.[127]

> When one's been used, where one's own work was concerned, to clearing away all obstacles often by means of one immense intellectual effort and in those 8 years found oneself constantly faced with new obstacles against which all thinking, all power of invention, all energy, all ideas, proved helpless, for a man for whom ideas have been everything it means

nothing less than the total collapse of things, unless he has come to find support, in ever increasing measure, in belief in something higher, beyond. You would, I think, see what I mean best from my libretto "Jacob's Ladder" (an oratorio): what I mean is—even though without any organisational fetters—religion. This was my one and only support during those years—here let this be said for the first time. (20 July 1922)

It was in December of the same year that Schoenberg wrote to Marya Freund, "I have never at any time in my life been anti-religious, indeed, have never really been unreligious either.... [128]

The three works mentioned in the letter to Berg, October 1933, with which this chapter began, represent the first expression of the earliest full formulation of Schoenberg's Jewish beliefs, which he incorporated into all his writings with remarkable consistency from that time until his death. The earliest of these to actually be put into writing were the *Vier Stücke für gemischten Chor*, Op. 27, which made use of two texts by Schoenberg and two texts by Chinese poets, translated by Bethge. The two Schoenberg poems, particularly No. 2 cited in the letter, "Du sollst nicht ... du musst" contain important religious themes: [129]

1.
Unentrinnbar

Tapfere sind solche, die Taten vollbringen, an die ihr Mut nicht heranreicht.

Sie besitzen nur die Kraft, den Auftrag zu konzipieren und den Charakter, ihn nicht abweisen zu können.

War ein Gott noch so ungnädig, ihnen Erkenntnis ihrer Lage zu gewähren, dann sind sie nicht zu beneiden.

Und darum werden sie beneidet!

2.
Du Sollst Nicht, Du Musst

Du sollst dir kein Bild machen!
Denn ein Bild schränkt ein,
begrenzt, fasst,
was unbegrenzt und unvorstellbar bleiben soll.

Ein Bild will Namen haben:
Du kannst ihn nur vom Kleinen nehmen;
Du sollst das Kleine nicht verehren!

Du musst an den Geist glauben!
Unmittelbar, gefühllos
und selbstlos.
Du musst, Auserwählter, musst, willst du's bleiben!

The only known sources for these pieces are single drafts, from September and October of 1925, respectively. [130]

Extant sources for *Der Biblische Weg* date from the following year.[131] The play is not only an expression of a religious vision, but a political (i.e., Zionist) statement about the formation of a separatist Jewish state of Israel as well. It is also a very strong statement of personal Jewish identity made long before Schoenberg's formal re-entry into the Jewish community.

Alexander Ringer links the conception of this play with a request made to Schoenberg by editor Rudolf Seiden for a contribution to a Viennese anthology of essays entitled *Pro Zion*. Ringer suggests that Schoenberg's work on this essay precipitated his direct interest and involvement in Zionism. Ringer also suggests that the hero of the play, Max Aruns, was actually modeled after the militant Zionist activist Vladimir Jabotinsky.[132] In the 1930s, Schoenberg continued to devote thought to the idea of a Zionist state in Palestine, as demonstrated in his "Four Point Program for Jewry," written in November 1938.[133]

The themes presented in the Op. 27 texts and more fully expounded in *Der Biblische Weg* were finally expressed at length in *Moses und Aron*. The main theological ideas which made up Schoenberg's religious thought from this period onward, drawn from his texts written in the 1920s, will now be examined.

The first of these theological concepts is that of the idea of the holy as inconceivable. This embodies the concepts of Idea and Representation in its theological form—the conflict of the inexpressible God-idea or Noumena with the possibility of revelation through word and image. An example of this may be seen in Op. 27, No. 2 (cited above). It is present again in "Einziger, ewiger, allgegenwärtiger, unsichtbarer und unvorstellbarer Gott!" (the opening of *Moses und Aron*); and in the final speech of *Der Biblische Weg*, where it is stated that "The Jewish people lives for one idea: the idea of a single, immortal, eternal and inconceivable God."[134]

The awareness of God may come through direct revelation, as in Moses' encounter with the Burning Bush, or by a slowly dawning intuition or instinct, particularly in modern times: "aus uns, im Masseninstinkt spricht für einen Gott, für andere der Urustand." (Op. 35, No. 3 "Ausdrucksweise"). Schoenberg, in a letter to Dehmel on 13 December 1912, discusses this notion:[135]

> ... modern man, having passed through materialism, socialism, and anarchy, and despite having been an atheist, still having in him some residue of ancient faith (in the form of superstition), wrestling with God... and finally succeeds in finding God and becoming religious. Learning to pray!

A second important theological concept of Schoenberg's religious thought is that of the prophetic call. Once revelation has occurred, refusal to accept the accompanying calling as a consequence of enlightenment is impossible. This notion is exemplified in "Du hast die Greuel gesehn, die Wahrheit erkannt: so kannst du nicht anders mehr: du musst dein Volk befrein!" (*Moses und Aron*, I, i); and can also be seen in "Du sollst nicht, du musst," cited above on page 84.

A third notion central to Schoenberg's Jewish consciousness was the idea of the exaltation of God's chosen people, and the price they would pay for salvation due to the incomprehension and envy of others. This is one of the earliest themes in Schoenberg's thinking about Judaism, reflected in the unpublished essay inserted into the Schopenhauer *Werke*, volume V (1914), in which he refuted the popular idea that Jews were materialistic by pointing out that they struggled endlessly with only hope of a spiritual, not material reward.[136] The letter to Kandinsky of 4 May 1923 also contained a description of the Jews' task, imposed by God, as "service in exile, uncorrupted and unbroken, until the hour of salvation comes!"[137]

In a lighter vein, Schoenberg wrote in "Brahms the Progressive" (1947),[138]

> Our Lord is an extremely good chess player. He usually plans billions of moves ahead, and that is why it is not easy to understand Him. It seems, however, that He likes helping in their spiritual problems those he has selected—though not enough in their more material ones.

The nuance of the German word "auserwählt" is, more precisely, "chosen *out*," which relates to the prophetic call. There are several manifestations of this idea in Schoenberg's texts of the 1920s, for example, the character "der Auserwählte" in *Die Jakobsleiter*. "*Du musst an den Geist glauben!... Du musst*, Auserwählter, musst, willst du's bleiben!" (Op. 27, No. 2) also illustrates this concept; as does "Dieses Volk ist auserwählt vor allen Völkern, das Volk des einzigen Gottes zu sein, dass es ihn erkenne, und sich ihm allein ganz widme: dass es alle Prüfungen bestehe, denen in Jahrtausenden der Gedanke ausgesetzt ist." (*Moses und Aron*, I, i). Yet another example of this idea of the chosen people may be observed in "War ein Gott noch so ungnädig, ihnen Erkenntnis ihrer Lage zu gewähren, dann sind sie nicht zu beneiden. Und darum werden sie beneidet!" (Op. 27, No. 1).

The concept of the Promised Land is also an important one in Schoenberg's religious thought. The people will be freed and led to the promised land by grace, at the cost of their suffering and their worship of the unknowable God. This notion is seen in *Moses und Aron* (I, i): "Und das verheisse ich dir: ich will euch dorthin führen, wo ihr mit dem Ewigen einig und allen Völkern ein Vorbild werdet." Essential to Schoenberg's concept of the Promised Land, however, is that it is not tangible or real, as a geographical place, but rather it is a state of being, made present by faith—"ein unwirkliches Land, wo Milch und Honig fliesst." This is critically different from the usual literal interpretation of the biblical promise of God to the patriarchs—crucial to Zionism—that they would be given the actual land of Canaan. We see this belief in *Moses und Aron* (III), when Schoenberg writes:

> Da begehrtest du leiblich, wirklich, mit Füssen zu betreten ein unwirkliches Land, wo Milch und Honig fliesst. Da schlugst du auf den Felsen, statt zu ihm zu sprechen, wie die befohlen, dass Wasser aus ihm fleisse... Aus dem nackten Felsen sollte das Wort Erquickung schlagen. . . .

A fifth important component of Schoenberg's religious philosophy is the idea of the Law. Obedience to God's commandments is the rule of life. God was sometimes thought of by Schoenberg as the Supreme Commander, as in "Composition with Twelve Tones" (1941).[139] An example of this may be seen in *Sechs Stücke für Männerchor*, Op. 35 (1930), No. 2, which is entitled "Das Gesetz," with text:[140]

> Dass es ein Gesetz gibt, dem die Dinge so gehorchen, wie du deinem Herrn, das den Dingen so gebietet, wie dir dein Herr: Dieses solltest du als Wunder erkennen! Dass einer sich auflehnt ist eine banale Selbstverständlichkeit.

The entire poem of Op. 27, No. 2 is a reinterpretation of the Mosaic commandments. The commandment to believe in an unknowable God which cannot be portrayed in names and images becomes the central law in Schoenberg's religious understanding. This is not inconsistent with the first three of the ten commandments in Ex. 20:3–4a, and 7a, which are the commandments meant to set forth humanity's proper relationship to God: "You shall have no other gods before me. You shall not make for yourself a graven image, or any likeness of anything that is in heaven above, or that is in the earth beneath, or that is in the water under the earth... You shall not take the Name of the Lord in vain."[141] The centrality of the mystery, the command to believe in the intangible, however, is Schoenberg's own emphasis, bearing Schopenhauer's stamp, on the unknowability of God.

Specific ethical commandments do not appear in Schoenberg's writings. Even the commandment to love God and one's neighbor is subsumed under the commandment to believe in the intangible God-idea. There is a hint of predestination in the language of *Moses und Aron*, which may relate to the idea of the chosen people. God's grace cannot be bought by acts or offerings, but only granted through recognition of the mysterious nature of God. Schoenberg demonstrates this idea as follows:

> Moses: Gnade schenkt dir aus Erkenntnis. (*Moses und Aron*, I, ii)
>
> Aron: Gerechter Gott: Du belohnst die, die deinen Geboten gehorchen!

Moses: Gerechter Gott: *Du hast gerichtet* wie alles geschehen soll... Gebührt dem Lohn, der gern anders möchte? Oder dem, der nichts andres vermag?

Aron: Du erhörst die Bitten der Armen, nimmst an die Opfer der Guten!

Moses: Allmächtiger Gott, *dich erkauften die Opfer der Armen, die du arm gemacht hast?* *Reinige dein Denken, lös es von Wertlosem, weihe es Wahrem; kein andrer Gewinn dankt deinem Opfer.* (*Moses und Aron*, I, ii; emphasis added.)

There is no punishment, but rather God demands a price for salvation, which all cannot endure to pay:

Aron: Du strafst die Sünden der Väter an den Kindern und Kindeskindern!

Moses: Strafst du? Sind wir fähig, zu verursachen, *was dich zu Folgen nötigt?* (*Moses und Aron*, I, ii)

Aron: Willst du mich morden?

Moses: Es geht nicht um dein Leben....

Moses: Gebt ihn frei, und wenn er es vermag, so lebe er.
(Aron frei, steht auf und fällt tot um.)
(*Moses und Aron*, III)

Alexander Ringer has written further on how Schoenberg's concept of Law relates to form in musical composition, as well as functioning as a moral principle.[142] For example, "the ancient 'eternal' laws of musical aesthetics" are discussed in "My Evolution."[143]

The final aspect of Schoenberg's religious philosophy is the concept of prayer as central to faith. While humanity can never come to know God in essence, the struggle to believe must be kept alive, by means of prayer as an active wrestling with the inconceivable God-idea, so uncongenial to the human mind which seeks to know with certainty. In the letter to Dehmel (December 1912) Schoenberg writes, "...Modern man...wrestles with God...and finally succeeds in finding God and becoming religious. Learning to pray!" He also writes in *Die Jakobsleiter:*[144]

Learn to pray: for "he who prays has become one with God" [quoted from Balzac's *Seraphita*]. Only his wishes separate him still from his goal. But this union must not cease, and will not be invalidated by your faults. The Eternal One, your God, is no jealous God of revenge, but a God who reckons with your imperfections, to whom your inadequacy is known, who realizes that you must falter and that your road is long. He listens to you on your way; you are eternally in His hand, guided, watched over and protected in spite of your free will, bound to Him in spite of your evil desire for sin, loved by Him—if you know how to pray. Learn to pray: knock, and the door will be opened to you. [quoted from the New Testament, Matthew 7:7]

The importance of prayer in Schoenberg's thought is most completely and poignantly rendered in later years in the first of his *Moderne Psalmen*, written in September 1950, within a year of his death:[145]

Psalm No. 1

O, du mein Gott: alle Völker preisen dich und versichern dich ihrer Ergebenheit.

Was aber kann es dir bedeuten, ob ich das auch tue oder nicht?

Wer bin ich, dass ich glauben soll, mein Gebet sei eine Notwendigkeit?

Wenn ich Gott sage, weiss ich, dass ich damit von dem Einzigen, Ewigen, Allmächtigen, Allwissenden und Unvorstellbaren spreche, von dem ich mir ein Bild weder machen kann noch soll.

An den ich keinen Anspruch erheben darf oder kann, der mein heissestes Gebet erfüllen oder nicht beachten wird.

Und trotzdem bete ich, wie alles Lebende betet;

trotzdem erbitte ich Gnaden und Wunder;

Erfüllungen.

Trotzdem bete ich, denn ich will nicht des beseligenden Gefühls der Einigkeit, der Vereinigung mit dir, verlustig werden.

O du mein Gott, deine Gnade hat uns das Gebet gelassen, als eine Verbindung mit Dir. Als eine Seligkeit, die uns mehr gibt, als jede Erfüllung. (29 September 1950; emphasis added)

We have seen that the roots of these ideas, and how Schoenberg arrived at them, may be sought not only in Jewish Scripture and tradition (which provided the rich mythic imagery for their expression), and in the Schopenhauerian epistemology, which provided the rational basis for their formulation, but also the profoundly disturbing social and political pressures against Jews by the 1920s which culminated in the Holocaust.[146]

Schoenberg's vision may be seen as prophetic, not only in his recognition of the seriousness of the persecutions occurring all about him, but also in his finding a personal answer to the theological problems raised by such suffering. He viewed it as necessary to accept suffering as the price demanded by God for salvation rather than as punishment for sins against an ethical law, and to acquiesce, in the face of incomprehensible evil and horror, to the incomprehensibility and mystery of a God who can be only dimly understood as the presence of a Transcendent, wholly beyond the power of names or images to comprehend. Schoenberg's faith was ultimately responsive to this pressing question of theodicy. The last of the characteristics of Schoenberg's religious thought, prayer, then, is seen as the correct human response to the problem of evil—the only possible active sign, during a time of persecution and hardship, of patiently awaiting an as yet incomprehensible liberation and fulfillment of divine promise.

3

The Text of *Moses und Aron*

Sources of the Text

Schoenberg's text to *Moses und Aron*, like *Der Biblische Weg*, is a highly personal blend of religious polemic and poetry. As described in chapter 2, it is seriously and scrupulously wrought in a style resembling that of Karl Kraus' *Die Letzten Tage der Menschheit*; and it reflects the themes of Schoenberg's Judaism which incorporated the nominalism of Schopenhauer and the importance of prayer and direct confrontation with the divine.

The work fits into a wider context of many biblical dramatic pieces and literary works by authors in the second and third decades of the century. Among these are Strindberg's *Jacob Wrestling* (1897), *To Damascus* (1912), and *Cosmic Trilogy* (1922), which included *Moses, Socrates,* and *Christ*; Kokoschka's *Brennende Dornbusch* (1917); and Walter Eidlitz's *Der Berg in der Wüste* (1923). Schoenberg owned and read not only the Strindberg works, but also was familiar with Eidlitz's work, having received a copy of it and *Kampf im Zwielicht*, a collection of poems, from the author himself in 1933.[1] Schoenberg also owned the Kokoschka work *Der Brennende Dornbusch* in an edition which included *Mörder: Hoffnung der Frauen*. This was also presumably a gift of the author, and had a dedication on the title page.

While Schoenberg mostly refrained from direct biblical quotations, the Bible nevertheless did serve as important inspiration. This was acknowledged in his letter to Eidlitz, where he appears troubled about seeming inconsistencies in the biblical narrative.[2] Biblical sources for the broad outline of the narrative, while not used verbatim, are Exodus 3–4 (the calling of Moses and God's promise; Exodus 20–31 (the giving of the law through Moses); Exodus 32 (the exodus from Egypt, falling away from God, and the Golden Calf); Numbers 20 and 24 (Moses barred from the Promised Land),[3] as well as the conflicting passages concerning Moses's striking the rock instead of speaking to it (Exodus 17:6 and Numbers 20:8), which particularly plagued Schoenberg in his work on Act III.

The biblical commandment against making false images and the proscriptions against Canaanitic idol worship provide the central theme of the opera, transformed from the biblical historical/religious context into the philosophical theme of the ineffability of God, defying all representation, all attempts to capture God in *Bilder.* This is very close to the original biblical context itself: God's enigmatic response to Moses's request for a name is "YHWH"—"I am what/who I am" (Ex. 3:14)—a non-name, beyond definition. Similarly, the mysterious "man" who wrestles with Jacob at the ford of the Jabok evades telling Jacob his name by saying "Why is it that you ask my name?" (Gen. 32:22–32).[4]

In his letter to Berg just after beginning the musical sketches (5 August 1930), Schoenberg himself described how he made use of the Bible in writing the libretto, and he acknowledged the relationship of his work to literary precedents.[5]

> So I also appreciate (your hint in your last letter, evidently meant to warn me in good time) that you are still anxious about my "Moses and Aaron." I suppose, because you have seen some similarity to some other work treating the same subject; something to which, as you write, thinking of Strindberg. A whole year ago I looked into that play for this reason. There is in fact a certain similarity in so far as we both go in for somewhat Biblical language and even use many outright quotations. As a matter of fact I am now, among other revisions, removing these Biblical echoes. Not because of the likeness to Strindberg; that wouldn't matter: but because I am of the opinion that the language of the Bible is mediaeval German, which, being obscure to us, should be used at most to give colour; and that is something I don't need. I cannot suppose, considering your thoroughness and the confidence that I am sure you have in my inventive gifts, that you have found any other similarity. I don't at the moment remember what idea Strindberg was presenting. But mine, both my main idea and the many, many subsidiary ideas literally and symbolically presented, is all so much tied up with my own personality that it is impossible for Strindberg to have presented anything that could have even an external similarity. You would have been sure to find this on looking through the work again, all the more if—which is, after all, as you know, absolutely necessary with my work—you had looked at every word and every sentence from several points of view. Today I can scarcely remember what belongs to me: but one thing must be granted me (I won't let myself be deprived of it): Everything I have written has a certain inner likeness to myself.

Comparison of Oratorio Draft and Published Libretto

Introduction to the Oratorio Draft DICH[tung] 20

A chronology of text sources has been constructed in the course of analyzing the genesis of *Moses und Aron* in chapter 1. (See Table 1 for summary.) The first mention of the work, in the letter to Webern of 1926, was as a projected "Kantate" entitled "Moses am brennenden Dornbusch;"[6] and when actual work on the text began, it was as an "Oratorium." It has been seen that

Schoenberg's work on the text through the completion of the music of Acts I and II in 1932 occurred in essentially two periods. The first of these periods comprises work on the oratorio version, from the time of *Der Biblische Weg*, ca. 1927 to the "DICH[tung] 20" typescript, the typed version of the text manuscript dated 3–16 October 1928. The second of these periods occurs when the work became an opera (after a hiatus of a year and a half), beginning with handwritten corrections to "DICH[tung] 20" and transferring to the *Kompositionsvorlage*, the working text draft during the period of musical composition from ca. July 1930 to March 1932, with final clean typescripts from March 1932 of Acts I and II. Further work on the text of Act III continued sporadically in 1934 and 1935, after which time it was apparently abandoned.

These two periods suggest a good comparison for an examination of the nature of the changes in both form and content between Schoenberg's oratorio and is operatic conception of the work. The typedraft DICH[tung] 20 represents the completion of the first layer of work on the text, the final oratorio version before Schoenberg began composing the music. The very act of musical composition caused him to make many revisions in both the broad concept and outline, and the small details of the work. As such, the version represented by DICH[tung] 20, with attention to the earlier typed layer associated most cleanly with the dated 1928 manuscript, is the logical choice for a comparison with the final published opera version. An analysis of the oratorio draft answers two important questions: first, how does the oratorio conform to characteristics of the oratorio genre as it was known by the late nineteenth/early twentieth centuries; and, second, what elements in the early oratorio draft already suggest a more operatic conception of the work?

The Oratorio Draft as an Oratorio

The oratorio version generally conforms to the formal structure of a nineteenth century dramatic oratorio, such as Mendelssohn's *Elijah*, which will be useful to illustrate some specific analogies. In choosing *Elijah* as an example for specific comparison, it is not implied that Schoenberg was directly modeling *Moses und Aron* on the Mendelssohn work in any way. *Die Jakobsleiter*, Schoenberg's own prior experiment with oratorio form, and the large-scale choral work *Gurrelieder* both stand as more immediate precedents for an oratorio on the story of Moses and Aaron. Rather, the choice is useful because it stands as the main link in nineteenth-century composition between Schoenberg's opus and earlier oratorios. Schoenberg certainly would have known the work, as it remained firmly in the standard concert repertoire from the time of its composition, representing then as it does now the distillation of the Baroque oratorio into nineteenth-century musical form and language. No other piece composed between *Elijah* and *Moses und Aron* presents itself as such a normative model. Also, the two stories have some intrinsic similarities, since in both cases in the Bible a prophet of God—Yahweh—must combat orgiastic worship of false (i.e., Canaanitic) gods.

Moses und Aron was not Schoenberg's first essay into the genre of oratorio: his *Jakobsleiter* occupied him ten to fifteen years earlier than his first work on *Moses und Aron*. The choice of oratorio as the medium for presenting the Moses story was a natural one, given the tradition of the oratorio from the Baroque period onward as the proper way to treat a Biblical subject dramatically.

The work that Schoenberg had in mind by 1928 conforms with the Baroque three-act oratorio format. Part I portrays the calling of Moses, then Aron, and then the people, and concludes with God's blessing and promises. Part II contains the central action—the breaking of the covenant by the people and the fall into idolatry; and Part III dramatizes the judgment, the re-establishment of the covenant, the deaths of Moses and Aron, and the redirection of the people toward the Promised Land. The form of the oratorio *Moses und Aron* may be outlined as follows:

Part I

Scene 1: Moses's dialogue with the Burning Bush;
God blesses the people from the Burning Bush.

Scene 2: Moses and Aron in dialogue, Moses correcting Aron, with a concluding duet.

Scene 3: The people (soloists and small groups) talk about Moses and Aron.
They see Moses and Aron approach (verse form).
Moses addresses the people and Aron interprets.
Aron performs wonders; the people react;
Aron explains the wonders in "sermons."
Final choral hymn: "Führe uns aus dem Land der Greuel!"

Part II

Scene 1: The people confront Aron with Moses's absence;
Aron allows them to have their old gods back.

Scene 2: Chorus sings "Juble, freue dich, Israel!"

Scene 3: Offerings to the Golden Calf—choral soloists;
Hymn of the Seventy Elders, "Heilig ist das Volk."
Choral hymn "Götter, Bilder unsres Auges und unsrer Phantasie...."

Scene 4: People see Moses approach.
Moses enters.

Scene 5: Moses confronts Aron; dialogue.

Scene 6: Resolution;
        Choral hymn "Ewiger, gütiger, allmächtiger Gott...."

Part III: "Arons Tod" (Aron's Death)

Scene 1: Moses confronts Aron with judgment; dialogue.

Scene 2: Moses gives a sermon to the people;
        Choral hymn "Segne uns, Moses, im Namen des Ewigen...des
        Allmächtigen...."

Certain elements easily conform to the oratorio tradition. For example, the first Part of the oratorio version ends with a traditional closing hymn,

> Führe uns aus dem Land der Greuel! Allmächtiger, ewiger Gott! Du sollst der Einzige sein, dem wir dienen. Alle Opfer wollen wir dir allein weihen. In Ewigkeit wollen wir dir dienen, der du uns durch die Macht deinen Knechte sichtbar und vorstellbar worden bist. Ewiger, einziger, starker, allmächtiger Gott!

The second Part ends with a similar choral hymn "Ewiger, gütiger, allmächtiger Gott....", and again, the third Part provides for a closing hymn of reconciliation, "Segne uns Moses ins Namen des Ewigen...." This is very similar to the function in Mendelssohn's *Elijah* of No. 20 "Thanks be to God" and No. 43 "And then shall your light break forth...Lord our Creator how excellent thy Name is!" In both works, the choruses were intended to round out the overall form and to create a sense of unity.

As is normal in an oratorio, Schoenberg makes greater use of the chorus throughout than would be expected in an opera. Choral numbers are frequent and placed regularly between sections of dialogue. The chorus fulfills more than one function—it can be both the omnipresent voice of God in the Burning Bush or the masses of the Israelites. The chorus functions very similarly to the chorus in *Elijah*, reacting to the changes which are brought about by the soloists and representing both good and bad mass actions. There is a also a number of smaller groupings and choral soloist roles which exploit the chorus members to fullest advantage: For example, the Seventy Elders, and four Naked Virgins, the Invalid Woman, the Beggars, and others are drawn from the choral group in the oratorio version.

Although it is impossible to project what the musical setting might have been like had Schoenberg retained the oratorio plan, it can be reasonably speculated that the orgy scene would have been carried by the singing of text by a chorus and choral soloists and not by long passages of instrumental music, since there would be no stage action and hence no dancing. In the oratorio version, the orgy scene is represented on a similar narrative scale as the performing of wonders in the first section. There are also similarities here to the test of the Baalites in *Elijah.* The scene is greatly expanded in the operatic version with many separate subscenes, but there is actually less text in all in the opera version: the action is carried by stage directions for acting and choreography which are set to long passages of instrumental music.

Long solo passages in the oratorio are often didactic addresses to the people, hence the label "sermons." While the chorus largely presents the narrative portions of the story and primarily represents the people and their changing attitudes and reactions (as in *Elijah*), there is no separate narrator part—the characters Moses and Aron present the philosophical substance of the work. Through Moses's homiletics and philosophical debates with Aron, the central conflict of the piece is presented. This conflict is itself thought-oriented rather than action-oriented, as it stems from the Schopenhauerian conflict between the Idea (in this case, the God-idea) and its Representation. In this respect it is even less operatic than Mendelssohn's dramatic oratorio, which presents an action-oriented biblical story in a simple series of episodes as given voice by chorus and soloists.

Operatic Elements Already Present in the Oratorio Draft

In addition to those elements which are consistent with the oratorio genre as Schoenberg received it in his time, DICH[tung] 20 contains characteristics common to staged operatic presentations.

While the work is sectional, it is not a "number" oratorio. Within large divisions there are some clearly defined subdivisions, as outlined above, but there are also many long passages of dialogue in continuous scenes (for example, between Moses and Aron, or between Aron and the people). This is quite atypical of the Baroque one-person-or-group-at-a-time "exit number" format of oratorios. A study of Mendelssohn's *Elijah* reveals that the closest this nineteenth century oratorio comes to including true dialogue is in the "scene" between the widow and Elijah. The widow and Elijah do directly address each other, but Elijah's response to the widow ("Give me thy son!") does not initiate a close alternating dialogue. Rather it provides a transition to his singing about the miracle he performs, which in turn provides the occasion for a concluding stable-affect duet. The presence of material like this is the reason for the term "dramatic oratorio;" but of course the whole sequence is short enough to be included under one number, and can be considered a sectional duet. By and large, *Elijah* is consistent with a Baroque number oratorio in structure and is unlike *Moses und Aron* in this respect.

That the chorus never narrates in the third person provides a further element of dramatic realism in *Moses und Aron*. Except at the beginning, when the chorus sings the part of the Burning Bush, the chorus consistently plays the role of the people; and in neither role does the chorus step *outside* the chronological time sequence to comment upon the action. Comments on action, such as on Moses's and Aron's first approach in Part I, are not made by the chorus as omniscient narrator but as the crowd of Israelites actually observing their arrival. This is comparable to the opening chorus of *Elijah*, "Help, Lord!" Choral advice or narration (found in *Elijah* in the style of Greek drama such as "Lift thine eyes" or the impersonal solo "O rest in the Lord") does not occur to interrupt the dramatic continuity of *Moses und Aron*. Hence, a dramatic flow at least equally suitable to an opera as to an oratorio is maintained consistently throughout.

Dramatic realism is also seen in *Moses und Aron* in that there is a more consistent chronological communication among all the characters. There are no time breaks, except between the three large sections. Story time is continuous within each major division.

Furthermore, although it might be supposed that an abundance of long soliloquies in the text would not lend themselves well to operatic presentation, Schoenberg's own concept of dramatic action (as influenced by Kraus) certainly did include long monologues, as in *Der Biblische Weg*. The presence of long philosophical solo passages were equally plausible in Schoenberg's own mind in an oratorio, a play, or an opera. The fact that many such long "sermons" were retained and even added in the opera version of *Moses und Aron* attest to this.

From Oratorio to Opera

The opera version retains many oratoriolike features in its published form— one reason, no doubt, why some critics of the opera have found certain passages too static. The long sermons discussed above account for this seeming inertia more than any other feature. They reduce dramatic action to long periods where the crowd, or one of the two protagonists, stands and listens passively. The long choral numbers (and the large amount of choral participation in general) are also more typical of oratorio than opera, although the story itself demands crowd scenes. However, if a comparison of this opera to nineteenth-century grand operas which also employed very large crowds—for example, Meyerbeer's *Les Huguenots*—shows that the emphasis in the nineteenth century is on the solo singing of leading characters, punctuated by spectacular choral effects. *Moses und Aron* is not by any means a virtuoso singer's opera: there is only one true leading singing role, that of Aron.

What features, then, do distinguish the opera version from the earlier oratorio draft; and how are these characteristics consistent with Schoenberg's decision to change his conception of the work from an oratorio to an opera? Certainly, the decision to change *Moses und Aron* into an opera was primarily intended to expand the scope of the work, to reach a larger, more general audience, and to make a more dramatic statement. A certain didactic aim may have been present in his thinking—Schoenberg could not have been unaware of the hot debate through the first three decades of the century on the state of opera, (and theater in general) in relation to the public. Particularly well known at the time were opera critic Paul Bekker's critiques on opera for being increasingly controlled by the financial realities of public theater and thereby losing its power to create new cultural history, and to teach as well as to entertain,[7] and Bertolt Brecht's theory of epic theater.[8]

The process by which Schoenberg changed *Moses und Aron* from an oratorio to an opera involved three specific areas: alterations in the gross structure of the work; smaller adjustments in language and diction; and changes in actual dramatic and philosophical content. The changes in the gross structure are the most readily apparent, and constitute the most radical elements in transforming the oratorio into an opera. These changes are mainly in the form of expansions of the more dramatic material already contained— at least germinally—in the oratorio version, and the condensation of some of the more rambling prose material. In comparison with the outline of the oratorio given above, the outline of the opera version is much more lengthy:

Prologue: God alone

Act I

Scene 1:   Moses' dialogue with the Burning Bush; God blesses the people from the Burning Bush.

Scene 2:   Moses and Aron in dialgoue, Moses correcting Aron, and leading to central conflict ("Darfst?... Reinige dein Denken. ... ");
A second section of Aron rhapsodizing with Moses interjecting comments.

Scene 3:   The people (3 soloists and then small group) talk about Moses and Aron, anticipate being freed;
The people are skeptical about the new god ("Blutopfer!");
Priest and people become increasingly hopeful;
They see Moses and Aron approach.

Scene 4:   The people address Moses;
Moses and Aron address the people and they respond;
Aron and the people in dialogue ("Schliesset die Augen, verstopfet die Ohren. ... ");
The people mock ("Bleib uns fern!");
Moses despairs;
Aron seizes power, performs wonders, the people react;
Aron explains wonders in "sermons," the people praise him;
Final choral hymn "Er hat uns auserwählt. ... "

Interlude (Zwischenspiel): People wonder where Moses is.

Act II

Scene 1: The priest confronts Aron;
          The Seventy Elders argue.

Scene 2: The people ask "Wo ist Moses?";
          Dialogue between Aron and the people;
          Aron gives them back their old gods;
          Final choral hymn "Jubelt, freuet euch!"

Scene 3: The Golden Calf scene—
          Aron speaks;
          Procession;
          Offerings;
          Dance of the Butchers;
          Invalid, Beggars and Elderly before the Golden Calf;
          The Seventy Elders sing;
          The Tribal Leaders and the Ephraimite in dialogue;
          The Youth is killed;
          Mutual gift-giving;
          Dancing and fighting;
          The Seventy Elders sing;
          The four Naked Virgins are sacrificed;
          General rape and mayhem;
          Final choral hymn.

Scene 4: Moses is seen approaching.

Scene 5: Moses confronts Aron.

Act III (unfinished)

Scene 1: Moses sentences Aron with judgment; dialogue
          Aron falls down dead.

The two most dramatic sequences in the story, the miracles of Aron in Act I and the orgy scene of Act II, were already planned in the oratorio version but are greatly expanded in the opera. These scenes, similar to the sacrifices to Baal in the *Elijah* story, would not have been impossible in an oratorio. But the orgy scene in particular lends itself more to choreography and colorful stage action than could easily be achieved in an oratorio.

Most of the expansions are related to structural changes in which the dramatic interplay between the main characters is amplified by the addition of several actions. This is especially true of the second act, where the most substantial changes in structure appear. Very little of the oratorio material is retained in the second act of the opera. Long passages are deleted from the oratorio text, and repetitive emphasis is given in the opera version to a few important words, for example, "Blutopfer!" which echoes the people's apprehension in the first act.

Much of the condensation of the text in the second act is for concision and dramatic impact, making room for the much expanded sections of untexted dramatic action. Many passages of text of the second Part of the oratorio which were redundant—repeating sentiments of the chorus from the first Part—are deleted from the opera version. The expansion of the orgy sequence with the addition of such spectacular stage actions as the killing of the Youth and the sacrifice of the four Naked Virgins is the most obvious transformation of the oratorio into a fully staged dramatic work.

Another structural change is Schoenberg's effort in the opera version to create a stronger sense of a continuous time frame within the world created by the drama. This clarified time frame is needed more in an opera than an oratorio, since narrative time need not be presented as strictly in a work which does not fully re-enact a story. The addition of the interlude between Acts I and II provides a needed bridge over the time gap between the initial acceptance of the new god by the people in Egypt in Act I and the period of wandering in the wilderness in Act II. The interlude immediately sets up the time reference for Act II: "Lange schon hat ihn kein gesehen!" It sets up the apprehension and growing resentment of the people toward Moses during his long absence, which provides an explanation for the return of the people to the old forms of worship in Act II: "Wo ist Moses? Verlassen sind wir! Nie, nie, nie kehrt er wieder! . . ." This explanation does not occur in the oratorio version until the dialogue between Aron and the people in Scene 1, and then it occurs less directly.

The third type of structural change has to do with reorganization of the material in the oratorio version. This, in combination with condensation of polemic and expansion of dramatic material, serves to improve the clarity and coherence of the story. The interlude itself represents one such instance of reorganization. The interlude is built from material drawn out of the second scene of Part II: "Nie, nie, nie kehrt er wieder! Verlassen sind wir! Wo ist dein Gott? Wo ist der Einzige? Wo ist der Allmächtige? Götter, hilft ihr uns!" becomes in condensed form the material which bridges the time between the first and second acts of the opera: The removal of "Wo ist Moses? Verlassen sind wir! Nie, nie, nie kehrt er wieder! Wo ist sein Gott? Wo ist der Ewige?" to before the second act not only provides an explanation for the people's restlessness and fear, but tightens up the dramatic tension in the second scene by creating a situation in which the people now seem to have been aroused for a longer time. The Elders' ensuing plea to Aron to help them—"Aron hilf uns! Sprich zu ihnen! Sie morden uns!"—is more dramatically real. The movement toward the denouement where the people conclude that Moses must have been destroyed by his God and Aron restores the old gods to them is intensified, culminating in the joyful chorus "Jubelt! Jubelt, freuet euch!" There is then a clear break, and the third scene begins the orgy.

The oratorio version of the same action is less clearly organized. The first scene is brief, consisting only of one long statement of the Seventy Elders and Aron's reprimand: "Geduldet euch!" This is unprepared from the hymn ending of the first act. In the second scene the restlessness of the people is heard for the first time, as quoted above, rather than at the beginning of the act as the basis for all ensuing action. Then, immediately after the people's outcry, the Elders go on to the "Aron hilf uns!" exclamation, in a statement similar to the opera version. As in the opera version, it is Aron who suggests that possibly Moses has abandoned the people, and the chorus at Aron's suggestion sings "Vielleicht hat Gott ihn verlassen, vielleicht hat ihn sogar getötet." An indication for a fugue "Die Götter haben ihn getötet..." then follows in the oratorio version, which is removed from the opera, probably because it is incongruous with the sequence of the story and out of keeping with the biblical style of the language. This fugue will be described below. At the end of this scene in the oratorio, Aron addresses the people and advises them to pray to the eternal gods: "Volk Israels, bitte die ewigen Götter!" At the end of his speech he makes clear why this is necessary: "In der *gewöhnlichsten Form* wollen wir *Gott sehen.*" This is replaced by the more direct, dramatic, "Volk Israels! Deine Götter geb ich dir wieder" in the opera.

The "Juble, freue dich Israel" chorus which follows in the oratorio corresponds well to the "Jubelt, freuet euch" chorus in the opera. In the opera version this chorus concludes the scene just before the orgy. In the oratorio, however, it is not as clear: "Verwandlung" is written above the chorus, but "3. Szene" is written in after the chorus. As in the opera version, the oratorio then proceeds to the orgy around the Golden Calf. From this point on, the structure of the opera is similar to the oratorio in its broad narrative outline, but the number of separate dramatic events in the orgy scene is greatly increased, as shown in the outline of the opera above.

Changes in language and diction are more subtle, but are also very important in streamlining the philosophical content of the work and contributing to a more dramatic effect. These changes nearly always take the form of increasing the dramatic impact of the text by condensing overly wordy passages and making the diction more emphatic. For example, Moses's question to God in the oratorio: "Wie sollen sie mir glauben was ich ihnen nicht beweiden kann?" is reduced simply to "Niemand wird mir glauben!" Through such changes in words, phrases, and sentences, the central conflict of the opera is more dramatically drawn, and the philosophical content is clarified.

The effect of such a change is seen in Act I, Scene 2. The dialogue begins in this scene of the opera in much the same way as in the oratorio, and remains similar until Aron's line in the oratorio "unvorstellbar-unsichtbar, Volk auserwählt den Einzigen zu lieben, wirst Du ihn unvorstellbar wollen, wenn schon unsichtbar?" This is replaced in the opera version by the more emphatic "Volk, auserwählt dem Einzigen, kannst du lieben, was du dir nicht vorstellen darfst?", intensifying the meaning of his statements. Moses' response in the oratorio "Wollen?" has the same structural purpose as the "Darfst?" in the opera text; but because Aron's initial statement in the oratorio is less emphatic, the impact of Moses' response is not as dramatic in the oratorio version as it becomes in the opera.

Moses' ensuing speech in the oratorio very much resembles in tone the kind of ironic querying found in biblical Hebrew wisdom literature. For example, in Job 38:1–7, Yahweh speaks from the whirlwind:

> Who is this that darkens counsel by words without knowledge? Gird up your loins like a man, I will question you, and you shall declare to me. Where were you when I laid the foundation of the earth? Tell me, if you have understanding. Who determined its measurements—surely you know! Or who stretched the line upon it?...

Moses' response to Aron in the oratorio is replaced in the opera by a different word structure, no longer with the tone of a Hebrew wisdom discourse, but clipped and emphatic: "Unvorstellbar, weil unsichtbar, weil unüberblickbar, weil unendlich; weil ewig; weil allgegenwärtig; weil allmächtig. Nur einer ist allmächtig." While the meaning of the passage remains essentially unchanged, the dramatic impact of this brusque, choppy speech is far greater.

All these techniques—the manipulation of word order to produce more striking rhythmic effects, use of short repetitive phrases, and use of a curt, almost telegraphic style—were also highly cultivated in some circles of expressionist dramatists, especially the *"Sturm"* circle. Examples of highly condensed sentences occur in Kokoschka's *Mörder, Hoffnung der Frauen*, and in Fritz Unruh's novel *Opfergang.*[9]

Another of Schoenberg's concerns in his work with the language of *Moses und Aron* was for the surface sound of words, and for the rhythms they would produce. Some of these changes correspond to the general trend toward condensing and clarifying. However, many of these changes also reflect the fact that once Schoenberg began to compose the music, he began to hear a need in the language of the libretto for verse form and for more dramatic and singable language.

Many text changes, therefore, reflect attempts to improve and make the versification more regular. Rhythmic verse tends to belong mostly to the chorus, in its role both as God in the Burning Bush and as the people. An example of such a change occurs in the first scene. God in the Burning Bush originally sings: "Du hast gesehen, dass mein Volk in Elend ist; dass sie in Greueln leben; Du hast erkannt/gesehen, dass es Greuel und Elend sind, so musst du sie befreien!" This passage is condensed and converted to metrical verse in the opera version as follows:

> Du hast die Greuel gesehn,
> die Wahrheit erkannt:
> so kannst du nicht anders mehr:
> du musst dein Volk daraus befreien!

A more subtle change on the same order occurs slightly earlier. In the oratorio version, the first statement of God in the Burning Bush is "Lege die Schuhe ab; Du sollst nicht weiter gehn! Du stehst auf heiligem Boden, nun verkünde!" The phrase "Du sollst nicht weiter gehn" is replaced in the opera by "bist weit genug gegangen!" Both phrases have the same rhythm, but the latter has the advantage of an alliterative ending and a more emphatic monosyllabic beginning.

The texts belonging to the Burning Bush and Moses are also differentiated metrically. While the chorus which sings the part of the Burning Bush sings mainly in iambic meter, Moses' lines are slightly less regular and approximate dactylic meter. For example, "Gott meiner Väter, Gott Abrahams, Isaaks und Jakobs," and in the next line, "Ich bin alt. Lass mich in Ruhe meine Schafe weiden," and "Wer bin ich mich der Macht der Blind-heit entgegenzustellen?" This last phrase is made more regular in the opera text, the oratorio version reading, "Wer aber bin ich, dass ich der Macht Pharaos entgegentretensollte?"

Another example of increasing attention to versification occurs in the third scene as Aron seizes the rod from Moses. In the oratorio version, Aron's first miracle is in the context of a long prose speech followed by a briefer choral answer. The chorus' response to Aron's statement "Seht hier den Stab den ich nehme aus Moses Hand. Der Stab soll euch führen! Seht hier, ich werf ihn zur Erde: seht die Schlange!" and subsequent miracle and explanations is as follows: "Wunderbar hast die Macht du gezeigt, die nur ein Gott dir gegeben. Moses, ist Aron dein Knecht und du des Gottes, so bist du gewaltig genug uns zu führen. Doch wie willst du Pharao zwingen dass er uns freilässt/(geistig)?" This passage is replaced in the opera in Scene 4 by Aron's more concise: "Dieser Stab führt euch: Seht die Schlange!" Much quicker dialogue ensues between the chorus and Aron, and concludes with Aron's triumphant brief statement "Erkennet die Macht, die dieser Stab den Führer verleiht!" The chorus' response is now entirely in verse:

> Ein Wunder erfüllt uns mit Schreken:
> Der Stab, der sich wandelt zur Schlange,
> zeigt Aron als Herrn dieses Volkes.
> Wie gross ist die Macht dieses Aron.
> Ist Aron der Knecht dieses Moses,

und Moses der Knecht seines Gottes,
durch den Stab, den sein Gott ihm gegeben,
ist mächtiger Moses als Aron?
So muss es ein mächtiger Gott sein,
der Starke zu zwingen vermag!
Wie gross ist die Macht dieses Gottes,
da mächtige Knechte ihm dienen!

The concluding trio of solo voices, the young woman, young man, and other man, also conform to this metrical scheme: "Er wird uns befrein!...Wir wollen ihm dienen!... Wir wollen ihm opfern!"

That this increased use of meter was a conscious decision in Schoenberg's mind is demonstrated by inscriptions on some of the handwritten leaves laid in the DICH[tung] 20 source, representing transitional work between the oratorio and the opera *Kompositionsvorlage.* These give brief phrases of text with long and short syllabification signs and vertical strokes marking the metrical feet. An example of this appears in figure 3-1.

In addition to use of meter, the opera text is full of alliteration like Wagner's use of *Stabreim.* This techinque is particularly applied to Moses' speeches, as in the example "Reinige dein Denken, lös es vom Wertlosem, weihe es Wahrem..." In the same example, internal sounds also echo in "Reinige dein Denken" and "lös es vom Wertlosem."

Finally, there are important changes between the oratorio and the opera version in content, both narrative content and philosophical content. None of these changes radically disrupts the original religious or philosophical conception of the work. Most of the changes represent a tightening of the drama or a clarifying of the philosophical thought expressed.

Story changes have the effect of making certain actions already present in the oratorio version more emphatic. For example, in the second scene, the structure of the conflict between Moses' and Aron's respective understandings of the Word of God is more tightly drawn in the opera toward the climactic moment in which Moses has his only sung statement in the opera: "Reinige dein Denken..." This story change is accompanied with a sharpening of the language as in other examples given above. The statement with its terse sentences in a nearly metrical verse setting and with touches of alliteration or *Stabreim* as mentioned above, is much more dramatically effective than the same statement in the oratorio: "Wer opfert reinigt sein denken, befreit sein Herz, seinen Geist vom Hang zu Wertlosen lässt es dem wahren Denken sich neigen. (Opfere nicht für an denn Gewinn, als diesen.)" (Words in parentheses are handwritten additions.)

The whole dialogue between Moses and Aron in the opera version is more concise; and rather than alternating speaking, the two points of view are presented simultaneously, with Moses' views serving as a constant corrective. Thus more immediate parallels between the two characters are created for the listeners.

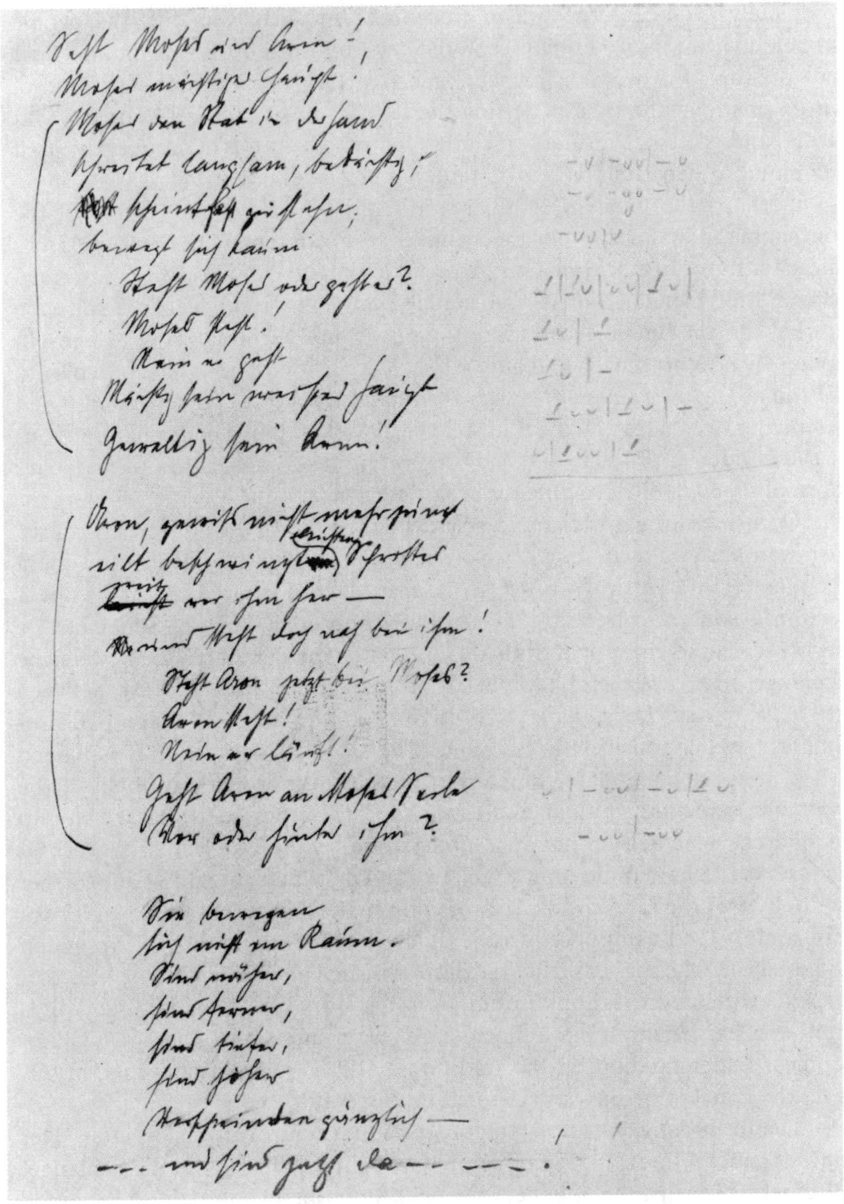

Figure 3-1. From DICH[tung] 20 Showing Metrical Markings (facsimile)

The concluding hymns of the acts in the oratorio are also made more dramatic in the opera. For example, at the end of Act I, rather than singing a completely God-centered prayer (as in the oratorio version), the people conclude with a more human-centered cry about their own plight and their own dream: "*Wir* werden frei sein, frei, frei, frei, frei!" Added repetition of words (made at the time of setting the text to music, since the straight text drafts and sketches do not include the repetition) is a frequently used technique of heightening the dramatic impact of the text.

Perhaps the most forceful dramatization in the opera version of the conflict in the first act involves a change in story content in the scene of Aron's miracles. In the oratorio version, Aron takes the rod from Moses, as described above: "Seht hier den Stab den ich nehme aus Moses Hand. Der Stab soll euch führen!" In the opera, Aron takes the power more dramatically to himself, saying "Das Wort bin ich und die Tat!..." Now the emphasis has shifted from the rod as the instrument of power from God, to Aron's possession of it and personal power. Story changes in Act II—the lengthening of dramatic actions in the Golden Calf scene and the corresponding condensation of text—are more obvious, and have already been described.

Occasionally word changes create changes in philosophical emphasis. For example, two intriguing key words appear in both the oratorio and opera versions in different ways: after Aron seizes the rod from Moses in the opera version, Aron goes on to say, "Dieser Stab führt euch: Seht die Schlange!... Im Moses Hand ein starrer Stab: das *Gesetz*; in meiner Hand, die bewegliche Schlange: die *Klugheit*" (emphasis added). Here the contrast between *Vorstellung* and *Darstellung* is brilliantly amplified by a second pair of concepts set in opposition: *Gesetz* and *Klugheit*. This opposition is explained in the context of God vs. humanity, or the unknowable absolute vs. the available, inadequate human expression of it. Law represents that which is to be obeyed, whether or not it is understood; while intellect or cleverness represents the human attempt to understand or, worse, to know. The further symbolism of the rigid rod vs. the writhing snake depicts the immovability of Law and of God as opposed to the fluidity and changeability of expression and intellect. The snake further recalls traditional and biblical associations of serpents with cleverness or wisdom, as in the story of Adam and Eve. This is another clear example of Schoenberg's superimposing of his own philo-sophical understanding on the traditional Old Testament concepts, in this case, the concept of Law as set forth in the Torah.

The term *Klugheit* already appeared in the oratorio version after "Der Stab soll euch führen."—"Seht hier, ich werf ihn zur Erde: seht die Schlange! Fürchtet sie? Sie ist die Klugheit die nicht Stab bleibt sondern drehend sich wendende Gestalt annimmt, wenn der Führer es will...." In both the oratorio and the opera versions, the term first appears when the voices out of the

Burning Bush sing to Moses: "Vor ihren Ohren wirst du Wunder tun....Von deinem Stab werden sie hören; Deine *Klugheit* bewundern...." [10] In this first reference to the rod, intellect and wonders or miracles are already linked and are already associated with the rod, no matter who wields it. The highly original contrasting of *Gesetz* with *Klugheit* as opposing ideas, however, does not appear until the opera version.

Most changes in the area of philosophical content represent a streamlining of ideas and a focusing in on the key concepts Schoenberg wanted to present: the unknowability of God, the mission of the chosen people to worship the unknowable, and the central combat against concrete, tangible forms of Representation of the invisible God Idea. One passage which appears in the oratorio version was completely excised from the final opera text because it did not contribute to this philosophical theme: in Part II, Scene 2 of the oratorio, after Aron has suggested that Moses may have been killed, there is an indication for a fugue with the text

> Die Götter haben ihn getötet,
> den Frevler!
> Pthah, Budda, Confutius,
> Zeus, Jupiter, Wotan,
> Allah, Zorraster, Manitu und Baal
> Straft den Frevler;
> Straft seine Priester
> Ihr mächtigen Götter!

This roster of gods has very modern overtones, and is quite removed from the biblical tone of most of the oratorio. There may be a connection between this list and the popular interest in Schoenberg's time in oriental thought, as in Confucius and Buddha. Wotan, of course, echoes Wagner; and Zorraster may be a reference to Nietzsche's *Also Sprach Zarathustra*, which Schoenberg owned. In the opera text, "Die Götter" are left unenumerated.

While in most cases the opera version represents a condensation from the philosophical prose of the oratorio, the concluding chorus of Act II, Scene 2 is an example of an expansion, with an elaboration of the philosophical content. The two texts are as follow:

Oratorio	*Opera*
Juble, freue dich Israel,	Jubelt! Jubelt, freut euch!
deine Götter sehen dich und	Juble, Israel! Jubelt!
du wirst sie wiedersehn	Götter, Bilder unsres Auges,
Lebet: Ihr werdet erhört!	Götter, Herren unsrer Sinne!
wenn ihr bittet und opfert!	Ihre leibliche Sichtbarkeit,
Ihr werdet gestraft,	Gegenwart,

wenn ihr sündigt.
Wenn Elend euch plagt, so
wisst ihr dass ihr einen
Gott beleidigt habt.
Wenn ihr Glück habt,
wisst ihr dass die Götter
euch lieben.
Bringt herbei was ihr habt.
Aron mag es gestalten, dass
wir den Gott unserer Wünsche
sehn, den Gott für den wir
alles geben.

verbürgt unsre Sicherheit!
Ihre Grenzen und Messbarkeit
fordern nicht, was unserm
Gefühl versagt.
Götter, nahe unserm Fühlen,
Götter, die wir ganz begreifen:
Tugend lohne Glückseligkeit;
Übeltat bestrafe Gerechtigkeit;
zeigend unsrer Taten Folgen,
Götter, stellt sich eure
    Macht dar.
Juble, Israel, freue dich,
    Israel!
Farbig ist diese Gegenwart,
düster ist jene Ewigkeit;
Lebenslust scheut ihr
    Ende nicht,
furchtlos sucht sie es
    freiwillig;
Lust grenzt an Leben und
    an Tod,
steigert zu dem von jenem sich;
Drohung entzündet Lebensmut,
Standhaftigkeit und Tapferkeit.
Deinen Göttern als Inhalt
    gabst du dein Innres,
    dein Lebensgefühl.
Deiner Götter Ausseh'n sichert
dein Gold: entäussre dich sein!
Mach dich arm, mach sie reich!
Sie werden dich nicht hungern
    lassen!
Juble, Israel, Juble!

It may be seen that the basic idea presented in the oratorio version is not changed, but is elaborated with greater detail. At the same time, it is made more metrical; and no doubt reflects the process of musical composition as well, during which Schoenberg heard a need for a longer, more structurally central piece. The oratorio already presents the most basic form of the philosophical statement intended by the scene: the people's need for and infatuation with a visible, tangible image to worship. The idea is similar to the abstract speeches of Moses and Aron in the oratorio's first Part, and is particularly close to certain speeches in *Der Biblische Weg*, such as the final speech, cited in chapter 2 above. The same ideas are presented in the opera version in a powerful, much more sensual way, going beyond the point of philosophical abstractions to dramatic events of sacrifices, sex, and murder. The dramatic nature of the philosophical ideas in opposition to Moses' vision of the unknowable God is also made more extreme in the opera version: "Heilig ist die Zeugungskraft! Heilig ist die Fruchtbarkeit! Heilig ist die Lust!" is heard as the culmination of the thought which is conveyed by the words of the Seventy Elders midway through the scene in the opera: "Sinn schenkt Seele Sinn erst, Seele ist Sinn. Götter, die ihr Seele schenktet, Sinne, Seele warzunehmen. Götter, sei gepriesen!"

The arousal of lust, greed, violence, and rapture in the opera are generated by the involvement with the senses; and the involvement with the senses is connected directly in the opera to the need for a god or gods which can be perceived by the senses. Self-worship and self-rapture are easily read into this picture. The operatic version represents a more colorful humanization of the rather dry, abstract philosophical concepts presented in the oratorio.

In Act II, Scene 4 of the opera, in keeping with this increased dramatization of philosophical concepts, Moses' horror with the concrete image of God is made more specific and amplified. In the oratorio, Moses simply says "Schweigt! . . . (Lange Pause) . . . "Vergeh, du Götzenbild!" In the opera this is expanded to "Vergeh, du Abbild des Unvermögens, das Grenzenlose in ein *Bild* zu fassen!" In addition, it was possible in the opera to have a stage direction that the Golden Calf should vanish. In both versions, the people lament the end of their joy and flee from Moses' strength.

Part III, or Act III, "Arons Tod," was never set to music. It represents the greatest divergence in both narrative and philosophical content between the oratorio and the version of Act III now published with the opera score. A complete translation of the oratorio version of this scene is provided in Appendix IV.

It is very important to note that the final version of this scene can never be known, since the very process of setting words to music influenced Schoenberg's process of creating the text, as described in chapter 1.

One major difference which has an important effect on content is that in the published version, only one scene is presented (the scene of Aron's death), while in the oratorio version a second scene is also presented where Moses speaks to the people and appoints successors to Aron and himself. A further difference is that the oratorio text is closer to the biblical narrative than the opera version. The idea that both Moses and Aron are forbidden to enter the Promised Land, and the Promised Land itself as a concept, are much more emphasized in the oratorio version. However, biblical language such as "the land of milk and honey" also appears in the opera version.

The first scene of Part III of the oratorio is similar to Act III of the opera. Aron's main point in both is "In Bildern sollte ich reden, wo du in Begriffen; zum Herzen, wo du zum Hirn sprichst."[11] The rest of the scene is amplified in the opera. In the oratorio version, Moses' interest in the conflict between speaking to the rock and striking the rock is mentioned. This material is enlarged in the published version of the third act:

> Moses: ...da genügte dir nur mehr die Tat, die Handlung? Da machtest du den Stab zum Führer, meine Kraft zum Befreier, und Nilwasser beglaubigte die Allmacht...Da begehrtest du leiblich, wirklich, mit Füssen zu betreten ein unwirkliches Land, wo Milch und Honig fliesst. *Da schlugst du auf den Felsen, statt zu ihm zu sprechen, wie dir befohlen, dass Wasser aus ihm fliesse...aus dem nackten Felsen sollte das Wort Erquickung schlagen....*
>
> *Aron: Niemals kam dein Wort ungedeutet ans Volk. Mit dem Stab deshalb sprach ich zum Felsen in seiner Sprache, die das Volk versteht.*
>
> Moses: Du sagst es schlechter, als du es verstehst, denn du weisst, dass der Felsen ein Bild, wie die Wüste und der Dornbusch: drei, die dem Leib nicht geben, was er braucht, gegen der Geist, der Seele, was deren Wunschlosigkeit zu ewigem Leben genug ist. *Auch der Felsen, wie alle Bilder, gehorcht dem Wort, daraufhin er Erscheinung geworden war.* So gewannst du das Volk *nicht für den Ewigen, sondern fur dich....*

The importance of images (*Bilder*) is spelled out precisely in this speech. The radical reinterpretation of biblical material is introduced in the opera version: "ein unwirkliches Land wo Milch und Honig fliesst." This is only implied in the oratorio when Moses says, "So you lost the Land, but you had already been in it." In other words, the Land is not a tangible place but a state of mind, an uprightness with God, perhaps. This is an idea with Eastern resonance, perhaps even reflecting the late-nineteenth century German fascination with Eastern philosophy.

The Chosen People is brought back as an image in Moses' speech in the opera version also: "dieses auserwählte Volk an die andern, das Aussergewöhnliche an die Gewöhnlichkeit." Similarly, "die Wüste" also represents a state of mind, that of renunciation of the truth of God, desolation due to separation from God. The paradox here is Moses' concluding statement: "Aber in der Wüste seid ihr unüberwindlich und werdet das Ziel erreichen: Vereinigt mit Gott." This is a mysterious ending, especially since it follows on the heels of Aron's being set free and then falling down dead.

Aron dies very differently in the oratorio version. He simply dies because his time is up. Moses says, "You have only too often allowed your own Idea to invade your God-concept and therefore you must now surrender—lie down low, die! I will reconcile you with God!" Punishment and reconciliation are both present. In the opera version it would seem that it is the shock of freedom after punishment which Aron cannot withstand, a very different circumstance.

A very important blessing in the second scene of Part III in the oratorio is not included in the opera version. It seems very unlikely that Schoenberg would have omitted this important dramatic moment of reconciliation between God and the people in the final opera version had it been completed, since this second scene contains ideas central to his religious thinking and important to concluding Moses' "business" with the people. In the final blessing of the people by Moses in the second scene, the idea of the Chosen People is most perfectly stated in terms which become extremely relevant in the light of the persecution of the Jews in Austria and German in the late 1920s: "So shall scorn attend you; persecution consecrate you; so shall sorrow sanctify you." These words are particularly poignant in the historical retrospect of the Nazi Holocaust. "Always will one be with you to keep the God-idea of your Chosenness clean/pure as I received it from the Eternal" echoes the Hasidic legend of the seven Just Men. An element of modern existentialism and the problem of doubt is also worked in: "And always even if all believe, you will be in doubt, and know the Right by which to believe your mission: the ungratifying, pure teachings of God." This is perhaps, in its dialectical tone, the most naked summation of the central God-concept of the piece. God, by being intangible and invisible, is therefore not easily accessible or gratifying. Rather, God is shrouded in mystery and demands blind obedience to the Law in return for being the Chosen People, the people called to carry out God's mission in the world.

In summary, Schoenberg's decision to change the oratorio on the subject of Moses and Aaron into a fully realized dramatic work obviously involved more than minor changes—it was a decision to greatly expand the scope of the work, to bring it to a wider audience, and to highlight the most powerful dramatic moments in the narrative by presenting them as theater, rather than in a concert format. The resulting conception was epic in scope, like a Wagnerian *Gesamtkunstwerk*, incorporating text, music, dance, scenery, and stage action, in an almost ritual work of art. It blends religious stage ritual as in *Parsifal* with spectacle as in French Grand Opera, and its presentation of the exotic ancient near eastern place and time rivals Verdi's *Aïda* and *Nabucco*.

The main differences between the oratorio and the published opera version are more formal than in content, but in the process of dramatization many of the religious and philosophical concepts expressed appear in the opera colorful and humanized. This is achieved partly, as shown above, by tighter organization of the formal structure of the work, and by attention to details of language as seen in the conscious manipulation of prose and verse format, and the careful patterning of word order and sentence structure to convey precisely the intended meaning.

The specific nature of the conflict between Moses and Aron is more clearly spelled out in the opera version, and obscure biblical references are made clearer. Changes in narrative and philosophical content serve to tighten the drama by condensing overly wordy prose passages and eliminating extraneous material. Content changes also to sharpen the focus of religious and philosophical material by either condensing or elaborating passages as necessary.

Finally, a comparison of the third acts of the two versions strongly corroborates Schoenberg's own insistence that the published version of the third act was not, by any means, a final version in his own mind—especially since only one scene appears in the published version, and the second scene in the oratorio presents a more fitting conclusion, incorporating ideas which were extremely important to Schoenberg's religious thinking. The integration of biblical time and nineteenth-century philosophical thought in this second scene aptly summarizes Schoenberg's own religious perspective.

4

The Music of *Moses und Aron:*
Compositional Techniques

Before investigating how the music of *Moses und Aron* expresses the text, it is necessary to examine the compositional techniques present. Certain of these are closely related to textual considerations; others are more or less purely musical decisions made by the composer for the sake of the organization of the musical materials, or the continuation and amplification of specific musical ideas.

The inner logic of the music of *Moses und Aron* depends on several important large decision-making areas on the part of the composer, within which more specific observations can be made. These decision-making areas are: the row and its basic properties, methods of dividing row material, some other specific techniques of row treatment and manipulation, methods of articulation of form, and the derivation and use of motivic material. These will now be examined in turn.

Terminology

Row forms will be labeled according to the "magic square" diagram in figure 4-1. The use of "P0, R0, RI0, and I0" differs from Schoenberg's own "T" (*Thema* or *Tonika*) and "T + 2," "T – 2," etc., and "U + 2," etc. *(Umkehrung)*, drawn in a simple linear chart (rather than in a "magic square" format as in figure 1-6, for example). However it is more consistent with current analytical practices and with important secondary literature. "P0" is the prime row form beginning on the pitch A, and is equivalent to the "T" (*Thema* or *Tonika*) of Schoenberg's own row charts described in chapter 1.[1]

"I0" begins on the pitch C, because the central semicombinatorial relationship of the opera, to be described later in this chapter, is between the prime row on pitch A and the retrograde inversion row on pitch A. This RI form becomes "RI0," and its retrograde then becomes "I0." This produces an aggregate A0 with consistent row contents P0, R0, I0, and RI0.

Figure 4-1.   Row Chart for *Moses und Aron*

		9	10	4	2	3	1	7	5	6	8	11	0		
P0	–	A	B♭	E	D	E♭	C♯	|G	F	F♯	G♯	B	C	–	R0
P11	–	G♯	A	E♭	C♯	D	C	|F♯	E	F	G	B♭	B	–	R11
P5	–	D	E♭	A	G	G♯	F♯	|C	B♭	B	C♯	E	F	–	R5
P7	–	E	F	B	A	B♭	G♯	|D	C	C♯	E♭	F♯	G	–	R7
P6	–	E♭	E	B♭	G♯	A	G	|C♯	B	C	D	F	F♯	–	R6
P8	–	F	F♯	C	B♭	B	A	|E♭	C♯	D	E	G	G♯	–	R8
P2	–	B	C	F♯	E	F	E♭	|A	G	G♯	B♭	C♯	D	–	R2
P4	–	C♯	D	G♯	F♯	G	F	|B	A	B♭	C	E♭	E	–	R4
P3	–	C	C♯	G	F	F♯	E	|B♭	G♯	A	B	D	E♭	–	R3
P1	–	B♭	B	F	E♭	E	D	|G♯	F♯	G	A	C	C♯	–	R1
P10	–	G	G♯	D	C	C♯	B	|F	E♭	E	F♯	A	B♭	–	R10
P9	–	F♯	G	C♯	B	C	B♭	|E	D	E♭	F	G♯	A	–	R9
		R19	10	4	2	3	1	7	5	6	8	11	R10		

This is borne out in the sources, because Schoenberg himself obviously identified this relationship between P and RI as a pair relationship. In Source Af, the small bound row sketchbook, Schoenberg writes the prime form beginning on A, labeled as "T$_a$," at the top half of the first opening, and the related inversion from "U + 6" on the facing lower half of the opening. (See figure 1-7) Each opening of the booklet contains only the next successive "T" and "U" forms with the same relationship to each other (e.g., opening 2 has "T – 2" and "U – 6," opening 3 has "T + 2" and "U + 5," etc.).

The semicombinatorial family made up of any P_x, R_x, I_x and RI_x will therefore constitute the aggregate which will be labeled A_x when referring to the entire group as one entity. Important divisions of row material will be labeled in subscript as follows (using P0 as a sample row form):

The two main hexachords: $P0_1$, $P0_2$

The four trichords: $P0_a$, $P0_b$, $P0_c$, $P0_d$

The three tetrachords: $P0_x$, $P0_y$, $P0_z$

The "inner hexachord" made up of two inner trichords: $P0_{b+c}$

Inner divisions: $P0_{1\ 2+4}$ represents the first hexachord, further divided into groupings of 2 notes plus 4 notes.

Basic Properties of the Row

Once the prime row form is identified, it is useful to examine its intrinsic properties for the compositional possibilities it offers.

The row is mainly constructed of whole steps and half steps, with two prominent tritones and a minor third interval. These larger intervals are positioned symmetrically, with one tritone in the middle, and a tritone and a minor third as the second interval from each end:

A   B♭   E   D   E♭   C♯ | G   F   F♯   G♯   B   C

mi2   TT   Ma2   mi2   MA2   TT   MA2   mi2   MA2   mi3   mi2

The predominantly stepwise character of the row actually generates much stepwise motion in the opera, for example, melodies like the *Hauptstimme* at m. 23 of Act I, Scene 1, shown in musical example 4-1.

Musical Example 4-1

l.Vcl

This emphasis on conjunct intervals is reflected in another way in the opening of Act I, Scene 2, to produce a stepwise melody accompanied by prominently heard minor ninths and major and minor sevenths, shown in musical example 4-2.

Since the minor third and particularly the tritone are so prominent in the row due to their placement among otherwise step intervals, these larger intervals are often highlighted. The minor third contained within the row becomes the basis for an important motivic idea, the triad, which will be discussed in much greater detail later. This motive is first introduced in m. 7 of Act I, Scene 1, but has its most audibly highlighted statement in Scene 2 at mm. 163–68, shown in musical example 4-3.

The tritone element of the row is employed consistently to produce an important vertical motivic sonority, the mysterious opening chords, shown in musical example 4-4.

It is the tritones which most audibly preserve the motivic identity of these chords as they are employed throughout the piece in various inversions, spacings and orchestrations, and through various motivic transformations.

2. Szene
Moses begegnet Aron in der Wüste

Musical Example 4-3

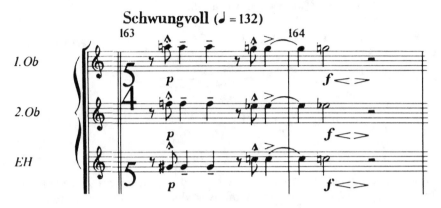

Musical Example 4-4

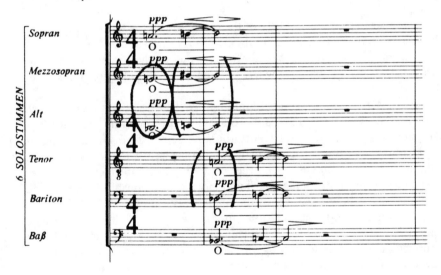

The division of the row into trichords produces mirrorlike symmetrical intervallic structures between trichords a and d:[2]

trichords b+c: D ∨ Eb ∨ C# ∨ G ∨ F ∨ F#

mi2 Ma2____Ma2 mi2

and

trichords a+d: A ∨ Bb ∨ E ∨ G# ∨ B ∨ C

mi2 TT........mi3 mi2

These similarities between trichords b and c, and a and d, generate the opening chordal vs. linear motivic sonorities, motives which, as it will be seen later, are among the most important motives in the structure of the entire opera. The opening bars are as follows, in musical example 4-5.

The mirror-image sound is particularly audible as it characterizes the first linear motive of the piece, constructed of trichords $P0_{1_{b+c}}$, shown in musical example 4-6.

Another important property of the row designed for *Moses und Aron* is the unique set of relationships among various row forms. These relationships are integral to the compositional working out of the piece, and may be expressed in simple equations, where "X" represents the transposition level of the row form.

First, PX = RIX semicombinatorially. That is, the tones of each hexachord of PX are the same as the tone of the corresponding hexachords of RIX, although they are in different order. These row forms usually appear together and function as an aggregate AX in the piece, with the PX and RIX components accompanying each other or serving to complement each other harmonically or contrapuntally. This important relationship is set up and exploited from the very outset of the opera. (See musical example 4-5)

There are several other relationships of row forms which involve specific materials shared by two or more row forms. These shared materials are frequently used by Schoenberg as common tones or common materials for the purpose of modulation from one row form to another. It should be explained that throughout this analysis, certain terms normally reserved for analysis of tonal music will be employed occasionally, including "modulation," "pivot chord," and "overall tonal plan," because the row forms of this opera are placed in an overall structure which functions exactly as the overall plan of keys of a nineteenth-century opera would be, with primary and secondary referential or home row areas and contrasting row areas. David Lewin describes Schoenberg's use of row areas as "very similar to that [way] in which a Tonal composer might use keys," including in his examples the opening of

Musical Example 4-5

Musical Example 4-6

Moses und Aron, Act I, Scene 3.[3] The word "tonal" in this context does not mean pertaining to this or that *tonic,* but rather pertaining to this or that *configuration of tones.* "Modulation" is a particularly appropriate term, because row areas are presented initially, and then they change, with an audible formal relationship as clear and directional as a shift from a tonic area to a mediant area or a subdominant area (although, perhaps no relationship in a twelve-tone piece is as immediately polar in sound as the tonic-to-dominant relationship). This is consistent with Schoenberg's insistence that his own compositional techniques, while employing his twelve-tone system, were still traditional in terms of formal manipulation of materials—and this manipulation pertains not only to motivic transformation, but also to the overall formal design of a work.

In addition, there is a separate relationship among row forms which have the same inner hexachord, trichords b+c, in common. Using the terminology again of PX, RX, etc., any PX will have the same inner two trichords b+c, in the same order of pitches, as the corresponding row form RIX–1. This relationship may be expressed by the following equation:

$$PX_{b+c} = RIX{-}1_{b+c}$$

An example of the usefulness of this relationship in modulating between the two row forms PX and RIX–1 using the shared inner hexachord b+c as common pivot material appears in Act I, mm. 50–54, shown in musical example 4-7.

The half-step relationship PX to RIX–1 is noted by David Lewin in his article, "Moses und Aron: Some General Remarks, and Analytic Notes for Act I, Scene 1."[4] It is in this article, however, that we see the danger of focusing too much on a single row property in abstract, as mentioned above, and thereby missing other more important points about how the music actually functions in context. The main point of Lewin's article, both in the introductory section where he describes the piece and later as he sets up a "metric analysis," is that this property is at work, for example, in mm. 50–54, 67–70, and m. 85. However, several questions arise from Lewin's discussion of

Musical Example 4-7

Musical Example 4-7 (continued)

this property of the row, especially as he focuses on it to the exclusion of other important aspects of the music. First, does this method of movement from one row form to another constitute a very important or frequently used method of modulation in the piece? Second, does it justify Lewin's metric analysis of the form of the scene? And, lastly, is the presence of this technique at specific points in the music the best description of what is really operating there musically, or are other explanations needed for an understanding of the way the music works as well?

To answer the first question, it is necessary to look at the junctures between disparate row areas and to see if the minor-second relationship pertains to many of them. In fact, the very first instance of the juxtaposition of two aggregates a minor second apart occurs at a place in which Lewin states "the function of neither the texture nor the row forms is clear to me."[5] This first modulation away from A0 is in m. 8 at Moses's entrance, where the notes in P0 of Lewin's "motive Y" (PX_{b+c}) are harmonized by the tetrachords of R11 and P10, as shown in musical example 4-8.

The relationship of A0 and A1 contains the relationship of P1 to R10. There is, in fact, a combinatorial interplay in this passage, but it is a different one: it is R10 and P1 which have the common inner hexachord b+c, but in this passage it is the inner hexachord of P0 accompanied by tetrachords of R11 — just the reverse of the relationship—which is stated. So in this case, two aggregates which contain the very row property under discussion are set up in m. 8, but the specific technique of pivoting on a shared hexachord is not exploited there.

In fact, this semitone relationship is not very frequently used on the large formal level, although on the local level it is used as in the measures which Lewin cites. It is not very frequently used at major junctures between row areas. For example, (as Lewin states) P1 does function to pivot to A0 in the motion from A8 to A5 in mm. 84–86 but the main row areas of this scene are P0, P5, and P8. None of these has hexachordal material in common with any other. There is something else, however, which they do have in common, namely, a shared tritone C♯–G, which occurs in P0, R15, and R18, and which is used frequently as a referential sonority. This property of shared tritones will be discussed shortly in more detail.

Imitation is combined with common tone motion as another often used method to move from one area to another. A good example is found in mm. 41–44, shown in musical example 4-9.

During the most modulatory part of the central conflict between Moses and the voices in the Burning Bush, in mm. 41–44, six tetrachords are heard in the chorus as follows:

$$P5: x \quad\quad y \quad\quad z$$
$$I5: \quad\quad x \quad\quad y \quad z$$

Musical Example 4-8

Musical Example 4-8 (continued)

* Anfangs schwach besetzt

Musical Example 4-9

The top notes in the soprano are, as Lewin points out, (D), C, B♭, B, which constitute the second half of the pervasive b+c motive, or the third trichord of the prime row form, trichord c. This is picked up in a sequential imitation in m. 43 in the strings as F, E♭, E, within a context of string and wind chords spelling P8$_{x,y,z}$. The next notes, which spell RI8$_{x,y,z}$ are hooked in by use of a chromatic line in the viola:

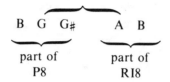

and even more important, by a repetition of the pitches F and E in the violins, forming a violin tune: F E♭ E F E C♯. Then the D–E♭ in the trumpet and the B♭–A♭ motion in the clarinet, which form part of the RI8 chords, are imitated in the same register by the oboe and the horns to form part of P3$_{c+d}$ as follows:

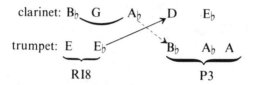

The inner trichords appear again in m. 44 in the voices as well, within a context of 2+4 grouping, and the motive continues to be repeated through m. 53. Another use of the techniques of sequence and repetition to modulate occurs at mm. 50–54, where the property of the row on which Lewin focuses is specifically used in the context of a repetition of the b+c motive as a pivot to the related aggregate.

There is one more common-material modulatory device used in the opera as well: relatedness through important common half-steps. The row is often divided dyadically, for example, at m. 366 in Act I, Scene 3, as well as earlier examples already cited, such as Act I, Scene 1, m. 21. Row identity is often signaled by prominent use of certain characteristic half-steps; and a shift from one form to another often involves transforming a medial half-step of one row by singling it out in the texture and turning it into the initial half-step of the new row. An early example of this technique occurs at Act I, Scene 1, mm. 43–44, as shown in musical example 4-10.

Certainly, then, Lewin's point about the usefulness of the shared inner trichords of aggregates a minor second apart is valid, particularly on the local level. But other methods of modulation are used more often at major

Musical Example 4-10

junctures of row areas which make up the large form of the scene; and simpler kinds of common tone modulation as well as imitation and sequence are also in frequent use in the piece.

A third type of relationship is generated by the prominence of tritones in the row. Each possible pair of tritones contained in a row is shared in groupings, or families, of row forms as follows:

D–G#, F–B : P1, P4, P7, P10, RI0, RI3, RI6, RI9
C#–G, E–B♭: P0, P3, P6, P9, RI11, RI2, I5, RI8
A–E♭, C–F#: P2, P5, P8, P11, RI1, RI4, RI7, RI10

It is easy to see how this relationship is associated with the relationship of shared inner trichords b+c described above, since one of the two possible tritones occurs in the center of the row, and is also part of the inner hexachord formed by the trichords b+c. Therefore, the same pairs which share inner hexachords also share tritones. In these pairs, the other tritone falls in the first trichord of the prime row form of the pair and in the last trichord of the retrograde inversion form, again reinforcing the relationship of trichords a and d among prime and retrograde inversion forms as in the opening bars of the piece.

These families with tritones in common function together in interesting ways in the overall "tonal plan" of the opera. For example, the three main aggregates in Act I, Scene 1—the main referential aggregate A0 and secondary aggregates A5 and A8—are unified by the shared tritones C#–G, and E–B♭ in P0, RI5, and RI8. The prime forms of secondary aggregates A5 and A8 are also unified by shared tritones A–E♭ and C–F#.

Row Divisions

The foremost division of the row is trichordal, as in the opening bars of the opera. The related division is into hexachordal formation, both by normally dividing the row into two halves, PX_1 and PX_2, and by dividing the row into trichords and grouping the two middle trichords into a hexachord PX_{b+c} (which has been demonstrated above). It is in this latter use that a hexachordal division is most prominently used motivically throughout the first scene. The transformations of this linear motive, together with the chordal motive of trichords a and d, are centrally important in providing motivic unity for the entire opera.

The more conventional division of P0 into hexachords $P0_1$ and $P0_2$ is also presented at the opening of the opera at the first complete linear statement of P0 in mm. 6–7, shown in musical example 4-11.

Two other divisions of the row are frequently employed. One is the division into tetrachords, $PX_{x,y,z}$, which is often deliberately employed to

Musical Example 4-11

achieve a contrasting texture. For example, the first tetrachordal division of the row has a definitely new sound at Moses' entrance in mm. 8–10, with vertical alignment of each tetrachord in long held chords, contrasting with the trichordal and hexachordal material of the preceding measures as shown in musical example 4-12. Tetrachordal material often appears in a vertical arrangement as a means of introducing change or tension into a largely trichordal/hexachordal context throughout the scene.

A second division of the row which has a similar disquieting or tension-building effect in the music is the division into dyads. These dyads may be formed by isolating two notes of a trichord in the orchestral texture so that the third note is heard as accompanying the dyad, or dyads may be pulled out of a tetrachordal setting. For example, the dyadic arrangement of notes in Act I, Scene 1, m. 16 is created by separating out notes of trichords

as shown in musical example 4-13.

This fragmented-sounding texture, with its ambiguity between groupings of twos and threes provides the first important structural break from a previous section of trichordal and hexachordal material predominating within a large block. It also presents a new motivic sound after the piling up of the two opening motives composed of chords (trichords a and d of P and RI row forms) and linear statements of the inner hexachord b+c in mm. 11–15, shown in musical example 4-14.

Later in the opera a tetrachord-plus-dyad division is also used, grouped from within a hexachord and occasionally even rotated (that is, $P0_{1\,2+4}$, $P0_{2\,4+2}$ becoming $P0_{1\,2}$, $P0_{2\,4+2}$, $P0_{1\,2}$). That such procedure was part of Schoenberg's conscious and intentional technique is demonstrated by many examples in the sources, such as in Source Ab, 2^v and also folio 1(2) and (4). An early example of this technique occurs in the final score in Act I, Scene 1 at mm. 44–45, shown in musical example 4-15.

A more complex example is found at mm. 79–80 of the same scene, with $RI8_{1\,4+2}$, $RI0_{2\,4+2}$ in the lower brass instruments, together with three purely dyadic divisions of $I0_2$, $I0_1$ in the horns. In addition to this already dense structure, there are chordal arrangements of hexachords $I0_2$, $I0_1$, all accompanying a *Hauptstimme* of the important b+c motive, now in inversion form, as $I0_{b+c}$. These measures are shown in musical example 4-16.

In the next two measures, this tetrachord-plus-dyad arrangement becomes rotated as shown in musical example 4-17.

Musical Example 4-12

Musical Example 4-13

Musical Example 4-14

Musical Example 4-15

Musical Example 4-16

Musical Example 4-17

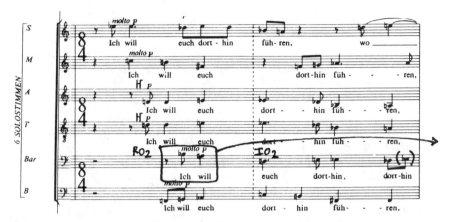

Articulation of Form

> *Form in music serves to bring about comprehensibility, through memorability.*[6]

> *Deviation from regularity and symmetry does not necessarily endanger comprehensibility.*[7]

Schoenberg described form in terms of grammatical principles—the connection of musical ideas, and the structure of musical phrases and sentences. In his essay "Brahms the Progressive" (1947), he used the term "musical prose" to refer to asymmetrical phrasing, avoidance of simple repetition, and other techniques of creating the directness of expression, the kind of emancipation of the rhythm at the service of the inner idea that he observed in the works of Mozart and Brahms.[8]

Schoenberg gave a detailed list of techniques of rhythm, phrasing, and other aspects which he would later include in his discussion of "musical prose" in the earlier essay "National Music (II)" (1931), outlining them in the context of describing his inheritance from Bach, Mozart, Beethoven, Brahms, and Wagner. This outline provides important information about Schoenberg's evolutionary compositional procedure, which remained undisturbed by his method of composing with twelve tones:[9]

From *Bach* I learned:
1. Contrapuntal thinking; i.e., the art of inventing musical figures that can be used to accompany themselves.
2. The art of producing everything from one thing and of relating figures by transformation.
3. Disregard for the "strong" beat of the measure.

From *Mozart*:
1. Inequality of phrase-length.
2. Co-ordination of heterogeneous characters to form a thematic unity.
3. Deviation from even-number construction in the theme and its component parts.
4. The art of forming subsidiary ideas.
5. The art of introduction and transition.

From *Beethoven*:
1. The art of developing themes and movements.
2. The art of variation and of varying.
3. The multifariousness of the ways in which long movements can be built.
4. The art of being shamelessly long, or heartlessly brief, as the situation demands.
5. Rhythm: the displacement of figures on to other beats of the bar.

From *Wagner*:

1. The way it is possible to manipulate themes for expressive purposes and the art of formulating them in the way that will serve this end.

2. Relatedness of tones and chords.

3. The possibility of regarding themes and motives as if they were complex ornaments, so that they can be used against harmonies in a dissonant way.

From *Brahms*:

1. Much of what I had unconsciously absorbed from Mozart, particularly odd barring, and extension and abbreviation of phrases.

2. Plasticity in moulding figures; not to be mean, not to stint myself when clarity demands more space; to carry every figure through to the end.

3. Systematic notation.

4. Economy, yet richness.

To observe how Schoenberg applied his own understanding of musical prose to the composition of *Moses und Aron*, the long vocal lines of Aron's first entrance in Act I, Scene 2, mm. 123–47 provide a good example for analysis.

The vocal line emerges on an unaccented beat from under 1½-measure *Hauptstimme* played by three trombones. Aron's three sentences divide into phrases as follows:

Sentence 1:
(row = P4)

Sentence 2:
(row = I4)   (row = R4)

Sentence 3:
(row = RI4)

```
            6½ mm. as 4 phrases                    2½ mm.
       ┌─────────────────────────────┐         ┌─────────┐
      1+½   ½+½+½+½    ½+¾    ¼ + 1 + ½      ½ + 2
       ⌣(rpt.)                                    (rest)
      139 140    141      142    143   144   145 146-7
```

This diagram shows the complexity of Schoenberg's layering of asymmetrical subdivisions: at the outset, the entire section is twenty-five measures long, not an evenly divisible number. There is no room for interpreting this length otherwise: the section is clearly demarcated on each end at the barline by a meter change (from 6/8 to 4/4(12/8) and from 4/4(12/8) to 3/4, respectively), and row change: from the modulatory "wasteland" music at the opening of the scene to Aron's series of clear linear statements of the four row forms of A4 in m. 123, and from A4 to A7 in m. 148.

Within the twenty-five measures, there are three main musical sentences, corresponding to Aron's three sentences of text. These contain totals of seven, nine, and nine measures, respectively. The division of the section into four row forms still corresponds with this structure: the first and last sentences contain P4 and RI4, and the middle sentence contains I4 and R4, dividing between the two where the next smaller subdivision of phrases occurs.

Within the seven-, nine-, and nine-measure-long phrases, subdivisions occur with no two alike: two subphrases within the seven-measure phrase as 4mm + 3mm; two subphrases within the first nine-measure phrase as 5mm + 4mm; and one long subphrase within the second nine-measure phrase, plus 2½ mm. of rest. The actual number of *smaller* subphrases which make up these subphrases is similarly varied: for example, in Sentence 1:

```
        4mm. 3mm.      ;   5mm.              4mm.       ;
                      ┌─────────┐      ┌──────────────────┐
#subphr:  3  2+½ rest   ;  ¼ rest+4    ¼ rest+2+½ rest;

          6½mm. 2½mm.
#subphr:    4    (rest)
```

An odd *Vierhebigkeit* thus emerges after the initial grouping of three phrases in mm. 123–26, where the number of phrases within larger groupings are in groups of two and four—but the interspersing of ¼-measure and ½-measure rests and the resulting avoidance of downbeat metrical accent renders this analytical detail inaudible.

The phrasing agrees well with Schoenberg's description of musical prose. It carefully accents the words and phrases of the text and the natural pauses among them. It is a highly accurate declamatory style, truly proselike in character, and would retain the proselike quality even if the text were absent. A relationship may also be observed between this declamatory style and Wagner's style of declamation, and between the proselike melodic phrasing and Wagner's *endlöse Melodie.*[10]

Schoenberg also uses the opportunity in this passage to apply his technique of musical prose to characterization, as he observed in the opening duet of Figaro and Susanna in Mozart's *Marriage of Figaro.*[11] Moses' *Sprechstimme* part has many more sentences than Aron's sung melodies; and while Moses' lines are short and rhythmically active, full of eighth and sixteenth notes, Aron's are long, declaimed at a languorous pace, and use mostly quarter notes with relatively much less use of eighth and sixteenth notes. Moses' lines further subdivide easily into one-beat units. They do not correspond with Aron's phrasing, expressing the tension between the two brothers: for example, in the first sentence:

Further, Moses, the lawgiver, intones phrases which do not subdivide the beats as much as Aron's do with dotted rhythms and ties, but rather adhere to the metrical barlines more easily. However, asymmetry, in the form of syncopation and avoidance of strong downbeat attacks, is still present in Moses' musical prose as well.

It is also important to analyze Schoenberg's manipulation of form on a larger level. It is particularly the larger structural divisions of *Moses und Aron* which contribute to the comprehensibility of the work, one of Schoenberg's greatest concerns.[12] The large-scale formal structure of the opera corresponds with blocks of music in certain row areas, which function referentially as key areas would in a tonal work. (This is shown in the formal diagram in Appendix 3.) Other elements function together with this "tonal" plan to create an audible impression of sectional form. These include both textural and temporal, i.e., rhythmic and metrical, changes between sections, which reinforce changes between large blocks of music in a given aggregate or row form. These changes, rather than being independent of the text, support its sectional and dramatic structure.

Large articulations are achieved by traditional cadences—not traditional in the sense of "V–I" tonality, of course. These are points of rest achieved by long chords or notes, sometimes held by a fermata and/or articulated by rests, including grand pauses. Schoenberg describes the grammatical usefulness of both grand pauses and direct juxtaposition of different materials as formal articulating devices in his essay "Connection of Musical Ideas" (1948).[13] As a simple example, a clear cadence occurs in Act I, Scene 1 at m. 15: the cadencing material is closed with a fermata, then at m. 16 there is a new instrumental texture, a new rhythmic figure, a new row—a new "tonality"— and a new section of text with a new character singing, shown in musical example 4-18.

Transformations of motivic material may also reinforce the articulation of form. For example, during Moses' argument with the voices in the Burning Bush, the long section beginning at m. 16 (see previous musical example) is shaped by all the contrast-producing devices listed above, and is supported by the manipulation of the opening motive of chords as well. From the very beginning of the opera, the expected motion of the opening chords is set up as $P0_a$–$P0_d$, and $RI0_a$–$RI0_d$. Moses' argument contains this expected motion in m. 17 as $RI5_a$–$RI5_d$. The Burning Bush responds with this motion in inversion at m. 23: $I0_a$–$I0_d$, then, overlapping with this statement, presents the motive in retrograde: $R0_a$–$R0_d$ in the second half of the measure, shown in musical example 4-19.

As resolution begins to take place, the original motion of trichord a to trichord d is restored in mm. 26–27, and a new section begins after a clear cadence on the single held high B♮ in the winds and violins in m. 28 (which itself is a heightened version of the melodic motive set up in the opening bars of the opera). This is shown in musical example 4-20.

Texture is a very important articulating device. Texture changes involving shifts of instrumental timbre and increasing or decreasing of overall density, usually in conjunction with changes in rhythmic configuration, account for the most audible articulations of section changes. Strictly homophonic passages are few, and have striking effect (for example, the passage of sustained tetrachords accompanying Moses's entrance in Act I, scene 1, mm. 8–10. (See musical example 4-8.) Here also, however, note the strong horizontal component of the important inner hexachord $P0_{b+c}$ in the English horn and tuba, which provides the actual motivic material from which the particular supporting tetrachords were chosen.

One last method of articulation of form which is employed at special places is change of meter. This is particularly true in the Golden Calf scene, Act II, Scene 3, where large form is defined by repetitions of certain dance rhythms in large sections. (For a formal outline of this scene, see Appendix 3.) On a smaller scale, a major articulation is made in m. 272 of the same scene by establishing a stable area of 3/4 meter after a long section of shifting meters from m. 253ff:[14]

Musical Example 4-18

Musical Example 4-19

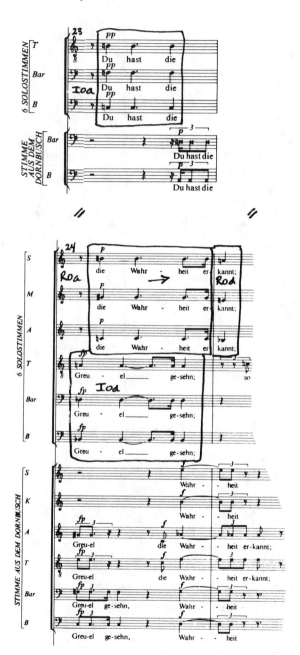

Musical Example 4-20

m.   253: 2/4 254–55: 3/4   256:   2/4   257: 4/4 258: 3/4
      259: 2/4 260–61: 3/4   262:   2/4 263–64: 3/4 265: 2/4
   266–67: 3/4   268: 2/4 269:   4/4   270: 3/4 271: 2/4
      272: 3/4 until m. 288.

Derivation of Motivic and Thematic Material

In a letter to René Leibowitz, 1 October 1945, Schoenberg wrote that the row
of any twelve-tone work has the property of providing motivic unity: "The
main purpose of the 'row' is to *unify the motival material* and to enhance the
logic of simultaneous sounding tones."[15] Two years later, Schoenberg wrote
again to Leibowitz: "The main purpose of twelve-note composition is:
production of coherence through the use of a unifying succession of tones
which should function at least *like a motive.*"[16] In the essay "Composition
with Twelve Tones" (1941), Schoenberg also wrote, concerning the
compositional process of *Moses und Aron* itself,[17]

> I found that ... the more familiar I became with this set the more easily I could *draw themes
> from it.* Thus, the truth of my first prediction had received splendid proof. One has to follow
> the basic set; but, nevertheless, *one composes as freely as before.* (emphasis added)

Moses und Aron, because it is composed entirely from a single basic row, is a
primary example in Schoenberg's œuvre of his use of twelve-tone composition
to generate a motivic and thematic whole. A chart of the main motives of the
opera is provided for reference in Appendix 2.

The genesis of the row itself and the first two motivic ideas of the opera—
the trichordal chords and the hexachordal linear gesture—were a single
creative act, as described in chapter 1. On the same day Schoenberg
constructed the row (paying a great deal of attention to the possibilities of row
divisions and the relationships possible among them), and jotted down the
opening chordal sonorities (Source Ab, 6[1] "Arbeit angefangen am 16/VII 30;
Reihe entworfen und I Skizze 7.V.30." The idea of chords as the opening
material then probably generated the second motive, made up of melodic
material left over from using the first and last trichords of the row in chordal
formation, which also exploited the semicombinatorial relationship of the
row. This was enough to generate the first music of the opera.

Another important motive of early derivation which has a melodic and
rhythmic outline contrasting to the opening materials suggests that some
motives were probably first conceived in terms of broad contour, rather than
in terms of specific notes as in the opening material of the opera just discussed.
The sources show that an important motive (first introduced in Act I, Scene 1,
but first highlighted in Act I, Scene 2, m. 123) was first invented with a slightly

different sonority in mind than the final version of the motive as it now appears. This motive is a melodic perfect fifth followed by a minor second moving in the opposite direction. The motive in its most common presentation is made up of the first, third, and fifth notes of a given row form, and typically is accompanied by the remaining notes of the first hexachord. Its striking and memorable contour suggests that Schoenberg may have wanted such a shape and then looked at the row to determine how to derive it. The early appearance of this motive in the sources in fragmentary form supports its early genesis—it is included in the *Thementafel* in Source Ab, folio 1.

The very first presentation of the motive in Act I, Scene 1 is not in its most characteristic form. It appears at mm. 32ff as the first, fourth, and fifth notes of P8, played pianissimo by the flute in a high register, and as the first, fourth, and fifth notes of I8 played in the high register of the violin. The whole configuration of this passage also incorporates the first and second trichords of the row, giving the effect of a wrong resolution of the first trichord, which would ordinarily be expected to move toward the last trichord instead. This passage is shown in musical example 4-21.

The next statement of the motive occurs at Act I, Scene 2, m. 123, Aron's entrance. This is quite transparent division of row material, with the very bold *Hauptstimme* statement of the motive played by three trombones, configured as the first, third and fifth of I4, and accompanied by the second, fourth, and sixth notes in the string basses. This is the first full statement of the motive with its characteristic accompaniment. The appearance of this motive was planned early in the compositional process. Originally, in the *Thementafel* sketch in Source Ab, Aron was to sing the motive in its ascending form as the first, third, and fifth notes of P0, shown in musical example 4-22.[18]

The motive became more highlighted in the next sketch version, pulled out to be played by three trombones and three contrabassoons. It appears in its descending form, which had to be derived from a different row, marked in the sketch by Schoenberg as T+3 (=P4), but which actually uses the first, third, and fifth notes of the related inversion form I4. The motive still accompanies Aron's first phrase, shown in musical example 4-23.[19]

The motive is given its strongest statement in the final version. Here it remains in the three trombones as the first, third, and fifth notes of I4, contrapuntally accompanied by the necessary second, fourth, and sixth notes in the string basses, heard slightly later. In this version, Aron does not sing until the entire motive is outlined first, as shown in musical example 4-24. Schoenberg's final choice for the motive of notes E,A,B♭ still refers back to P0, because the three notes also constitute the first trichord of P0.

By tracing this compositional process, we can see the importance of the motivic idea in Schoenberg's thought in shaping the rest of the material around it. As with other compositional techniques described above, this

Musical Example 4-21

Musical Example 4-22

Musical Example 4-23

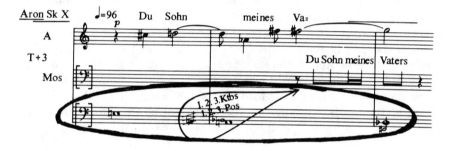

Musical Example 4-24

practice again shows the debt which Schoenberg owed to classical and nineteenth-century composition. This may be seen not only in his use of "musical prose" as he observed it in Mozart and Brahms, but also in his composition of motivic and thematic material, and in his use of motives to unify and direct the continuation of a piece. The motive itself, while carved out of the row as the first, third, and fifth notes, has an intended striking and memorable contour which could conceivably be found in any row. Schoenberg treats it within the bounds of serial theory by handling it consistently and accompanying it with the notes necessary to complete the row. Therefore, while the specific notes of this important motive were certainly drawn out of the row, it is likely that the basic idea of a contrasting and memorable melodic motive pre-existed the actual notes.

In summary, then, the row was most likely drafted before any actual musical material was sketched, but in very close association with the first sketch for the opening chords of the opera. Subsequent motivic invention was drawn from the notes of the row and may have been suggested by a number of factors. These include notes left over from another motive or motives (as is likely in the case of the six-note linear motive which follows the opening chordal motive in Act I, Scene 1), and notes available in a given row or hexachord to produce a desired preconceived melodic contour, as in the case of the three-note motive highlighted in Act I, Scene 2, m. 123. In all cases, Schoenberg's statement is borne out that in composing *Moses und Aron* from a single row he was not limited, but was able to compose as before.

5

Musical Text Expression

The final task of this book is to explore the intimate relationship of music and text; and to begin to address the question of how Schoenberg, with his concern for the concepts of Idea and Representation, dealt in his own work with the constant struggle between the elusiveness of the Idea and the impotence of expression to capture it, not only in the realm of theological reflection on the God-Idea, but also in the realm of his work as a composer.

It is well known that Schoenberg was a composer with a high degree of concern for expressing both the overall meaning and the individual words of texted works.[1] Schoenberg's methods of expressing the text often avoided literalistic tone painting, and tended more toward creating a total inner mood (as in expressionist drama which creates an entire world within the work of art). In his own discussion of the Four Orchestra Songs, Op. 22, Schoenberg wrote that he avoided literal text painting and preferred more subtle portrayal of meaning of a whole thought.[2] He explained, "Apparent superficial divergences [from text painting] can be necessary because of parallelism on a higher level."[3]

He discussed inner resemblance between text and musical composition as follows: "I am aware that it is mainly a concern with the art of variation, which allows for a motif to be a constant basis while, at the same time, doing justice to the subtlest nuance in the text."[4] He gave examples of his technique of text expression by describing his uses of color, vocal registers, and transparency of texture particularly in writing song no. 4, "Vorgefühl."[5] Finally, he also refuted the idea that a piece could avoid being expressive, even if the composer intended it to be:[6]

> In the preface to *Pierrot Lunaire* I had demanded that performers ought not to add illustrations and moods of their own derived from the text. In the epoch after the First World War, it was customary for composers to surpass me radically, even if they did not like my music. Thus when I had asked not to add external expression and illustration, they understood that expression and illustration were out, and that there should be no relation

whatsoever to the text. There were now composed songs, ballads, operas and oratorios in which the achievement of the composer consisted in a strict aversion against all that his text presented.

What nonsense! . . .

Songs, operas, and oratorios would not exist if music were not added to moods and actions.

Besides, how do you make sure that your music does not express something—or more: that it does not express something provoked by the text?

Characterization

One of the most basic means of portraying the text of any dramatic work in music is in differentiating the main characters musically. This is done by means of such elements as voice type, range and tessitura, melodic style, rhythmic style, and characteristic features of accompaniment.

The most striking technique of characterization in *Moses und Aron* is an effect immediately apparent to almost every listener. The ineloquent Moses, who tells the Burning Bush in Act I, Scene 1: "Meine Zunge ist ungelenk: ich kann denken, aber nicht reden," is cast as a *Sprechstimme* role, and never sings except at the one crucial line "Reinige dein Denken. . . ." Though his voice type is given as "*Sprechrolle*" rather than given as a singing range, a deep voice is called for in Schoenberg's instructions ("tiefe, sehr grosse Stimme"). This is also demonstrated in the very low tessitura of the *Sprechstimme* notation written in the bass clef. For example, at the line "Ich kann denken, aber nicht reden," the last note in the *Sprechstimme* is a growling low F♯, shown in musical example 5-1.

Musical Example 5-1

The eloquent character ordained as mouthpiece for the God idea, Aron, is cast as a tenor, with long virtuosic singing lines which touch both high and low extremes of his vocal range within very short spans of time. The contrast between Moses and Aron is clearly heard at the opening of Act I, Scene 2, where the brothers engage in their philosophical dialogue. Here, their vocal lines are juxtaposed as Moses' expressive deep *Sprechstimme* provides a constant corrective to Aron's roller-coaster rhapsodizing. The two parts are also differentiated rhythmically here: Aron's lines are smooth and long with mainly quarter- and eighth-note motion and a few brief melismas, while

Moses' speech is strictly syllabic, rhythmically emphatic, and in short note values, as shown in musical example 5-2.

Musical Example 5-2

As a third contrast, the Burning Bush is also characterized very clearly in musical terms. Karl Wörner (among others) has commented on the mysterious quality of the opening bars of the opera.[7] The humming energy of the opening wordless chords represent God's own self. As soon as interaction with the human world and Moses takes place, the chordal singing sonority of the six-voice choir is combined with a rustling *Sprechstimme* choir not heard before. The two choral groups voice the same words at different times in a transparent but polyphonic texture to create the other-worldly effect of an omnipresent voice which is located in the bush but is mysteriously at the same time all around Moses. The serene, slow harmonic motion of the chordal texture of the bush, which returns over and over to create a motivic transformation of the opening chords (the meaning of this motivic material will be discussed again below), is contrasted with Moses' straightforward statements, in quicker note values. Moses' declamation is closest to the Burning Bush's (God's) at the very beginning as he speaks the words which for Schoenberg are treated, as in *Der Biblische Weg*, almost as an incantational name of God: "Einziger, ewiger, allgegenwärtiger, unsichtbarer und, unvorstellbarer Gott!" Here his rhythm is very close to the *Sprechstimme* part of the Burning Bush in the next measures, shown in musical example 5-3.

Moses' rhythms diverge more sharply from the smooth continuity of the Burning Bush's rhythmic motion in his first long speech (mm. 16–22) when the conflict is initially introduced. Compare the static quality of Moses' speech in mm. 16ff, accompanied by long sustained chords, with the preceding rhythm and texture of mm. 13–15 as shown in musical example 5-4.

Accompanimental textures, enriched with highly varied orchestral colors, also support the musical characterization. Orchestration is, perhaps, the most prominent feature of characterization which is readily accessible to the listener. For example, in Act I, Scene 1, the Burning Bush generally appears in horizontal slow-moving configurations of polyphonically arranged blocks of sound, each of which is set in homophony or animated (i.e., slightly broken) homophony. While the text expresses a state of rest and resolution, this texture prevails. Division of row materials is primarily trichordal, strongly related to the opening chordal textures ($P0_{a,d}$ and $RI_{a,d}$).

When Moses enters, however, and the basic conflict of the scene (and the opera) is to be set in motion, Schoenberg employs a vertical texture—large choralelike chords in the orchestra using a tetrachordal arrangement of row material (mm. 8–10; see musical example 4-12.)

The prevailing row aggregate also changes on the harmonic level at this point from A0 to RI1 and P10, although the top line of the chorale texture spells out $P0_{b+c}$ so that the section remains within the A0 family on one level. The change of texture and row strikes the ear as something distinctly different from the prevailing slow-moving trichordal, block-polyphonic texture of the Burning Bush; and introduces tension which, as the scene continues, is extended in each successive confrontation of Moses with the bush. Real tension is brought about at Moses's long speech at mm. 16–22, in which more vertical and tetrachordal sonorities are employed, together with the first extensive use of dyads, creating a feeling of further tension and fragmentation, as shown in musical example 5-4.

The Burning Bush then responds to the mounting excitement of Moses' objections. The effect is similar to the quicker motion of molecules in a heated liquid—both choral and orchestral textures become more broken up, more contrapuntal within the larger groupings of voices, and with more varied divisions of row material. This effect is intensified throughout the scene with each ensuing confrontation—the textures of Moses' speech at mm. 16ff are picked up again in his next speech at mm. 29–30, and again at mm. 47–50 where wide spacings of chords and repeated chords in pairs (mm. 51–53) continue the same vertical textural feeling, although now that Moses has hit on the main problem, the opening chords are heard in inversion, along with the opening motive $P0_{b+c}$ (mm. 48–49ff).

Musical Example 5-3

* Anfangs schwach besetzt

Musical Example 5-4

In response to these passages, the chorus also begins to use tetrachordal structures, and the 2+4 grouping of row material described in chapter 4 is used (mm. 44ff). After Moses' critical speech at mm. 47–53, the chorus is whipped into its most contrapuntal response, with the three-part blocks broken up into contrapuntal voices with varying internal pairings. Here the row is treated entirely tetrachordally until, at m. 59, the solution is reached and the opening chords and blocks of three voices plus three voices in the singing choir return. The accompanying orchestration is similar to the opening, using brass and winds. Only the transposition of the chords to P8 and RI8 keeps this arrival from being a complete return of opening material, which is utterly consistent with the text—the pure, perfect state of the motive representing God alone cannot be communicated within the human context—the perfect version of God's essence cannot be used in connection with Aron, or in the light of the conflict with Moses.

The ensuing blessing section at m. 71 is again polyphonic, now incorporating dyadic, widely spread sonorities (m. 71 in the winds), with opening motivic material (m. 71 in the strings).

There are also a few examples of quite literal text painting in the opera. One of the most delightful examples, and one which interrupts the dense mood of the instrumental music of the opera with a markedly different sound, occurs at the opening of the Golden Calf scene (Act II, mm. 320–70) to accompany stage action of a procession of animals being brought for ritual slaughter, shown in musical example 5-5 (mm. 334–37). Exotic rhythms are used to convey a vaguely Near Eastern sound and to produce the jostling of herds of large animals; and special glissandi in strings, winds, and brass (especially the trombones) imitate the sounds of the animals with striking realism.

Musical Example 5-5

*Das gliss. sehr gut hören lassen; die ganze Saite herunter!

Leitmotive

Can the term *Leitmotiv* justifiably be applied to an analysis of *Moses und Aron*? Karl Wörner has written:[8]

> In considering the symbolism of musical themes and their recurrence, we must not think of Wagner's *Leitmotiv* technique. The musical symbols in Schoenberg's opera, and Wagner's leading-motives, merely rest on a common basis: the ability of music to act as the expressive form (symbol) of a given conceptual and affective content. Certain contents and musical themes present themselves simultaneously, and blend, in a new unity, in the listener's mind. With Wagner, the themes themselves are symbols for ideas, objects, external events, sentiments or dramatic impulses. ... With Schoenberg, on the other hand, there is only *one* spiritual idea. Its name is God, and it is in the summons to Moses, and the promise to the people, that this idea manifests itself. It is the focus of the work, and not a *Leitmotiv*, either in its spiritual or in its musical significance; it is the life of the spirit itself.

In fact, *Leitmotive* do function in *Moses und Aron*, as in Wagner's operas, just as Wörner describes them.[9]

Schoenberg himself referred to his own use of *Leitmotive* in the much earlier work *Verklärte Nacht*, in his essay "Heart and Brain in Music" (1946),[10]

> ... it will be astonishing to you as it was to all my friends when I came with the score of *Verklärte Nacht* and showed them one particular measure on which I had worked a full hour, though I had written the entire score of 415 measures in 3 weeks. This measure is indeed a little complicated since, according to the artistic conviction of this period (the post-Wagnerian), I wanted to express the idea behind the poem, and the most adequate means to that end seemed a complicated contrapuntal combination: a *leitmotiv* and its inversion played simultaneously.

If we consider the unifying element of the row as it is used to generate an overall "tonal plan" as described above, it becomes comparable to the key plan of a Wagner opera, within which the *Leitmotive* may then be seen to provide the actual musical substance over the skeleton of the tonal scheme, as Schoenberg himself remarked in "Brahms the Progressive":[11]

> Dramatic music resembles in its modulatory character the modulatory elaboration (*Durchführung*) of a symphony, sonata, or other rounded form. Wagner's *Leitmotive* usually contain some germinating harmonies in which the urge for modulatory changes is inherent. But simultaneously they fulfil another task, an organizational task, which shows the formalistic side of Wagner's genius.

In both Wagner's operas and in *Moses und Aron*, the tonal scheme is related to the motivic plan of the opera, because certain motives are, at least initially, identified strongly by the ear with a certain key or row. For example, the rolling opening E♭ chord of the Rhine in *Rheingold* which belongs to a family of "nature" *Leitmotive* in E♭ may be compared to the opening chords of *Moses und Aron* with P0 and RI0 as their proper pitch level. The tonal plan of the operas, therefore, may both shape and be shaped by the needs of motivic transformation, as the ideas and characters represented by the motives change and progress through the course of the opera. A table of *Leitmotive* is provided in Appendix 2.

The first scene is very important, because it contains, at least germinally, most of the important motives and themes which are developed throughout the opera. The main musical materials and textures are all contained in three important scenes: Act I, Scene 1, Moses with God; contrasting with Act I, Scene 2, Moses with Aron; and the very long Golden Calf scene, Act II, Scene 3, where the musical elements representing conflict with God are given their fullest development. A complete motivic analysis of the opera, showing corresponding row areas and important text and dramatic action, is given in Appendix 3.

It is clear by the context of the first scene that the opening music of the opera, preceding the curtain, is intended to be associated with God.[12] The same opening material is used as the initial calling of the Burning Bush to Moses in mm. 11ff, but now words are added in order to communicate.

The two motives introduced in the opening of the opera, the central unifying motives of the entire opera, labeled in Appendix 2 as M1 and M2a, are the chordal motives $P0_{a,d}$ (=M1) and $RI0_{a,d}$ (=M1'), and the linear motive $P0_{b+c}$ (=M2a) and $RI0_{b+c}$ (=M2a').

Wörner, while rejecting the use of the term *Leitmotiv* in connection with *Moses und Aron*, suggests the symbolism of God alone in the opening chords, and God reaching out, God's will, in the subsequent six-note motive.[13] He describes the chords as a representation of pure calm, and compares them to Schoenberg's use of similar chords in similar programmatic contexts in the String Trio at the moment of calm following the crisis of the first movement; in *Herzgewächse* at the last bars at "Ihr mystisches Gebet;" and in *Erwartung*, the single moment of calm at the words "der Weg ist breit." In fact, in his musical example from *Erwartung*, the chords to which he refers clearly begin not with the text "der Weg ist breit," but with "*Gottes willen...*"!

Wörner describes the second motive, the six-note linear motive, as God reaching out to humanity, or God's will, in the following words:[14]

> In disclosing Himself to Moses, God emerges from His infinity, becoming will and thought. At this point a theme arises, a self-contained melodic inversion of six notes, cast in mirror-form, the fourth, fifth and sixth notes of which are the retrograde of the first three notes. Thus the theme becomes a symbol of order and divine will.

He goes on to trace this theme through the opera.

The way the motives associated with God undergo transpositions, inversions, and melodic transformations throughout the opera is consistent with the central idea of the text. God's Word is being interpreted and transmitted through Moses, through Aron, to the people, in increasingly changed form. Also, God's music is associated with the row structure in a special way: both motives are based on trichordal divisions of the row which have already been identified on solely musical grounds in chapter 4 as A0.[15]

Trichordal and hexachordal motives are the most simple, natural division of row material within Schoenberg's own twelve-tone system, and are particularly suggested by the trichordal mirror patterns built into the row of the opera, described in chapter 4, producing Schoenberg's favorite tritone and quartal chords, so characteristic of atonality because of their symmetrical balance and avoidance of any traditional references to a tonic-dominant polarization. It may be observed that Schoenberg intended the purest use of his own system, the twelve-tone system, to represent God, while its distortion is meant to represent the distortion of the God-Idea. Schoenberg most likely viewed the row itself as a compositional rule parallel to the Law (Torah) or the Commandments.[16]

The M2a motive may be divided into two related motives: first, the six-note arpeggios based on trichords b and c of P0 and R10 (which also appear in transposition later in the opera, as may be seen in the motivic analysis in Appendix 3) are labeled M2a and M2a', respectively. Later in the opera M2a is also heard as a natural row hexachord, stated linearly, and is labeled M2a''.

A second M2 motive, M2b, derived from the first, consists of only half of M2a—either trichord b or c, also presented linearly. This motive makes up a special "motto" motive, or a motive intended to be a musical signal for a central word in the text, in this case "Verkünde." It appears near the end of Act I, Scene 1, after the relative resolution of the conflict between Moses and the Burning Bush, where Moses is sent out on his prophetic mission with the word "Verkünde!", shown in musical example 5-6.

This motto motive is foreshadowed in m. 70 at the word "gesegnet" (blessed), and is accompanied by two motives, one belonging to Moses (M4d) and one belonging to Aron (M5), as shown in musical example 5-7.

It may be inferred from this textual association with the M2 motive that while M1 represents God's presence in essence, the M2 motives represent God's word, or even more specifically, God's word being sent out through the chosen prophet.

As discussed above, Wörner has written that the God-music (here labeled M1 and M2) constitutes the only text-expressive idea or theme and dominates the whole opera. In relation to Aron, he writes, "Twice only does he have a theme of his own," referring to the opening of Act I, Scene 2 as a depiction of

Musical Example 5-6

Musical Example 5-6 (continued)

Musical Example 5-7

"he floated rather than walked," and the melody at m. 163, "auserwähltes Volk...."[17] However, musical materials which work clearly as *Leitmotive* are also present to represent Aron, Moses, and other characters and ideas.

Contrasting music and contrasting ideas are represented by the third motive family, labeled M3. The first of these motives, M3a, a triad, is introduced very subtly in Act I, Scene 1, m. 7, as a moment of foreshadowing of the motive's first truly audible arrival in Scene 2. It is brought out as a *Hauptstimme*, played by three trombones; but its subtle connection with tonality is disguised by the clearly atonal vertical sonorities in which it is couched, as shown in musical example 5-8.

Musical Example 5-8

1.2.3. Posaune

The motive is presented again in the bass strings in mm. 17–18,, somewhat buried in a dense texture of motivic material mainly related to M1 and M2, shown in musical example 5-9.

The first pronounced presentation of the M3a triad which establishes its connection with Aron is in Scene 2 at mm. 163–68. Aron is accompanied by chords which are heard as related to the opening chordal textures while he sings "...einen einzigen Gott...." As the chords move from one to the next, however, they sound like deliberate distortions of the opening "God" chords of M1. This is precisely the intended effect—Aron's God-idea can only be a distortion of the "real thing." The second of these chords is the M3a triad; the first contains a third also, at the top, combined with a seventh. The two chords together are labeled in Appendix 2 as M3b, as shown in musical example 5-10.

It is significant that the distortion of the pure, logically row-related quartal chords of M1 should involve chords with intervals of thirds and sevenths—intervals much closer to traditional tonality, even going so far as actual root-position triads as in mm. 163 and 167–68. If the purity of the atonal row represents God, then the hint of tonality is given by Schoenberg as moving away from God—perhaps a hidden strike against tonality? To take the parallel even further, the newness and daring of Moses' quest to obey an unknowable God may be seen in Schoenberg's mind as forging of new paths in composition, with tonality being portrayed by the sensuality and weak backsliding into the easier, old accessible religiosity represented by the Golden Calf: if twelve-tone composition is difficult and visionary, then traditional tonal composition is easy and idolatrous.

Musical Example 5-9

Musical Example 5-10

*mit vollem Ton, jedoch ohne den Sänger zu decken

Yet it is also important to remember that the first subtle presentation of M3, the seeds of Aron's wrongness, are found within the setting of God's own music as early as m. 7. Is Schoenberg suggesting that everything, even the potential for human disobedience and error are foreknown, even preordained in God?

The fourth family of motives, labeled M4, belongs to Moses. All the M4 motives have in common a dyadic and/or tetrachordal division of row material, and many are vertical in textural arrangement as well. As has already been observed above in the discussion of characterization, Moses tends to be accompanied by vertical textures as distinct from the horizontal, contrapuntal textures of God's music. Even the chords of M1 are not strongly vertical in their impact on the listener: they are sustained for a long time and progress in pairs from one to the next, and they overlap with other chords and with the M2 motive in a contrapuntal organization, as in the opening bars. Moses also tends to be accompanied by nontrichordal but logical divisions of the row: dyadic and tetrachordal textures, as in the appearance of Moses' first motive, M4a, already described as the tetrachordal accompaniment of his first statement in mm. 8–10, first introduced under the umbrella of the M2 motive in the top voice. These tetrachords are also heard as different from, but related to, the opening chordal structures since they contain somewhat similar quartal sonorities. But compared to Aron's distorted chords at mm. 163–68, they sound much closer to God's chords. They are still nontriadic and largely quartal in sound, even including the B♭–E tritone of M1 in the first chord of m. 8. They are drawn from a natural, logical division of row material, and are still connected to P0 by the overlying presence of M2 at P0 pitch level.

On the other hand, Aron's chords at mm. 163–68 are produced by a much more contrived method of row division, shown in musical example 5-11.

This chordal structure is also connected to the rising perfect fifth and falling half-step motive mentioned above under the discussion of derivation of motivic material. This very important motive is also associated with Aron, as will be seen.

The difference between Moses' dyadic motives and the previous "God" music is, then, mainly textural and rhythmic. As described above in the discussion of characterization in the music, the effect of this different texture is to introduce tension and to depict the conflict between Moses and God. The tetrachords at mm. 8–10 are still tied to the sound of the opening chords; but at m. 16 a second motive crystallizes out of the melodic gesture of jagged leaps and the contrapuntal division of material into groupings of two in an open, exposed texture. These seemingly dyadic divisions, however, produce on a vertical level the opening chords in inversion, with the two inner trichords now between the first and last trichords so that the characteristic motion from trichord a to d is not heard.

Musical Example 5-11

Moses' second motive, M4b, is introduced as a special inversion of God's music—not as a distortion of actual pitch content as in Aron's chords at mm. 163–68, but as a special inversion texturally broken up to disguise its motivic connection to the opening material. The actual distinguishing feature of this M4 motive, then, is the leaping melodic character and the dyadic sonority produced by the rhythmic structure, rather than the motive's actual pitch content.

The next M4 motive, M4c, utilizes the dyadic characteristic of M4 in a semitone presentation, shown in musical example 5-12.

Musical Example 5-12

The stepwise motive is native to the abundance of major and minor seconds of the row itself. M4c evolves into several variant versions throughout the opera. The first, M4c′, is a single sustained chromatic dyad, first appearing in Act I, m. 64 pianissimo in the strings, and then emphatically in Act II, mm. 45–47, opening Act II on the theme of Moses' prolonged absence, shown in musical example 5-13.

M4c″, the second development of M4c′ appears as four chromatic notes in succession in Act I, Scene 4, m. 656, highlighted in the upper register of the piccolo, shown in musical example 5-14.

Another version of M4c″, now with two different semitone dyads in alternation, appears in Act II, Scene 2, just before the Golden Calf scene, in m. 293, as shown in musical example 5-15.

It should be noted that these brief appearances of variant versions of M4c do not replace appearances of M4c, but rather are developed from it in a cumulative fashion, as may be seen in the motivic analysis in Appendix 3.

M4c in m. 21 is followed in the next measure by M4d, dyads played as a *Hauptstimme* within the vertical context of a tetrachordal arrangement of notes which form a configuration of parallel sevenths, played by the horns. This configuration appears with a variant of the parallel sevenths, a linear statement of ninths and sevenths played by a solo cello as a *Hauptstimme* within a tetrachordal context, shown in musical example 5-16.

Musical Example 5-13

II. Akt
1. Szene
Aron und die siebzig Ältesten vor dem Berg der Offenbarung

Musical Example 5-14

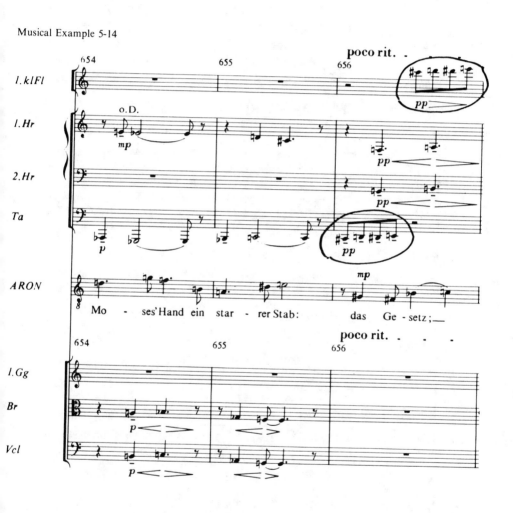

Musical Example 5-15

Musical Example 5-16

Later in the opera, the same motive M4d′ generates the "wilderness" texture of the opening of Act I, Scene 2, shown in musical example 5-17. This

Musical Example 5-17

scene is rich in associations—the appearance of sevenths and ninths at m. 22 may be foreshadowing the wilderness text: "lass mich in Ruhe meine Schafe weiden!" (making the association between the wilderness and the nomadic sheep herding across wilderness areas). Since, at the opening of Act I, Scene 2, it is Moses who now is in control and has the message to convey, trichordal and contrapuntal textures of the Burning Bush disappear just as God has withdrawn. Moses goes alone to obey the command to prophesy, signaled by the development of motive M4d at the beginning of the scene. As the scene unfolds, and conflict of interpretation ensues between the brothers, Aron's motives and textures become increasingly dominant. The end of the scene, shown in musical example 5-18, does not, in fact, result in a restoration of Moses' music (much less God's). The music here is a kind of amalgamation of

Musical Example 5-18

Musical Example 5-18 (continued)

all three, with the suggestion of God's music at the end buried within the rest of the texture as a reminder that in some sense God is still at work in the whole process.

A later version of M4d, labeled M4d″, which also makes use of parallel sevenths, appears in Act I, Scene 4, mm. 487ff, as an agitated accompaniment to further conflict between Moses and Aron. This immediately follows Moses' words to Aron: "er will nicht den Teil, er fordert das Ganze;" and accompanies Aron's looming into the foreground as Moses stands behind him in the background, shown in musical example 5-19.

The next M4 motive, M4e, occurs at m. 44, expanding the idea of dyadic and tetrachordal arrangements of pitch content into a 2+4 arrangement of notes and creating a new variation on the sonorities already established as belonging to the M4 family of motives, shown in musical example 5-20.

The last of the M4 motives, M4f, is a "motto" motive, associated with the single word "auserwählt." It is closest to motive M4c, oscillating half-step dyads, now made up of a half-step motion up and back down again (or down and up as it evolves). For this reason it could be considered another M4c motive; but because it has a special motto relationship to the text, it has a separate label under the general umbrella of M4 motives. It is also heard as related to motive M2b, the "Verkünde" motto motive, and therefore has a textual connection to God and the idea of prophecy as well as to Moses.

The concept of the chosen people is extremely important in Schoenberg's religious thinking, as described in chapter 2. The word "auserwählt" is first set in Act I, Scene 1, mm. 71ff, in a very special way. Surrounding this little motto, in m. 71, which eventually undergoes many transformations, are several divisions of row material. These include as a *Hauptstimme*, R01 which sounds melodically very much like a variation on M2, which it also resembles rhythmically. This is doubled by the altos. There is also a contrapuntal distribution of the notes of P01 in baritone and bass to complement and complete R01, which emphasizes the important initial A–B♭ dyad of P0 by repeating it, as well as an arrangement in the horns of P8$_2$ in a 4+2 grouping (separated by a rest) with a tritone leap linearly reminiscent of Moses' conflict music, M4. The first chord is repeated to create another rocking linear half-step motion, which generates the "auserwählt" motive in the tenors. The word "Volk" in the altos is highlighted by an imitation in the oboe on the last beat of the measure.

The measure is clearly dominated here both by Moses' motives and his sonorities: the dyadic figures (M4c), the 4+2 division of hexachordal material (M4e), the rocking stepwise figure in the motto of "auserwählt" itself, relating back to M4c. "God" music is also present, but varied from its original statement: now M2 is presented altered and in retrograde form, as R01 instead of P0$_{b+c}$. The same texture is retained up to m. 79, as long as the "auserwählt"

Musical Example 5-19

Musical Example 5-20

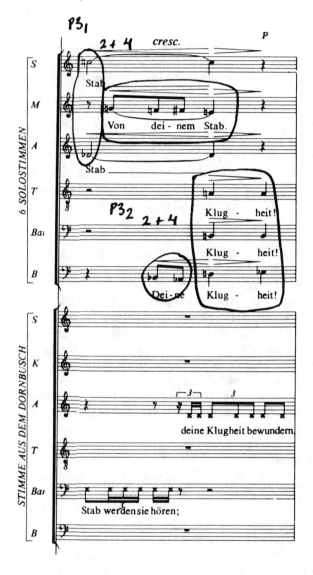

idea is being set in the text. So the music informs the text by conveying that the people, though blessed, are already removed one step from God's original essence, and their chosenness is already tempered by Moses' character.

The "auserwählt" motive begins in this way as an outgrowth of Moses' music M4c, the half-step motive. It also, as it undergoes development, shows itself to be very close in sound to the two mirrorlike inner trichords of the row which themselves depend on not one but two stepwise intervals for their identity (later becoming motto motive M2b). At the words "des einz'gen Gotts, zu sein" the "auserwählt" motive is heard in eighth notes on the words "Gotts, zu sein," immediately following a real statement of P0$_b$, also in eighth notes. Measures 71–78 are shown in musical example 5-21.

The audible relationship, as well as the differences, are clear. Chosenness is an idea close to and even generated from God (M2). However, as it also depends on human agency for fulfillment, it cannot quite achieve in the music a trichordal status, and falls back instead into a repetition of a note from the dyad.

The opening God idea of M1 is heard in the next section of the promise "Das verheisse ich dir..." (mm. 79ff), followed by a contrapuntally very complex statement of "Ich will euch dorthin führen" again related to Moses' music. This involves a rotation of material from hexachords based on the 2+4 division (see above, chapter 4) and develops the linear half-step dyadic sound into a last motive, related to the PX$_{b+c}$ idea, and therefore labeled M2b, the "Verkünde" motive. It has already been suggested that while M1 probably represents God in essence, M2 represents God's communicating to human beings. The "Verkünde" motto is half of M2 at a time, being heard as both I0$_c$ and P0$_c$. The word is also set as inversions of the M1 chords: I9$_c$ accompanied by RI9$_c$ and P0$_d$. I9 in this system of labeling row forms is the exact inversion of P0 beginning at pitch level A, as opposed to the semicombinatorial inversion form labeled I0 which begins on the pitch C, and, hence, is still related strongly to A0 materials.

The entire final "Verkünde" section is composed of trichordal sonorities, very much again in God's sound world, but not left unchanged by Moses' resistance. Moses' motives are now completely fragmented, without a complete statement of M2 and with the opening material mainly heard in inversion. There is also a linear *Hauptstimme* in the harp underlying the last statement of God's chords, with a pair of Moses-type dyads, first D–E♭, then E–E♭, accompanied by a D♭–G tritone and a D–G♯ tritone in the flutes. This final E♭ carries over into the *Hauptstimme* in the flute at the opening of the next scene where Moses holds sway and God has withdrawn—Moses' musical materials remain and are developed, while the trichordal God music disappears for a time.

Musical Example 5-21

Musical Example 5-21 (continued)

The fifth motive, M5, is the important musical motive of a perfect fifth (or fourth in some versions of the motive), followed by a minor second moving in the opposite direction (Aron's motto *Leitmotiv*). The genesis of this motive from a gestural contour to its final form is described in chapter 4. It first occurs in the dialogue between Moses and the Burning Bush as the *Hauptstimme*, already described as a distortion of half of M2, played in m. 29 by the bass clarinet. In this appearance it does not really have its characteristic shape yet (here it is presented as I2$_a$), since the large interval is the tritone rather than a perfect fourth or fifth, and it begins with the minor second. It is immediately followed by minor seconds in dyadic pairs (motive M4c); and in this context, especially as the minor second is heard first, it still belongs to Moses's conflict, close to the M4 family. This passage is shown in musical example 5-22.

Musical Example 5-22

Motive M5a appears in its true shape very soon after this in mm. 32–33, shown in musical example 5-23.

It is still in this context, foreshadowing its true textual association which is presented in Act I, Scene 2. At this early point in Scene 1, it accompanies the words "dem einzigen Gott verbunden, mit dir einig, entzweit, Pharao entzweit... " with a juxtaposition of "verbunden" in the upper voices with "entzweit" in the lower. (This is perhaps meant to represent a dialectic in which Aron could go either way in relation to God, i.e., be bound to God or torn loose from God.) The motive is clearly set apart to flag the listener's attention for future reference. In this presentation, the motive is constructed

Musical Example 5-23

of the first, fifth, and eighth notes of row P8. The association with Aron is clearer in the motive's next two appearances, but these are modified appearances which still foreshadow the motive's first big appearance in Scene 2. The motive appears at m. 62, immediately following the text "Aron soll dein Mund sein," and accompanying the text "aus ihn soll deine Stimme sprechen." This time the motive is constructed of the first, second, and fourth notes of R8, and sounds like a kind of inversion of its appearance in m. 32, shown in musical example 5-24.

Next the motive appears, slightly modified at the word "Aron!" in mm. 88–89 as a trichord (P5$_a$) with a tritone in it (as at m. 29) and as a complex arrangement of pitches within a 2+4 division of row material related to motive M4e (row P5), shown in musical example 5-25.

Motive M5a is more audibly identified for the first time as Aron's *Leitmotiv* at Aron's appearance in Act I, Scene 2 at m. 123. Here in a strong *Hauptstimme* statement by three trombones, the motive appears in its most usual configuration from this point on as the first, third, and fifth notes of I4. It is here that Aron's long discourse in all of the four row forms belonging to aggregate A4 begins, as shown in musical example 5-26.

It is significant that this motive never appears in connection with any row form of A0—Aron's row aggregate is A4, as distinct from God's A0 and from the two secondary row areas of Scene 1, A5 and A8 which are related to Moses' conflict and are also related by shared tritones to A0. The notes themselves in this statement, however, as noted in chapter 4, do equal the notes of the first trichord of P0, and therefore do retain a subtle association with God's music.

Musical Example 5-24

Musical Example 5-25

Musical Example 5-26

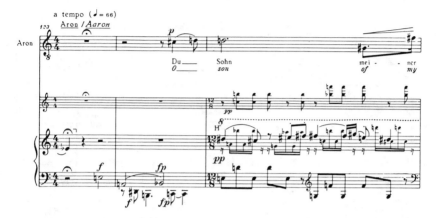

Aron's *Leitmotiv* is also made up of prominent intervallic components of two other motives—the half-step of M4, Moses' conflict, and the perfect fifth, which is the primary component of motive M6 representing disobedience. The possible interpretation of the meaning of these interrelationships will be discussed below.

A variation of M5, called M5b appears in the context of the *Jüngling*, the *Mädchen*, and the *Mann* at the beginning of Act I, Scene 3, at m. 279 at the words "Ich rief ihn" and repeated in slightly varied form in the next measure at "aber er beachtet...," shown in musical example 5-27.

Musical Example 5-27

The sixth motive, M6, is composed of parallel perfect fifths, and its initial appearance in Act I, Scene 1 is also an example of the foreshadowing of its main context of meaning. It first appears at m. 47 in the winds and brass, accompanying Moses' statement "Meine Zunge ist ungelenk," shown in musical example 5-28. This motive is identified with disobedience, to be discussed further below. The moment of foreshadowing is appropriate, since it occurs at the moment of Moses's first rebellious statement toward the Burning Bush. It is foreshadowed even earlier in Act I, Scene 1, m. 6, by a *Hauptstimme* statement of linear fifths in the violins, as the curtain rises on the opera, shown in musical example 5-29.

Musical Example 5-28

Musical Example 5-29

Again, musical elements which are to depict unrest and disobedience, like the triad in m. 7, appear within the earliest "God" music, just as the curtain rises—the human aspect of the drama begins, and with it the potential for disobedience.

The motive M6 appears in its most striking and meaningful context in Act II, Scene 3 (the Golden Calf scene), where it becomes the foundation for the shockingly un-Schoenbergian sound of the ostinato orgy music in mm. 371ff, shown in musical example 5-30.

The twelve-tone row itself is virtually unrecognizable at this point, but by observing the appearance of fifths within P0 passages in Act I, Scene 1, and carefully examining the division of material, P0 can be identified as the row form in this passage, as shown in musical example 5-31.

It may be noted also that the *Hauptstimme* is a variant of Aron's motive M5a at the same time.

The meaning of the parallel fifths is made clear in this longer passage as the *Leitmotiv* for total disobedience, associated with the orgy itself. It may even have been meant to suggest associations with the demonic because of its presentation as open string fifths reminiscent of the playing of Paganini, whose virtuosity was rumored to be diabolic. The same use of open string fifths is used in both the Liszt and the Rachmaninoff rhapsodies on a theme of Paganini, in the Liszt even in combination with quotations of the "Dies Irae" sequence. A similar reference to open string fifths is made in the Liszt "Mephisto Waltz." The presence of this association of open string fifths in the common repertoire of the nineteenth century with the demonic very likely inspired this passage. The Stravinskian sound of the widely spaced chords and the hypnotic rhythmic ostinato also calls to mind the orgiastic sound of Stravinsky's *Le Sacre du Printemps*, completed in 1913 and well known all

Musical Example 5-30

Musical Example 5-31

over Europe by the mid-1920s. It is impossible to tell whether *Le Sacre du Printemps* is a direct influence on this passage, or even an intentional reference (perhaps not altogether flattering to Stravinsky in terms of its context). In any case, however, throbbing ostinati are an appropriate device to portray an orgy.

The last motive, M7, is a thematic type of motive associated consistently with the *Jüngling*'s theme (M7a) and the *Mädchen*'s theme (M7b) first presented in the beginning of Act I, Scene 3, shown in musical example 5-32.

M7a and M7b almost always appear in the opera in the same way, and are always connected with one of these two characters or both. They are inversions of each other. M7 is therefore really a single motive, and is tuneful

Musical Example 5-32

and memorable. Beyond representing the characters themselves, M7 seems to represent a youthful innocence and hopefulness in the Volk. Appearances of M7 throughout the opera will be discussed at greater length below.

Two additional motives which appear infrequently need to be mentioned. These motives, M8a and M8b, are both motto motives for the word "Blutopfer." The first motto, M8a, appears in m. 340 in the soprano, as shown in musical example 5-33.

Musical Example 5-33

The second "Blutopfer" motto, M8b, appears in mm. 356–61, as shown in musical example 5-34.

Motives M8a and M8b become more distinctly separated later in the opera, often losing their pitch content and becoming identified only by rhythm.

From the above discussion, it becomes clear that not only are there musical motives which have specific textual connotations, working symbolically and within the tonal plan as *Leitmotive*, but that some of these seem to relate to one another in sound and function. A chart may be drawn up of the various families of these *Leitmotive*, based upon similarities in texture and textual meaning, melodic and rhythmic gesture, and association with related row forms. Two polar extremes may be identified in the text toward which the motives may also be seen to tend: God in essence on the one hand, and total disobedience on the other. The motives distribute themselves according to similarity of both motivic shape and characteristic association

Musical Example 5-34

with a particular row or aggregate in a continuum which corresponds well to the continuum of characters and ideas between the two extremes of God and disobedience, as shown in figure 5-1.

A few observations may be made from this chart. First, the identification of the demonic with God's home aggregate A0 seems to be the only discrepancy in meaning. It is possibly intended to mean that all things, even evil, are contained and foreknown within God, while the human characters Moses and Aron—since they do not fully comprehend—are further away and have different home aggregates.

Aron's motive is made up of both Moses' half-step dyad (Moses' conflict), and the perfect fifth of disobedience. The relationship between the motives representing the peoples' innocent hope (particularly as expressed by the *Mädchen*), and the "Blutopfer" motives, is also a clear reflection of the dramatic content of the opera.

This extreme care in the construction of motives sheds more light on the questions raised above concerning the derivation of motivic material. Certainly, motives are not arranged haphazardly in the opera, but are chosen carefully both for their individual sounds and for their possible interrelationships. This, combined with the fact that all these motives are either stated or foreshadowed in the first scene of the opera, strongly suggests that the motivic materials were chosen early on in the compositional process, most likely as part of the exercise of constructing the row itself, particularly in the case of motives like M1, M2, and the M4 family which relate to natural divisions of row material. This also helps to explain the early appearance in the sources of a *Thementafel* in Source Aa, which also included motives not to be fully exploited until Act II.

Interpretation of *Leitmotive* through the Opera: Some Examples

The true test of the real presence or absence of *Leitmotive* as a guiding structural principle in an opera goes beyond the immediate identification of motives with ideas or characters as they first appear. It is also necessary to trace the relationships of these motives as they are developed and transformed further in the course of the opera. To function as *Leitmotive*, the motives must consistently continue to refer to the concepts and characters with which they are initially associated. Measure-by-measure analysis demonstrates that this is indeed the case, as shown in the motivic analysis in Appendix 3. Furthermore, many of the motives presented early on evolve during the opera through normal procedures of motivic transformation into families of closely related motives which continue to carry the original asssociation, sometimes with subtle variations in specific meaning.

Figure 5-1. A Continuum of *Leitmotive*

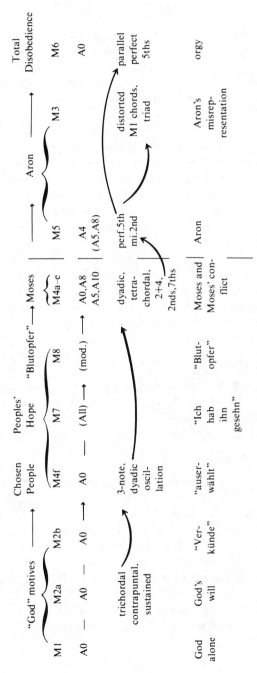

As the motives function throughout the opera, two types of *Leitmotive* occur: first, a more simple "motto" use, where a motive does not undergo significant transformation, but generally appears with the same relative pitch (sometimes with exaggerated contour) and rhythmic configuration each time it is presented. It functions as a "motto," much like some of the shorter simpler *Leitmotive* in Wagner's *Ring* cycle, such as the sword, or Hunding, to herald or to remind of the previous occurrence of its associated idea or character. M7 provides a good example of this motive type. Unlike other more complex motives or motive families, M7 takes only two related forms, M7a and b; and the relationship is simply that of retrograde, with intervallic and rhythmic identity otherwise intact. In either version M7a or M7b, this motive is clearly recognizable in its appearances throughout the opera, and is consistently associated with the youthful, innocent religious hope—especially as connected with longing for freedom—expressed in its first use and epitomized at the end of the same scene before the final chorus, as shown below. Both forms, M7a and b, are first present in the beginning of Act I, Scene 3 (see musical example 5-32). M7 reappears as the chorus sings "Moses" in mm. 294ff, representing again the idea of innocence or hope, now transferred to the whole Volk, as shown in musical example 5-35.

It is summed up in this section by the Man, who sings "Er wird uns beschützen" in mm. 305–6, shown in musical example 5-36.

The final text of that small section (mm. 294–305) retains the characteristic rhythm of the M7 motive and textually relates a hopeful idea. M7a,b and M5b are combined at mm. 325–34, as the three characters sing together. Here the M7 motives again have a thematic quality as in the beginning of the scene, shown in musical example 5-37.

The M7a and b motives are next taken by the choral voices, incorporated into a motivically complex choral fugue in mm. 335–46, accompanied by motives M4c in winds and brass and M4d in piano and xylophone. The fugue itself is a double fugue, using as the first version of the subject a statement of R1 complete, beginning with M7a; and as countersubject a melody using the notes of RI_2. The first notes of the hexachord are repeated, creating a stepwise oscillation heard as motive M4c, followed by a tritone version of M5a as the last three notes. The subject is also heard in inversion, first in the mezzo-soprano voice, beginning with motive M7a. The opening of this section, with motives labeled, is shown in musical example 5-38.

The relationship between M7 motives and the M8 "Blutopfer" motives is also made clear in this section: M8a appears first in m. 340, and consists of the first three notes ($=RI1_a$) of the four notes of M7b ($=RI1_x$). It is first stated as part of the fugal subject as an independent tag to the subject in mm. 341ff, shown in musical example 5-39.

Musical Example 5-35

Musical Example 5-36

MANN
Er wird uns be- - schüt-zen!

Musical Example 5-37

JÜNGLING
Wie er wohl aus - sehn mag, der

MANN
Der neu - e Gott, __ viel-leicht ist er

JÜNGLING
neu - e Gott? Er schwebt wohl, da auch A - ron

MANN
stär-ker als Pha - rao, stär-ker als un - se - re

schweb - te!

Göt - ter?

MÄDCHEN
Ich glau - be,

MANN
Die an - de - ren

Musical Example 5-37 (continued)

Musical Example 5-38

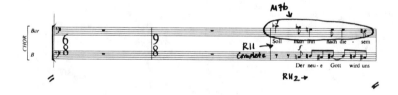

Musical Example 5-39

The priest interrupts the fugue in mm. 347–66, during which time the M8b "Blutopfer" motto motive is introduced. The soloists reiterate their themes simultaneously in counterpoint in mm. 366–76, accompanied by vigorous statements of M4d. The fugue then returns in mm. 381–88, with the subject shortened just to the four notes of M7a and b, shown in musical example 5-40.

The whole section ends with a dramatic shift in m. 389 to *Sprechstimme*, reducing M7 to a purely rhythmic motive. It concludes with a last statement of M7a by the Young Girl in mm. 397–98, shown in musical example 5-41.

Overall, Act I, Scene 3 is remarkable for its motivic streamlining and textural consistency. This is due to the many appearances of these M7 motives, and also to its large blocks of varied repetition. Basically one consistent group of accompanimental figures and one consistent set of tunes (M7a, M7b, and M5b) govern the musical material of the scene. These are accompanied motivically mainly by use of M4c, d, and some M4b leaps. M7a and b and M5b function as themes—or, more precisely, as incipits to themes—and also are motivically developed by diminution and repetition, especially in the last sections, mm. 377ff in the instrumental accompaniment. They never lose their signal or motto quality throughout the scene, however.

In the following scene, the M7 motive undergoes some transformation as various reactions of the people to Moses' and Aron's prophecy are heard (see the motivic analysis in Appendix 3). Important occurrences appear at m. 442 to the words "Sie sind jetzt da!" expressing the people's hopeful vision of the arrival of Moses and Aron; at m. 490, which is also connected with the experience of the first meeting of Moses and Aron with the Volk; at mm. 568–69, an exact quote of M7b on the words "So wollen wir knien!"; and again at m. 552, "Ich sah seinem Glanz." Rhythmically, M7 is referred to in m. 685 at the words "Ein Wunder erfüllt uns...," still related to hope. After much turbulent interaction between the Volk and the two main characters, the Young Girl, the Man, and the Other Man make a final reference to their motives, stated together, in mm. 706ff, shown in musical example 5-42.[18]

The rhythm of M7 is picked up again at another dramatic ending of a musical section, at m. 821 in *Sprechstimme*, "Alles für Freiheit!", which again expresses hope and has a specific emphasis on freedom.

M7 appears almost not at all again until the Golden Calf scene, where the M7 motto of innocence and hope, also linked with motives M8a and b ("Blutopfer") occurs, first in m. 551 when the Youth enters and faces his murder, shown in musical example 5-43. M7 continues to govern mm. 552–85. Brief references to M7, particularly rhythmically, appear in mm. 630, 657, and then, in its most climactic statements, M7 appears for one last section, finally reinterpreted as the innocence of the four naked virgins. This section begins—

Musical Example 5-40

Musical Example 5-41

Musical Example 5-41 (continued)

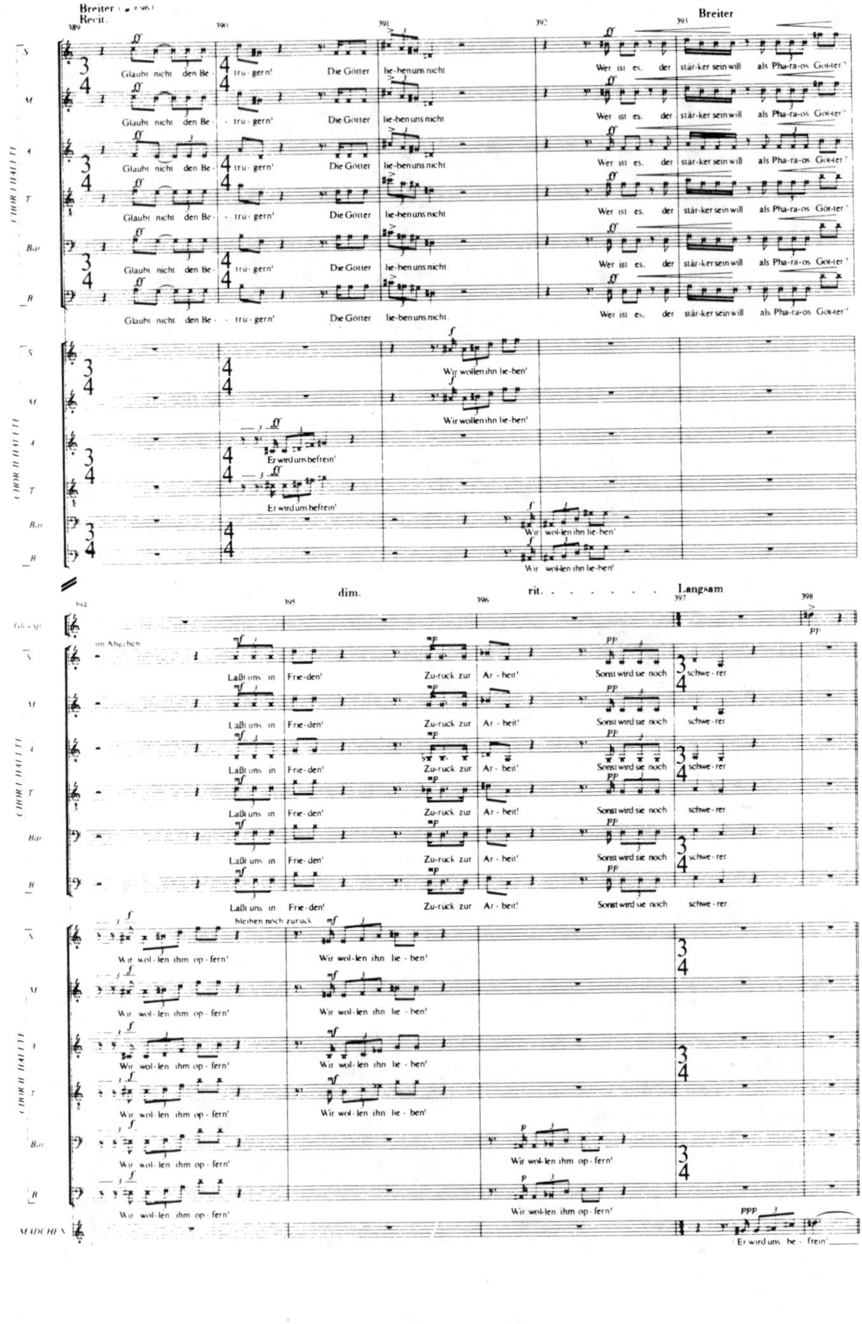

Musical Example 5-42

using M7b with one note missing in mm. 662–70 as a musical introduction to
the scene of the sacrifice of the four virgins and then presents the virgins in m.
748. The motto becomes associated with the text "du goldener Gott!" in Act
II, mm. 754–63, shown in musical example 5-44.

Fragments of M7 continue through mm. 769–87. The four virgins sing it
at their joint entrance in m. 780, shown in musical example 5-45; and it
appears again in mm. 802–23 when the virgins are actually killed.

The quick transition to the "Blutopfer" M8b motive, as in the murder of
the Youth, happens again in mm. 816ff. The motive appears a final time in a
fertility chorus, "Du goldener Gott!" This is the last reference to motive M7.

The second type of *Leitmotiv* used in *Moses und Aron* may be termed a
"transformational" *Leitmotiv*. These motives are more frequently present—
some almost always—and constitute the unifying melodic and rhythmic
elements of the entire opera. Though always retaining certain identifying
structural features, these motives are transformed or developed during the
course of the opera, generating families of related motives as initially
described above. The different forms of these motive families may represent
different aspects of the general category of meaning with which they are
associated. Some of these motives may also appear, especially initially, in
order to establish a reference point of meaning, as "motto" motives. For
example, M1 chords often appear as a clear reminder of God in Act I, but are
later incorporated, transformed, into the more complex developmental music
of Act II. The motive M2b, initially identified with the word "Verkünde," and
linked with the specific commandment of God to prophesy, first reappears as
a motto as Moses and Aron begin to address the Volk in I, iv, mm. 442 and
again at m. 523: "Schliesset die Augen..." etc.

Not surprisingly, the best example of this process and the most
elaborated motive family is that of Moses' motive family M4. Among God,
Moses, Aron, and the *Volk*, it is Moses who undergoes the most internal
change in the opera. God and Aron stand for the more unchanging poles on

Musical Example 5-43

Musical Example 5-43 (continued)

Musical Example 5-44

Musical Example 5-45

* I.Sopran = MÄDCHEN

either side of Moses' internal struggle, with God representing the inexpressible Idea and Aron embodying the material Word, while the *Volk* come to every experience in the opera with the same basic attitude of fear and lust ("Blutopfer"), gullibility and hope ("Er wird uns befrein!"). It is Moses' task to mediate between the inexpressible Idea (God) and its Representation (Aron), and to lead the people with their unenlightened or innocent hopes and fears.

The introduction of various individual elements within the M4 family is described above and illustrated in Appendix 2. Some of the M4 motives are more generally associated with Moses, while others seem to carry more specific meanings. For example, M4b' appears infrequently and seems to have a quite specific meaning as a motto for Moses or Moses' name. The parallel sevenths motive M4d, which is a central unifying musical motive throughout the opera, is early in the opera linked to the idea of the wilderness, especially in its form as M4d' with sevenths and ninths. M4f is specifically linked to the word "auserwählt" in another motto, and is only used in that context. M4a, b, and c, on the other hand, refer throughout the opera to Moses' idea, but are not further differentiated. The M4 motives—b, c, and d together—are important unifying structural components of the opera in purely musical terms. They are dyadic and tetrachordal sonorities clearly complementary to the trichordal motives of God's music (motives M1 and 2) and in direct tension with the motives carved out of the row to create Aron's motives (M5a, triadic M3a, and disruptive chord M3b). The traditional tonal implications of M3, M5a, and M6, with emphasis on thirds and fifths, are strongly opposed by Moses' strict and upright-sounding dyadic materials, whether expressed in stern leaping figures or in agitated semitone oscillations.

Aron's motives, like the M4 family, also are "transformational." However, like some of the M4 motives mentioned above, M5a and M3b may also speak as mottos (for example, see uses of M5a in I, ii, m. 123 and II, iii, mm. 308ff; and M3b in I, ii, m. 163 and II, iii, m. 308). The tension between the two brothers' conceptions (Moses' insistence on the ineffable Idea vs. Aron's constant efforts to turn the Idea into something tangible for the sake of the people's desires) is expressed throughout the opera both in the acute tension of simultaneous statements by the brothers, entangled in counterpoint, and also in other places in strict alternation between the two contrasting characters. By carefully reading through the motivic analysis chart, the reader may see these various techniques at work as Schoenberg creates a close correspondence between the relationship of the brothers' words in the text and the interplay of their motives. As an example, it may be seen in Appendix 3 that in the dialogue in Act I, Scene 2, Moses' and Aron's motives appear first in alternation as they speak. Aron sings alone in mm. 163–177, accompanied by a texture of M3 and M5a motivic material, then quotes the original revelation to Moses using M2b with added notes and embellishments corresponding to his own adaptations and elaborations of the revelation. Moses interrupts with a corrective "Darfst?" (M4b′) accompanied by M4d and M4b dyads in m. 182; and as Moses and Aron continue to dialogue, mm. 187ff, M4 dyads dominate the texture but combine with M5a in the accompanimental material. At Aron's "Du belohnst . . . " in m. 195, M5a is played as a *Hauptstimme* by three celli and a varied M5a is also played as a *Nebenstimme*. The combination continues through m. 207, building to Moses' dramatic outburst, his only sung passage: "Reinige dein Denken . . . " The row forms change briefly at this point from A7 to I2 with the melody strictly drawn from it, with a purely M4a and b tetrachordal accompaniment. But Aron's succeeding solo shows that he is unperturbed: A7 returns, with strong M3b and *Hauptstimme* and M5a statements as Aron continues to sing his elaborations of the original God-Idea.

In Scene 3, as the people anticipate the coming of Moses and Aron, M4 is the symbol of the revelation to Moses traveling along its assigned route of communication. It dominates the accompanimental texture, but it is secondary in importance in the entire scene to the thematic motto motives of the Young Man, the Young Girl, and the Other Man (M7a and b and M5b). Moses' and Aron's motives only appear at the end of the scene to herald their arrival. As they are seen approaching in the final chorus of the scene, "Seht Moses und Aron," mm. 399–442, the initial melodic leap on the word "Seht Moses" sounds clearly derived from the M4b′ "Moses" motto; and both it and the continuation of the phrase "und Aron" uses a variant of the M5a idea, shown in musical example 5-46.

Musical Example 5-46

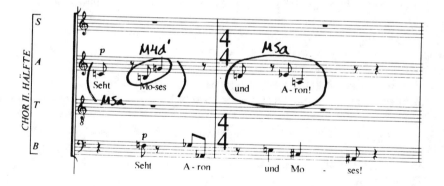

These two motives are then developed and transformed as the basis for the chorus, mm. 399–418. A fierce "motive war" then begins between inversions of M1, the God-Idea, and the distorted chords of Aron's M3b in mm. 419–42. This "war" ends in huge tetrachordal chords which seem to incorporate M4a, M1, and M3b at "Sie sind jetzt da!"—a useful and dramatic sonority for Moses and Aron bring the Word of God, as shown in musical example 5-47.

A battle ensues in Scene 4 as Aron gains control and Moses' vision slips away from the crowd. At first, in mm. 443ff, inversions of M1 dominate while the God-Idea is fairly faithfully described and well received. However, even the opening is not clearcut. The opening measures are shown in musical example 5-48.

A very complex opening texture prevails, one which Schoenberg labored over in the sketches. It is comprised of several transformed motives, combined to create melodic themes and accompaniment. The motives are God's M1a and b and M2b, plus Aron's thirds, fifths, and triads (M3a and b). Two main choral melodic lines combine to form a complete row. The *Hauptstimme* melody moves mainly in quarter notes (doubled initially in the clarinets), and does not have a "pure" atonal sound. Thirds and fifths are emphasized, plus semitone motion from subphrase to subphrase. The whole melody stays within the range of a perfect fifth. Only one traditionally dissonant interval, the tritone at the end of the first half of the line, occurs, punctuating a question phrase. It is answered at the end of the line by a perfect fifth descending. In the accompanimental melody there is also a great predominance of thirds and use of repeated notes which state the thirds as well. These thirds, and fifths, with their tonal implications, are linked to Aron's material—M3a and b, and also to the repetition of notes in his speech in Scene 2 at mm. 178ff. These lines are doubled in the accompanimental texture. In addition, the accompaniment includes two other motivic gestures: first, in the strings, then in the horn, and later (mm. 448–49) in the winds, a staccato presentation of M2b; second, chordal music, with the first chord repeated, presenting M1 (first chord) transposed up a whole step. This is also possibly related to M1 (second chord), as the inner note is different. The second chord of M1 also begins to appear in mm. 448ff. The next two chords, in the winds, form first-inversion triads (M3a), the lower two notes of the winds together with the horns form other triads (M3a inv.). In addition, there are isolated minor sixths separated out in the orchestra in the oboes. Altogether, they sound amazingly like unresolved appoggiaturas within a tonal chordal context.

Throughout the scene, Moses' and Aron's motives again are presented in opposing alternation or entangled in battle (e.g., M3 and M5a dominate during Aron's miracle of turning the Nile water into blood in mm. 877–93). The people's response is to return to their receptivity to God—not a

Musical Example 5-47

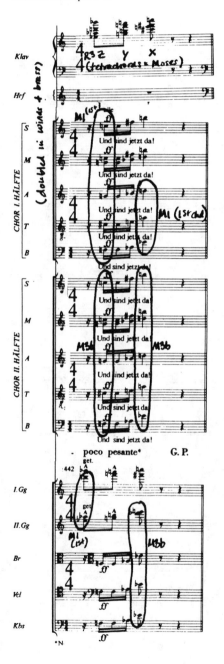

Musical Example 5-48

4. Szene

Musical Example 5-48 (continued)

thoroughly bad response, although ill-motivated in Moses' eyes—and a combination of M4, M1, and M2 motivic material returns. However, the scene closes dominated by Aron's music as the people cry "Frei, frei, frei!" in mm. 957ff. M3b and a *Hauptstimme* M5a statement return in m. 958, and the scene closes on an M3a triad in mm. 968–70, foreboding the dissolution and loss of the revelatory vision to come in the second act.

It may be seen that Act I, Scene 4 presents a more complicated set of dramatic relationships, with Moses, Aron and the vacillating people all interacting. In keeping with this, the motivic content of the music of the scene is also more complex, with many combinations of motives hitherto presented in a more transparent manner. The complexity of motivic content naturally progresses through the act from Scene 1 to Scene 4 as more characters are introduced and increasingly interact with each other. This process culminates in the fourth scene, where Moses, Aron, and the *Volk* (who vacillate between acceptance and rejection of the new God), plus references to God, are all combined in the dramatic action. In the motivic analysis outlined in Appendix 3, the multiple combinations of motivic material previously identified with God, Moses, and Aron, can be seen sensitively presenting the precise nuances of textual meaning in the music phrase by phrase.

The *Zwischenspiel* (II, mm. 1–42), is a short, highly unified introduction to the chaos and frenzy of the second act. In it, the people express their anxiety about the absence of their prophet or their link to prophetic wisdom—the two growing motives are M5a and a new version of M2a as natural hexachord M2a′ and M2b′. The seeds of suspicion to be sown by Aron are represented by motive M5a, and we see the last glimpse of desire for Moses' prophecy. M2a″ becomes increasingly scrambled, as in the technique used for Aron's carved-out motive M5a. In the last three measures a sparse texture of Moses's M4c and d underlies the last dramatic whisper "Wo ist Moses?"

In Act II, Scene 1, the ensuing discussion of Moses' disappearance by the Seventy Elders and Aron is accompanied by M4 material. But in the striking moment in mm. 173ff when Aron seemingly caves in to their pressure and returns the worship of the old gods to the people, it is Aron's music which prevails: M3 and M5a, full of tonal implications with triads and thirds. These tonal implications are a good example of how tonal references are used by Schoenberg as the musical equivalent in the opera to the old pagan ways of the Hebrew people. The rest of the scene, the long choral section "Jubelt, freuet euch," is a complex intertwining of M3 and M5a with M4 motives—in continual transformation and development. The consequences of the encounter between Moses and Aron, and between the two brothers and the people, culminate in that moment.

However, the long choral section from mm. 200–307 is remarkably unified motivically. Melodic material is consistently built on units of seconds and thirds, and accompanimental material is dominated by a complex of a few consistent motivic figures which are melodically and rhythmically all in the M4 family—mainly M4b, c, and d, plus references by frequent use of thirds to M3 motivic material. About halfway through this section, at mm. 246ff, Moses's motive M4b begins to dominate. Aron's motive M5a, and isolated dyads, M4c′, are also heard as signals in certain measures. This is the music of humans—Moses and Aron. God's music is notably absent in this passage.

Aron's motives M5a and M3b are heard most prominently near the end of the section: M5a in mm. 283 and 286, and especially strikingly in m. 307; and M3a and b frequently from mm. 275 to the end. These lead into the prominent use of M5a and M3 at the outset of the Golden Calf scene, where now Aron's more materialistic interpretations reign supreme. In mm. 308ff, A4, Aron's original row aggregate, from his discourse in I,ii, mm. 123ff, also returns. Moses' M4 dyadic materials drop away at this point, and Aron's music now predominates as the people give in to their old ritual practices: the worship of a tangible, definable idol, rather than the inexplicable God of Moses' vision.

Schoenberg makes it clear that while Aron is responsible for his own actions in miracles and in returning the old tangible gods to the people, the people are influenced by both Moses and Aron. They are constantly in a state of flux and confusion, embedded in the drama of the struggle between their two leaders.

Act II, Scene 3, the Golden Calf scene—as a development and elaboration of the consequences of Aron's action and an interpretation of Moses's prophetic vision—most appropriately contains the most complex intertwining of the opera's transformational motives. M5a and the M3 motives strongly dominate at the outset as Aron establishes the worship of the Golden Calf, the ultimate symbol of tangibility and concrete knowability.

Particularly striking, at the end of Aron's short speech at the opening of Act II, Scene 3, preceding his exclamation "Verehrt euch selbst in diesem Sinnbild!", Aron's motive M5a is heard prominently twice, played by horns and winds, reminiscent of the first bold statement of the *Leitmotiv* as *Hauptstimme* before his first entrance in Act I, Scene 2 (see musical example 5-49).

His motives continue to provide the underlying material for motivic development and transformation throughout the long scene. Moses' motives also appear from time to time, for example, in connection with the Seventy Elders in mm. 697ff. Moses himself is not without culpability for the orgy. The God-Idea gesture M2b relating back to the prophesy "Verkünde" is also heard in the scene—again, relating to the *Zwischenspiel*, as a reminder that the events are distortions of the true yearning for prophetic wisdom, frustration with its absence, and an inevitable chain of events set in motion by the original

Musical Example 5-49

Musical Example 5-49 (continued)

initiative of God's revelation out of the Burning Bush to human agents. Fleeting references, one chord at a time, of the serene chordal motion of the original God music is heard in the orgy scene—even God, then, is involved in the situation. In the darkest of moments in the text of the scene, a glimmer of the original prophecy is still occasionally heard.

The complex motivic development of M3, M5a, and M4 motives is broken not only by the formal divisions of different narrative sections (represented by changes in row area, in meter and rhythm, and texture) but by the pointed appearance of certain motto motives as well. For example, in mm. 548ff, the Youth, in his innocence, tries to protest in favor of the new God's prophecy and is brutally slaughtered. Throughout the passage, mm. 548–96, the *Leitmotive* relating to innocent hope (M7a,b), God's prophecy (M2b), and blood sacrifice (M8a) are all woven into the music. At the Ephraimite's cruel joke "Hier blick nun zur Ewigkeit, wenn du Lebens nahe so wenig ist," a brief reference is made to the second chord of M1, perhaps a reference to "Ewigkeit," the Youth's truth of vision. References to M7a and b, M2b, and M8a continue to appear in the music, representing the ensuing wild drunkenness and dancing in mm. 605–70, combined with M4 dyadic material, as shown in the motivic analysis in Appendix 3.

A similar use of motto occurs during the sacrifice of the four virgins, as described earlier, when, predictably, the Young Girl's thematic motto M7b is again used and elaborated. The section of the scene is introduced in m. 746 and presents M7b as a *Hauptstimme* in combination with other prominent motives of the larger scene, mainly M4 and M5a, also M3. As the priests embrace the maidens and the sacrifice takes place, the "Blutopfer" motive M8b appropriately begins to be heard once again, and continued through to the end of the section at m. 823.

While reference is made to the prophetic motive M2b ("Verkünde") throughout the scene, the number of appearances of the motive increases markedly during the transition at the end of the scene, mm. 945–66, to Moses' return. After a last flicker of M3, 4, and 5 together as the fire is dying (mm. 942ff), the musical texture thins to reveal the return of M1 and M2b together again for the first time since the first act, with a sustained M1 and *Hauptstimme* M2b in the last four measures of the scene (mm. 963–66). Moses' return is heralded in the brief Scene 4, which consists of these motives giving way again to a texture saturated with only Moses' M4c and d motives. The calf vanishes as the M1 chord sounds, embedded in a larger M4 texture which represents Moses and God combined.

The ensuing confrontation between Moses and Aron is parallel to their first confrontation in the wilderness. The motivic fabric of the music simplifies from the elaborate combinations and transformational development of the orgy scene. There is once again much clearer alternation between Moses' M4 motives and Aron's M3 and M5a motives as they engage in dialogue, as shown in the motivic analysis of Act II, Scene 5, (mm. 984ff) in Appendix 3. Moses' final cry of despair and confusion begins with the desolation of wilderness music M4d' against the Aron-related choral material built on thirds (M3), and refers to M5; then moves to a poignantly sparse texture of long sustained leaps (M4b), in utter solitude, a last dyad as he speaks "O Wort, du Wort das mir fehlt!"

The opera cries out for musical completion—the process has begun, back from the motivic complexity and contrapuntal density of the inner scenes I,iv to II,iii to clearer textures as in Act I,ii and iii. But resolution, the return of the peaceful self-sufficient God-music in both motive and row area from the opening, is, finally, left unaccomplished by the composer.

Conclusion

It has been seen that, for Schoenberg, the years prior to the composition of *Moses und Aron* were rich in sources of intellectual influence. Schoenberg's thinking was formed out of close involvement, especially ca. 1909–11, with the expressionist movement, particularly in connection with Kandinsky and the *Blaue Reiter*. He was concerned with theosophy and mysticism, particularly after the move to Berlin in 1911, and he had a fascination for the mystical writings of Balzac and Strindberg. Schoenberg was also interested in the philosophical thought of Schopenhauer before the 1920s and through the rest of his life, and was influenced by the biting literary style of Karl Kraus and his sharp observations of Viennese society and letters. Finally, Schoenberg's growing awareness of anti-Semitism, particularly after 1922, greatly influenced his thought during this period. It has further been seen that this rich philosophical and literary background deeply informed the creation of Schoenberg's first oratorio text for *Moses und Aron* and continues to be reflected in the published libretto of the opera version.

This richness has its parallel in the complexity of the musical procedures, and the minute attention to detail which Schoenberg applied to expressing concepts from the text in his music. These include the careful use of twelve-tone techniques, orchestration, vocal registration, and other compositional procedures in order to create a subtle and complex system of *Leitmotive*, which not only reflect simple ideas and characters as motto motifs, but also echo finer details of the philosophical and religious content of the opera. Nor was text expression achieved in spite of, or independent of, the twelve-tone structure of the work. On the contrary, it has been seen that Schoenberg's use of twelve-tone techniques was integral to the derivation of motivic material, and thus to the overall dramatic and formal structure of the opera.

Schoenberg disclaimed on many occasions the primacy of the method of composing with twelve tones, and insisted that he was a composer dealing with the same structural and functional principles as any tonal composer. He argued against the commonly held understanding of so-called new and old

music, pointing out in "New Music, Outmoded Music, Style and Idea" (1946),
with Bach as an example, that compositions which may seem to one's
contemporaries to be "outmoded" may in fact contain progressive new
elements unrecognizable to the composer's own generation, while some
seemingly "new" music may simply be superficially different in style but not
innovative in important ways—in content, in Idea.[1] He insisted over a span of
many years beginning around 1922—and thus coinciding with both his return
to Judaism and his period of twelve-tone composition—that he owed a great
debt to the masters of classical composition, and that his own creative work
was evolutionary, rather than revolutionary:

> The artist who has courage submits wholly to his own inclinations. And he alone who
> submits to his own inclinations has courage, and he alone who has courage is an artist. The
> literature is thrown out, the results of education are shaken off, the inclinations come
> forward, the obstacle turns the stream into a new course, the one hue that earlier was only a
> subordinate color in the total picture spreads out, a personage is born. A new man! This is a
> model for the development of the artist, for the development of art.
>
> That is called revolution; and artists, those who submit to such necessities and cherish
> them, are accused of all possible crimes that can be culled from the rubbish of the political
> vocabulary. At the same time, however, it is forgotten that one may call it revolution, if at
> all, only in a comparative sense, and that this comparison has to hold only with respect to
> the points compared, i.e., points of similarity, but not in every respect. An artist who has a
> good, new idea is not to be confused with an arsonist or a bomb thrower. Any similarity
> between the advent of the new in the spiritual and intellectual sphere and in political
> revolutions consists at most in this: the successful will prevail for a period of time, and in the
> light of this prospect, the older will feel under threat from what is new. But the fundamental
> distinctions are greater: the consequences, the spiritual and intellectual consequences of an
> idea endure, since they are spiritual and intellectual; but the consequences of revolutions
> that run their course in material matters are transient. Besides: it has never been the purpose
> and effect of new art to suppress the old, its predecessor, certainly not to destroy it. Quite
> the contrary: no one loves his predecessors more deeply, more fervently, more respectfully,
> than the artist who gives us something truly new; for respect is awareness of one's station
> and love is a sense of community. Does anyone have to be reminded that Mendelssohn—
> even he was once new— unearthed Bach, that Schumann discovered Schubert, and that
> Wagner, with work, word, and deed, awakened the first real understanding of Beethoven?
> The appearance of the new can far better be compared with the flowering of a tree: it is the
> natural growth (*Werden*) of the tree of life. But if there were trees that had an interest in
> preventing the flowering, then they would surely call it revolution. And conservatives of
> winter would fight against each spring, even if they had experienced it a hundred times and
> could affirm that it did become, after all, *their* overthrow; they suffice for believing that
> when the new shoots emerge from what was once new the destruction of the old is at hand.[2]

> Nothing collapses so completely as renovation through bad growth. And, on the other
> hand, all revolutions simply bring reaction out into the open and can threaten what took
> years to grow. *I was never revolutionary.* ("*New Music,*" 1923; emphasis added)[3]

> It is a remarkable thing, as yet unnoticed by anyone—although a thousand facts point to it,
> and although the battle against German music during the war was primarily a battle against
> my own music, and although... nowadays my art has no line of succession abroad;

remarkably, nobody has yet appreciated that my music, produced on German soil, without foreign influences, is a living example of an art able most effectively to oppose Latin and Slav hopes of hegemony and derived through and through from the traditions of German music.

This has remained unnoticed, not only because my scores are hard to read, but, even more, because those sitting in judgment are lazy and arrogant. For it can be seen.

But for once I will say it myself.

My teachers were primarily Bach and Mozart, and secondarily Beethoven, Brahms, and Wagner.... I also learned much from Schubert and Mahler, Strauss and Reger too. I shut myself off from no one, and so I could say of myself:

My originality comes from this: I immediately imitated everything I saw that was good, even when I had not first seen it in someone else's work.

And I may say: often enough I saw it first in myself. For if I saw something and I did not leave it at that; I acquired it, in order to possess it; I worked on it and extended it, and it led me to something new.

I am convinced that eventually people will recognize how immediately this 'something new' is linked to the loftiest models that have been granted us. I venture to credit myself with having written truly new music which, being based on tradition, is destined to become tradition. ("National Music (2)," 1931)[4]

It is remarkable that my most revolutionary steps (I have always thought them evolutionary) have never had a destructive effect. What could be preserved (and what was important could always be preserved; what had to go was only the incidental, the fashionable) I always preserved. ("Revolution—Evolution, Notation (Accidentals)," 1931)[5]

It is seldom realized that a hand that dares to renounce so much of the achievements of our forefathers has to be exercised thoroughly in the techniques that are to be replaced by new methods. It is seldom realized that there is a link between the technique of forerunners and that of an innovator and that no new technique in the arts is created that has not had its roots in the past. ("A Self-Analysis," 1948)[6]

Source-critical examination of Schoenberg's religious and philosophical development, his sources of intellectual influence, and the genesis of the concept and the evolution of the text and the music of *Moses und Aron* in a synthetic fashion (whereby each area of investigation has been found to shed light on the others) has yielded a new confirmation of Schoenberg's insistence of that, in spite of the seemingly revolutionary nature of its twelve-tone structure, the opera *Moses und Aron* is actually within the mainstream of nineteenth-century operatic compositional techniques.

The philosophical streams investigated show that Schoenberg was not influenced by the more "progressive" logical positivist school of Wittgenstein and others, in vogue in Vienna in the second two decades of the twentieth century. Rather, his thought was formed by the nineteenth-century philosopher Schopenhauer and the related philosophers Kant and Nietzsche.

The composition of the libretto itself was first conceived as an oratorio; and the opera as it evolved still belonged formally more to the nineteenth century (borrowing Baroque forms via the dramatic oratorios of Mendelssohn and others) than to contemporary progressive, experimental operatic models, such as *neue Sachlichkeit* (e.g., Hindemith), or Berg's experimentation with instrumental forms and almost cinematic dramatic structure as in *Wozzeck*. The musical compositional procedure (as seen in the source study in chapter 1) was not focused on detailed row manipulations, but was within the practice of nineteenth century tonal composition, focusing on the creation of melodies, motives, and textural sonorities. Finally, musical analysis of the piece shows that to focus primarily on the row and its properties causes the analyst to miss more centrally important ways in which the inner musical logic of the piece is developed, i.e., the overall and local "tonal" planning and motivic structure of the opera.

It has also been demonstrated (in chapter 5 and in appendix 3) that the piece functions musically as a *Leitmotiv* opera. As such, the music is inextricably entwined with expressing the meaning of the text, both reinforcing narrative details and also conveying subtle nuances of philosophical content. This is the primary structural/functional logic of the music of the opera, which transcends the issue of whether the piece is written as a tonal, freely atonal, or twelve-tone composition. The twelve-tone structure of the opera is at the service of this more central structural principle, just as the key plan and motivic development of a tonal opera would serve the same ends. In this way, *Moses und Aron* stands firmly in the mainstream of late-nineteenth-century German opera composition with Wagner, and uses the late-nineteenth-century compositional procedures of thematic transformation and motivic development as the primary governing procedures for the unfolding of musical form.

The present synthetic study of the various aspects of the genesis and structure of *Moses und Aron* reveals that, in spite of its seemingly revolutionary nature as the earliest-conceived twelve-tone opera based on a single row, the opera is from this perspective a conservative artwork, conceived, generated, and brought to its present—only nearly completed—form via the philosophical thought, the literary and musical compositional procedure, and the musical form and function of the late nineteenth century.

As a concluding note, it has also become clear in the course of this study that *Moses und Aron* is not complete as it stands. The central conflict of *Moses und Aron* itself, the war between Idea and Representation, becomes a metaphor for the creative process—the translation of the Idea into a text and the text into a musical setting. Only the Idea remains unchanging, while text and setting may mutually influence each other as the composer strives to come closer and closer to a true Representation, which in this case is Schoenberg's personal religious testament: the very impossibility of the task at hand bears witness to the inconceivability of God. Perhaps a new answer can thus be suggested to the ever-intriguing question, why was *Moses und Aron* left unfinished? The answer is in the opera itself, as Moses cries "So bin ich geschlagen! So war alles Wahnsinn, was ich gedachte habe, und kann und darf nicht gesagt werden! O Wort, du Wort, das mir fehlt!"

Schoenberg strongly desired to finish the work, and did not ever view it as a completed effort. It is a mistake to view the published version of the text to Act III as a final one, especially since study of the text sources reveals that the process of musical composition powerfully changed his concept of the text in Acts I and II; and also since the presence of fragmentary sketches for Act III, Scene 2 suggest that a further development of the concluding portion of the work was in Schoenberg's concept. (See the translation of "Arons Tod" from DICH[tung] 20, Appendix IV.)

This older version of Act III, particularly the later unrealized second scene, provided resolution for many religious themes which were important to Schoenberg. However, he did not find a way of incorporating them into the present published version of Act III. Traces of Schoenberg's Zionism appear in the words, "you are nearing the Land that you should have enjoyed so long, until the Lord spread you out in other lands." His continual concern for the Chosen People, and their eternal duty and struggle, is expressed in the words: "filled with sorrow and joy, as long as there are people on this earth, and as long as enemies are found to Him [God] and you." In this second scene, Schoenberg came closest to expressing outright the difficulty in following an ineffable God, "the *ungratifying* pure teachings of God (*Gotteslehre*)." Schoenberg's understanding of the sufferings of the Jewish people, which was not only biblical in perspective but also was an expression of the turmoil of the Jews in his own time and included his own sense of persecution as both an artist and a Jew, was finally expressed in terms of this mission to believe in the unknowable God: "So shall scorn attend you, persecution consecrate you; so shall sorrow sanctify you!"

The second scene of the oratorio version of Act III ends with a hopeful, nearly messianic vision:

> Consecrate us, Moses, in the name of the Eternal, the Almighty, who led us out of the Land of Horror, and will bring us into the Land of Desirelessness, where milk and honey flow, and the pure Idea of the One God will be thought and felt by all.

It is inconceivable that, in a finished version of the conclusion to the opera, such crucial personally and profoundly felt ideas would not have been brought to some form of poetically and musically satisfying resolution.

Musical analysis also reveals the incompleteness of the work. The motivic structure of the music itself requires a return of opening material with the denouement and reconciliation of the people with God which Moses finds inexplicable. Hermann Scherchen's performance solution in the second staged production of the opera, to accompany the spoken third act with music from Act I, Scene 1,[7] followed the logic of bringing back the music representing God to accompany God's leading of the people on toward the Promised Land, once again reconciled, chosen, and blessed. No such return is achieved by the end of Act II. Surely, based on the present *Leitmotiv* analysis, a conclusion to the opera would have necessitated that Schoenberg compose a complex structure interweaving the motives of the people, Moses, and God (e.g., the motto motives "auserwählt"; God's motives M1, M2a, and M2b; and Moses' family of motives M4). Nor could the music representing God return pure and intact, since the opening of the opera represents God before any interaction with humanity, and therefore the first statements of M1 and M2 could never return in their pure, solitary state. Similarly, the judgment of Aron and concluding dialogue between Moses and Aron would require some resolution of Moses' (M4) and Aron's (M3, M5) musical materials. Perhaps a union of these motives, and a union of the people with God, was intended. In any case, such complex musical matters are clearly left unresolved in the opera in its present state.

On the basis of these speculations alone, it is no wonder that Schoenberg found it too difficult to pick up the thread of his earlier compositional activity and complete the work. Schoenberg's earnest desire was to achieve the ultimate expression and to complete the opera. But, like the "tenth symphony" to which he referred in his essay "Gustav Mahler" (1912/1948),[8] it eluded him. Though it was not complete (and he knew it), it never could be, even if the final double bars were applied by his hand. The sense of resignation which one senses from the final letters that he wrote concerning its final incomplete form was connected to his vision that, like that tenth symphony, it could not be grasped. He felt that it required a greater knowledge than was humanly possible according to his own religious and philosophical beliefs— ultimately, the Idea could never be perfectly expressed, captured in Representation. The artistic Idea, like the God "I am" to whom Schoenberg prayed, was greater than the human power to grasp it.

The opera was, for Schoenberg, even in its unfinished state (or perhaps even consonant with it) a profoundly personal masterwork which had meaning for every aspect of his existence. Metaphors exist on many levels in the opera: for Schoenberg's own creative consciousness, for his self-image as a musical prophet, for his political vision of a free Jewry, for his reclaimed identity as a Jew, and for his own theology which drew freely from biblical, philosophical, and literary sources. Just as no one element in the opera itself— historical background, text, or musical techniques—can be singled out to provide an adequate, even preliminary understanding of the work, so, too, do the many meanings of the opera require a synthetic perspective.

Moses und Aron is, finally, a mirror of Schoenberg himself, his life, his world, his thought. In it, the clash of the spiritual, the creative/artistic, and the material (which Schoenberg first expressed in the earlier autobiographical dramatic work, *Die Glückliche Hand*) is brought closer to resolution through religion. The distinction between religious prophet, like the character Moses, and artist as prophet is, finally, unnecessary. The two merge in Schoenberg's thinking:[9]

It is a well known fact that already in the culture of even primordial peoples music's mysterious appeal to man adorns worship of the divinity, to sanctify cultish acts with primitive peoples it is perhaps even rhythm or sound alone which casts enchantment. But even the culturally high-ranking Greeks ascribed mysterious effects to simple successions of tones, such as expressing virtues and their contrary. The Gregorian chant does not profit as much from the meaning of the words as does the Protestant chorale; it lives on music alone.

Considering these facts, one might wonder whether the subsequent higher art forms were indispensable for religious ceremony. Whether or not art of a primitive or higher kind enhances the enchanting effect of music, one conclusion seems inescapable: *there is mystery*.

My personal feeling is that *music conveys a prophetic message revealing a higher form of life towards which mankind evolves*. And it is because of this message that music appeals to men of all races and cultures. (emphasis added)

Moses und Aron was never surpassed by any of Schoenberg's other efforts to express his religious and artistic ideas in music, and his later religious works continue to frame ideas already explored in the opera. The opera remains as a mirror for Schoenberg's artistic and religious development, and its creation came at a time when Schoenberg's religious and philosophical seeking came to a point of resolve which was never again shaken.

Ernest Becker has written of personal heroism in the form of creativity, a description which matches Schoenberg's artistic and religious personality:[10]

The key to the creative [personality] type is that he is separated out of the common pool of shared meanings. There is something in his life experience that makes him take in the world as a *problem*; as a result he has to make personal sense out of it. This holds true for all creative people to a greater or lesser extent, but it is especially obvious with the artist. Existence becomes a problem that needs an ideal answer; but when you no longer accept the collective solution to the problem of existence, then you must fashion your own. The work of art is, then the ideal answer of the creative type to the problem of existence as he takes it in—not only the existence of the external world, but especially his own: who he is as a painfully separate person with nothing shared to lean on. He has to answer to the burden of his extreme individuation, his so painful isolation. He wants to know how to earn immortality as a result of his own unique gifts. His creative work is at the same time the expression of his heroism as the justification of it. It is his "private religion"—as Rank put it. Its uniqueness gives him personal immortality; it is his own "beyond" and not that of others.

Schoenberg's statement to Berg about the genesis of his opera then, provides a more profound insight into the nature of Schoenberg's own creativity and the nature of *Moses und Aron* than the letter at first suggests. The work represents a synthesis of all Schoenberg's learning, with no meaningful influence lost along the way:

> ... [In *Moses und Aron,*] both my main idea and the many, many subsidiary ideas literally and symbolically presented, are all so much tied up with my own personality that it is impossible for Strindberg to have presented anything that could have even an external similarity. You would have been sure to find this on looking through the work again, all the more if—which is, after all, as you know, absolutely necessary with my work—you had looked at every word and every sentence from several points of view. Today I can scarcely remember what belongs to me: but one thing must be granted me (I won't let myself be deprived of it): Everything I have written has a certain inner likeness to myself.

Appendix 1

Sketch Types in the Sources to
Moses und Aron

Source labels are consistent with those in Schmidt/KB. For the purpose of this chart, however, Schmidt's breakdown of sketches was considered too fine. Here a single listing is used to refer to each coherent, unified sketch for a single version of a continuous grouping of measures, identified by corresponding act and measure numbers in the final score. Particularly early versions, and final versions ("Erstniederschriften") are identified. When a sketch does not take up an entire source sheet, the location on the sheet is designated. Pages of sources at the Arnold Schoenberg Institute Archive are further identified by archive number.

THEME TABLES

Source Ab:

$1_4^{1,2,4}$ (#2969,2970,2971)
$6_4^{2,3,4}$ (#2982,2984,2985) with 7^r (#2983) inserted

SOLO MELODY WITH LITTLE OR NO ACCOMPANIMENT:

(1) Solo Melody Only, No Accompaniment

Source Aa:

3_4^1 middle I,I,mm.163–179 (early version)
3_4 I,mm.123–45
4^r top I,mm.179–185 (=final)
4^r bottom I,mm.218–33 (early version)
7_3^1 bottom I,mm.177–81
7_3 top I,mm.199–202
7_4 mid-bottom I,mm.218–23 (early version)
7_4 top c.I,mm.222–33 (early version)
8^v I,mm.218–33 (3 incomplete versions)
10^r top and continuation pasted on bottom I,mm.255ff (early)
11^r I,mm.260–88 (with mm.265–6 left blank)
26^v bottom I,mm.879–94 (=final)
32^v I,mm.94–108

Source Ab:

3^r (#2975) II,mm.189–90, 191–4

6^1 (#2981) top I,mm.6-8
8^v (#2987) top II,mm.308-16
8^v (#2987) mid-bottom, II,mm308-19 (=final)
9^r (#2988) top II,mm.173-90 (very early with early text)
14^1 (#2998) top II,mm.943ff (early version)
18^v (#3005) mm.524-37 (continuation from sketch with
  some accomp.)
19^r (#3006) middle II,mm.448-89.
Source Ac:

(2) Solo Melody with Incomplete Accompaniment

Source Aa:

3^1 top I,mm.148-52 (early; one-line accomp.)
6^r I,mm.123-38 (text not written in)
6^v_1 top I,mm.140-5 (vocal melody plus Hauptstimme)
7^1 middle I,mm.171-6 (continued from complete mm.163-70
  at top)
7^2_2 middle I,mm.187-98 (almost complete)
7^3_3 middle I,mm.203-7 (almost complete)
11^r I,mm.255-9 (almost complete final version)
11^v top I,mm.290ff (false start)
11^v bottom I,mm.297-301 (incomplete final version)
22^v_1 I,mm.667-72
28^1 middle I,mm.738-41
30^r I,mm.936-62 (=final)

Source Ab:

2^r (#2973) II,mm.173-87 (begins complete, becomes
  incomplete)
3^r (#2975) II,mm.195-8 (continued from melody only
  mm.191-4
5^r (#2979) II,mm.702-5 (melody + Hauptstimme), +
  5 mm. (early), some accomp. indicates rhythm only
10^3_3 (#2992) II,mm.934ff(?) (early)
15^r (#2999) top II,mm.1108-36 (almost complete early
  version)
15^v (#3000) II,mm.1064-83 (no accomp. after m.1072 but
  shifting meters indicated)
18^v (#3005) II,mm.524-37 (melody =final, some mm. no
  accomp.)
21^r (#3009) middle II,mm.524-37 (accomp. often rhythm
  only)
22^v (#3012) II,mm.702-31 (melody =final); continues to
  732-9 (earlier version)

Source Ac:

10 (#3029) I,148ff (accomp. only)

10^{3b} (#3032 right) I,mm.547-50 (accomp.only)
16 (#3035) I,mm.552-4 (counterpoint only)
18-19, 20-21 (#3037-8, 3039-40) across bottom I,mm.564ff (counterpoint)
20 (#3039) top I,mm.629-31
22b (#3042 right) I,mm.552-4 (counterpoint)
23 (#3046) bottom II,mm.136-40

CHORAL PARTS WITH LITTLE OR NO ACCOMPANIMENT

(1) Choral Parts with No Accompaniment

Source Aa:

1^4 bottom I,mm.54-8
2^V Zwsp.mm.5-7 (contrapuntal studies)
12^r I,mm.335-44 (early, crossed out)
12^V I,mm.335-46 (=final; continues mm.347-50 with
  accomp. at bottom)
13^r I,mm.335ff (contrapuntal studies)
13^V I,mm.403-18,419-30
15^r I,mm.399ff (four versions, first at top =final)
15^V I,mm.427-8
16^r I,mm.421-2 (early)
16^V mid-bottom I,mm.443-73
17^r I,mm.429-42
17^V I,mm.443-7
20^V I,mm.508-22
21^r top I,mm.491ff
21^r middle I,mm.506-7 (=final)
21^r bottom I,mm.513ff (early, crossed out)
22^r top I,mm.566ff (early)
22^r bottom I,mm.573-81 (continued from complete
  mm.563-72 at top)
23^r top I,mm.585ff (early, crossed out)
23^r bottom I,mm.582-94
23^V top I,mm.595-9 (sop. only, then 2 parts)
23^V mid-bottom I,mm.600-15
24^V top I,mm.689ff
25^V bottom I,mm.798ff
28^2 top I,mm.762-6
29^r top I,mm.894-5
29^r top-mid I,mm.929-30 (=final)
29^r mid-bottom I,mm.936-9
29^V I,mm.937ff (canonic counterpoint)
33^V II,mm.114-28 (fragments)
34^r bottom I,mm.798-9 (continued from choral sketch with
  accomp. at top, mm.780-98)

Source Ab:

1³ (#2971) II,mm.200-39 (no accomp. except for a single
   chord in m. 204 which does not appear in final version)
4ᵛ (#2978) II,mm.273-88 (2 early, contrapuntal versions)
7ʳ (#2983) Zwsp.mm.20-23 (inserted in theme table of
   folio 6)
15ʳ (#2999) bottom II,mm.1102ff
21ʳ (#3009) bottom II,mm.538-43
42ʳ (#3015) II,mm.151-65
24ᵛ (#3016) II,mm.200-69 (early version)

Source Ac:

1 (#3020) I,mm.366ff (early, text not included)
2 (#3021) I,mm.366ff (early, counterpoint)
3 (#3022) I,mm.366ff (early, counterpoint)
4 (#3023) I,mm.380,401ff (early)
5 (#3024) I,mm.377-81 (early)
6-7ᵦ (#3025-6) unaccomp. single-line tenor melody
10²ᵇ (#3031 right) I,mm.366ff
23 (#3046) I,mm.366ff

(2) Choral Parts with Incomplete Accompaniment

Source Aa:

2ʳ₂ I,mm.54-64 (close to final)
3²₂ middle I,mm.72-6
3²₂ bottom I,mm.77-81 (accomp. only)
3³ I,mm.81-85
12ᵛ bottom I,mm.347-50
16ᵛ top I,mm.443ff (early, accomp. only)
20ʳ I,mm.491-505 (m.498 left blank; mostly choral parts
    only with instrumental parts to fill in interludes; =final)
21ᵛ fragment: accomp. idea only: 7ths on a staff
24ʳ mid-bottom I,647ff
25ʳ top I,mm.685-92
25ʳ top I,mm.817ff (fragmentary, accomp. only)
26ʳ I,mm.815-40 (almost complete, close to final)
28¹ I,mm.796ff (3 early versions, accomp. only)
30ᵛ I,mm.956-7
31ʳ I,mm.956ff (2 early versions)
34ʳ top I,mm.780-98

Source Ab

3ᵛ (#2976) top II,mm.219-25, 219-223
4ᵛ (#2978) top II,mm.241-3 (early)
6¹ (#2981) middle I,mm.11ff
8ᵛ (#2987) top II,mm.300-7
13ʳ (#2996) bottom II,mm.780ff (early: different rhythm,
    different text)

13^v (#2997) II,mm.200ff(?) (no text, accomp. only)
23^r (#3013) II,mm.1084-98 (at times only sop. melody)
23^v (#3014) II,mm.1084-99 (at times no accomp.)
24^v (#3016) II,mm.200ff (early)

Source <u>Ac</u>
6 (#3025) top I,mm.689ff (continues unaccompanied)
8 (#3027) I,mm.443ff
9 (#3028) I,mm.443ff
22 (#3041) I,mm.735-6
22g (#3045) II,mm.129-30 (fragment; accomp. rhythm only)

<u>TEXTED, COMPLETE</u>

<u>(1) Complete Solo Vocal Passages</u>

Source <u>Aa</u>:

6^v_1 mid-bottom I,mm.148-62
7^1_2 top I,mm.163-70 (continues incomplete)
7^2 top I,mm. 181,183-5
7^3 top-mid I,mm.208-14
7^3_4 bottom I,mm.230-33 (without text)
7^4 I,mm.234-43 (early version but complete)
8^r I,mm.234-43 (=final)
10^v I,mm.306-24 (=final)
11^v middle I,mm.290-6 (continues incomplete)
19^r top I,mm.481-3 (crossed out)
19^r bottom I,mm.484-8 (=final)
22^v I,mm.654-60 (continues incomplete)
24^v bottom I,mm.675-84
26^v top I,mm.870-8 (continues incomplete)
27^r I,mm.716-34
27^v I,mm.840-69
28^1 bottom I,mm.738-41
28^2 I,mm.736-61
28^3 bottom I,mm.767-78
28^4 I,mm.779-90
29^v I,mm.910-18 (continues incomplete)
32^r II,mm.43-62
33^r II,mm.71-93

Source <u>Ab</u>:

4^r (#2977) top II,mm.143-50 (=final)
8^v (#2987) bottom II,mm.308-19 (=final)
20^r (#3008) top II,mm.490-96; 497-518 without text

Source <u>Ac</u>:

10^{1a} (#3030 left) I,mm.523-35
10^{2a} (#3031 left) I,mm.553-4
10^{3a} (#3032 left) I,mm.547-50, 541-6
22^a (#3042) I,mm.642-6 + 1 m. contin.

(2) Complete Choral Passages

Source Aa:

1_r^1 I,mm.1-14
1_r^2 I,mm.15-18
1_r^3 I,mm.29-49
1_2^4 I,mm.50-53 (continues with vocal melody only)
3^2 top I,mm.67-61 (continues incomplete)
14^r I,mm.351-66
18^r I,mm.443-73
22^r middle I,mm.563-72 (continues incomplete)
25^r bottom I,mm.818-31
25^V top I,mm.791-5

Source Ab:

Source Ac:

Source Ad:

2^r, 3^r, 2^V present Zwsp.mm.1-42 consecutively (=final)

UNTEXTED, MAIN MELODY COMPLETE, SUPPORTING MATERIAL INCOMPLETE

Source Aa:

4^V I,mm.102ff
5^r I,mm.102ff (fragmentary)
5^V I,mm.102ff (fragmentary; melody =final)

Source Ab:

5^r (#2979) II,mm.598ff (fragmentary)
5^V (#2980) top II,mm.331-46 (early, notations of row
   forms T, U+6, U+1, U+2; Hauptstimme only from m. 336)
8^r (#2986) II,mm.824ff, 860ff
10_2^1 (#2990) top II,mm.975-83 (fragments)
10^2 (#2991) II,mm.881-902 (some accomp. rhythm only)
11^r (#2993) II,mm.861-70, 907ff (some accomp. rhythm only)
11^V (#2994) II,mm.842-57 (two versions plus add.
   fragment; some accomp. rhythm only)
12^r (#2995) "Anfang des III Aktes" (fragment)
13^r (#2996) II,mm.821-3 (4 early versions with stage
   directions)
16^r (#3001) I,mm.320-82 (long section drafted mostly by
   main melody with varying amounts of supporting material)

19^r (#3006) II,mm.448–89 (mostly main melody)
19^v (#3007) II,mm.524–37 (contin. from 18^v; crossed
   out)
21^v (#3010) II,mm.828–33 (early; some accomp. rhythm
   only; rhythm =final but melody does not)

Source Ac:

17 (#3036) fragments (c. I,mm.550ff? 716ff?)
22c (#3043 left) fragments of accomp. motives
22d (#3043) bottom, unidentifed fragments
22e (#3044 left) unidentified fragments
22f (#3044 right) unidentified fragments

Source Ae:

pp.[2–3] Act III, 5–m. fragment "Aron wird
   hereingeschleppt" (appears nearly complete)
pp.[4–5] top, Act III, 3–m. fragment (appears nearly
   complete)
pp.[4–5] bottom, 2 contrapuntal fragments

UNTEXTED, COMPLETE

Source Aa:

4^v top I,mm.98–101 (early)
10^r top I,mm.244–55
24^r top I,mm.621–3

Source Ab:

(N.B.: Recto sides only of Source Ab, sheets 16–22 contain some broadly
drafted sections and some fairly complete drafts of II,mm.320–626 (scene
3)—a major portion of the Golden Calf scene. They are the only long
section in Source Ab of this kind.)

5^v (#2980) top II,mm.331–43
13^v (#2997) II,mm.749–58
16^v (#3002) II,mm.627–66 (continuation from Source Ac?)
17^r (#3003) II,mm.382–414 (continues on 18^r)
18^r (#3004) II,mm.415–47
20^r (#3008) bottom II,mm.497–518 (continued from texted
   mm.490–96 at top
21^r (#3009) top II,mm.519–28 (gap between mm.528–538,
   continues on to choral parts mm.538–43)
22^r (#3011) II,mm.585–626 (laid out on page in
   fragments: mm.585–8,589–91,592–6,297; mm.595–6 Hauptst. and
   Nebenst. only)

Source Ac:

10^{4a} (#3033 left) I,mm.148–62 (=final)

15 (#3034) II,mm.605-15 "Tanz II-Akt" (=final)
17 (#3036) top I,mm.716-18 (=final)
18 (#3037) top I,mm.563-5 (early)
22d (#3043 right) II,mm.49-52 (=final)

ROW CHARTS

Source Ad:

1^V Complete row chart
Source Af (bound booklet of row forms):

Openings 1-12 (#3047-59) give one prime and one related inversion row
form per opening; after opening #12 various rows appear on last page
together.

Source Ag (row charts):

Loose sheets (#3060-2) show three more row relationships, related to
Source Af.

SPECIFICALLY ROW-RELATED SKETCHES

Source Aa:

3^1 bottom, related to sketch for I,mm.163-79, (blue and
  red pencil T5, U+2, T5K, U+2K)
5^V bottom I,98ff with blue and red row sketches
9^r chart of transpositions of hexachords
9^V I,mm.1ff opening chords and linear hexachord motive
  as "T,U,K" forms
15^r I,mm.399ff marginal notes of row forms

Source Ab:

2^V (#2974) 2+4 tetrachords of T-5,T-7,T+2 showing
  relationship among them
3^V (#2976) unlabeled hexachords in mainly diatonic scale
  formation
4^r (#2977) same tetrachords as in 2^V in use in I,mm.166-72
5^V (#2908) bottom, trichordal motives in 6/8 time[1]
10^1 (#2990) middle hexachords as 8th-notes, labeled
  T-3,U-s,T-6,U-2
25^r (#3017) top trichordal divisions of two rows

Source Ac:

1 (#3020) hexachordal row division with order of notes rotated

---

[1]Schmidt, KB p. 212, relates these to I,mm.371-96, but this is ques-
tionable.

10^{1b} (#3030 right) I,mm.1ff manipulation of motivic
material
10^{4b} (#3033 right) two mm. from mm.148-62(?)

Source Ad:

1^{r} Row sketch showing relationships between T+7 and U-5;
U5 (T+2), U8 (T+6) and U-2; and U+2 and U-6.

Source Ae:

VERBAL SKETCHES

Source Aa:

none
Source Ab:

7^{r} (#2984) note for Zwischenspiel
23^{v} (#3014) bottom "Canon...und hinter der Szene..."

Source Ac:

none
Source Ad:

3^{r} bottom, note for continuation of Zwischenspiel

REFERENCES TO SKETCHBOOK (Source Ac) IN OTHER SOURCES:

Source Aa:

2^{r} "SK IV", "Nie, nie, nie, SK IV"
4^{r} "SK X" (I,mm.163-77)
4^{r} "SK XII" (I,mm.199ff)

Source Ab:

1^{2} "Siehe SKb"
1^{4} "SK 22ef"
6^{2} "SK I"
6^{3} "6^{3} Nr. 8"
6^{4} "SKb 6/7"
7^{r} "SkV Doppel-Fugenthema"

Source Ac:

$10^{2b,5-7}$ "Siehe 19", refers back to Source Ac page 19.

UNTEXTED, UNIDENTIFIED MATERIAL, NOT RELATED TO
MOSES UND ARON

Source Aa:

Source Ab:

9^r (#2988) bottom (upside down)
9^v (#2989) two-part counterpoint, a row other than the
   row for the opera
10^1 (#2990) bottom
12^v (#2995) tonal melody, cadenza from Monn Concerto
14^1 (#2998) mid-bottom, tonal fragments
25^r (#3017) tonal fragments
25^v (#3019) fragments

Source Ac:

54 (no archive #) fragment
55 (no archive #) fragment

Source Ae:

p.[1] unrelated 12-tone row
p.[6] unrelated tonal melody
pp[7ff] unrelated prose: "The Art of the Caricaturist," UCLA
   notes, etc.

SUMMARY

Types of Sketches:

Theme Tables: 2 (Ab only)

Texted: Solo (incl. ensemble solo)
   Melody only: 19 (Aa=12, Ab=7)
   Melody + partial accomp.: 27 (Aa=12, Ab=9, Ac=6)
   Accomp. only: 2 (Ac=2)
   Complete: 29 (Aa=22, Ab=3, Ac=4)

Texted: Choral
   Choral parts only: 42 (Aa=27, Ab=7, Ac=8)
   Choral parts + partial
      accomp.:   24 (Aa=11, Ab=8, Ac=5)
   Accomp. only: 4 (Aa=3, Ab=1)
   Complete: 10 (Aa only)

Untexted:
   Main melody complete +
      partial accomp: 21 (Aa=3, Ab=13, Ac=5,

		Ae=3)
Complete:	16	(Aa=3, Ab=8, Ac=5)
Row charts:	2	(1 sheet, Ad[1];
		1 booklet, Af and Ag)
Specifically row-related sketches:	14	(Aa=5, Ab=6, Ac=3)
<u>Verbal</u> <u>Sketches</u>	3	(<u>Ab</u>=2, <u>Ad</u>=1)

Appendix 2

Leitmotive in *Moses und Aron*

M1   "God," P0_{a,d}

I. mm. 1-2

M1′

I, mm. 2-3

M2a   "God's will," P0_{b+c}

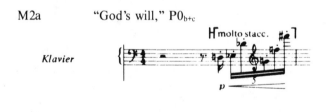

I, m. 3

M2a′   "God's will," RI0_{b+c}

I, m. 5

M2a″   "God's will," P/RI₁ or 2

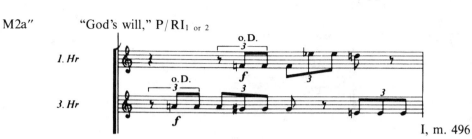

I, m. 496

M2b   "Verkünde!" P/RI_b or c

I, m. 94

M3a   "Aron's misrepresentation," triad

I, m. 7

M3b   "Aron's misrepresentation," "wrong" chord + triad

I, mm. 163-4

M4a   "Moses," sustained tetrachords

EH

I, m. 8

M4b   "Moses," wide dyadic leaps

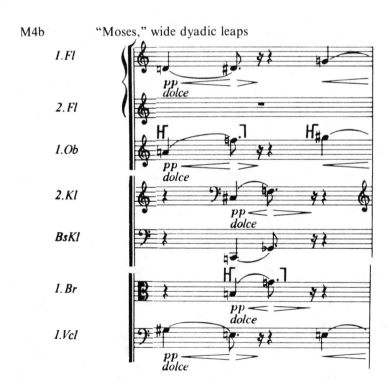

I, m. 16

M4b′   "Moses' motto," single dyadic leap of a mi7th

MOSES

Darfst?

I, m. 182

PRIESTER

Mo - - - - - ses?

I, mm. 290-91

M4c   "Moses," stepwise dyads

I. Vcl

I, m. 21

M4c′   "Moses," sustained chromatic dyad

I, m. 64

I. Geige

II, mm. 45-47

M4c″   "Moses," two alternating stepwise dyads

II, m. 50

II, m. 293

M4d   "Moses in the wilderness," parallel 7ths

I, m. 22

becomes 7ths
and 9ths in
I, mm. 98ff.

M4d′   "Moses in the wilderness," tremolo parallel 7ths

I, m. 487

M4e   "Moses," 2+4 structures

I, m. 44

M4f   "auserwählt" motto

I, m. 71

M5a   "Aron" (I4, notes 1, 3, 5)

3. Pos

I4, notes 1, 3, 5   I, m. 123

BsKl

2. Fg
                                                        foreshadowed
                                                        in I, m. 29

M5b   "Mann"

MANN

Ich rief   ihn,

I, m. 279

R5, notes 1, 3, 6

M6   "Orgy," Parallel 5ths

II. Gg

II, 371ff.

I. Geige

foreshadowed
in I, m. 6

M7a   "Jüngling" (hope) I5x

I, mm. 248-50

I, mm. 267-8

Bei mei - nem   Haus —

M7b   "Mädchen" (hope) RI5x

I, m. 255

Ich hab ihn ge - sehn,___

M8a   "Blutopfer, I" (I5a)

I, m. 340

Blut - op - fer

M8b   "Blutopfer, II"

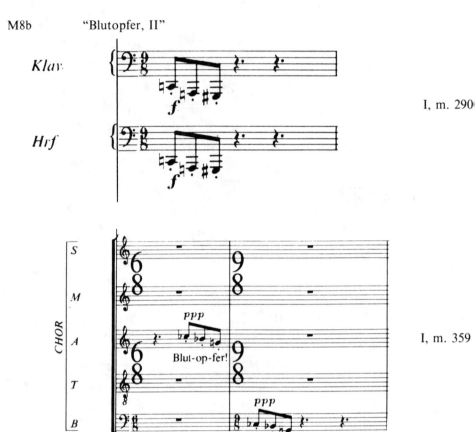

I, m. 290

I, m. 359

Appendix 3

Analytical Diagram of *Moses und Aron*:
Row Forms and *Leitmotive*

Meas.#:	Row/Aggreg.	Leitmotiv(e)	Text/Action

Prologue

Meas.#	Row/Aggreg.	Leitmotiv(e)	Text/Action
1	A0 (P0)	M1	God alone
2	(RI0)	M1´	in Burning
3	(P0)	M1,M2a	Bush
4	(P0)	M1´	
5	(RI0)	M2a,M1´	
6	A0	M6 foresh; M1,M2a;	
7		M3a foresh; M1, M2a´´	

I,i

8	RI1x,y	M4a	Moses speaks
9	RI1z, P10x,y	↓	
10	P10z		
11	A0	M1,M2a	God speaks
12			
13		↓	
14			
15		↓	
16	I9-R8	M4b	Moses
17	R8-RI5		
18	A5		
19		↓	
20			
21	A8	M4c	
22	A9	M4d	
23	A0	M1,M2a´	God
24		↓	
25		M1,M2a´	
26	A5		"dein Volk
27		(M5a foresh?)	befrein!"
28		↓	
29	A7-I9	M5a foresh; M4d,c	Moses "Wer bin ich?"
30	I9-P8	↓	
31	A8	M1,M1´,M2	incr. stress
32		M5a	"verbunden;
33		M1´	entzweit"
34		M1,M2a´	
35		M4a,d;M1,M2a	
36		M1,M1´(R)	"Der Ewige..."
37	A7		

38		M1+M1´	
39		M2a´´	
40		M1,M1´,M2a´´	
41	A5	M1+M4a	"vor Ihren Ohren..."
42		↓	
43	A8	M5a exagg.; M4a+M2a	
44	A3(2+4)	M4e(2+4)	"Von deinem Stab"
45		↓	
46	A9		
47		M4d	"Meine Zunge ist
48	A0	M1,M2a´	ungelenk..."
49		↓	
50		M1(M5a exagg.)	
51	A1	M1´,M1 as ostinato	
52	A7		
53	A5	M4a	God "Wie aus
54		M4a	diesem Dornbusch..."
55		M4a,M4c	
56			
57			
58		↓	
59	A8	M1,M1´ strong	God "Aron soll dein Mund sein"
60		↓	
61		M4a	
62		↓	
63	A7		
64		M4c´	
65	A8	↓	
66		M4b,d	
67	A0	M2a,M1inv	God blesses
68		M2a´	
69		↓	
70		M2b;M4d clar: distorted M5	"gesegnet"
71		M2a´´,M4d,f	"auserwählt"
72		M4d,f	
73		M4d,f	
74		M4d,f;M2a´´	
75		M4b,d,f; M2a´´;M5a	
76			
77		M4a,b,f;M5a	
78		M4a,b,d,f	
79		↓ +M1´	
80		↓	
81	(rotation)	M4d;M5a	
82		M5;M4d	
83		M4c;M2a´´	
84		M4c;M5;M2a´´	

85	A1	M2a´,M1(R);M4c´	
86	A5	M1	
87		M1;M4d; Haupt.M4b/c	
88		M1´;M5	
89		↓	
90	A0	M2b,M1, M1´inv.	"Verkünde!"
91			
92			
93			
94		↓	
95		M1,M1´;M2 broken into TT dyads(M4); Haupt.M4f; Haupt.M4c´´	final resolve: comb. of God + Moses
96			
97		↓	

I,ii

98	modulatory	mel=M4c/M5; accomp=M4d´	wasteland scene
99			
100			
101			
102			
103			
104			
105			
106			
107			
108			
109			
110			
111			
112			
113			
114			
115			
116			
117			
118			
119			
120			
121			
122			
123	A4 (P4)	+Haupt.M5a	Aron´s entr.
124			
125			
126		+M2b	"Väter"
127			
128		↓	

```
129
130            (I4)                                    |
131                                                    |
132                                                    |
133                                                    |
134                                                    |
135            (R4)                                    |
136                                                    |
137                                                    |
138                                                    |
139            (RI4)                                   |
140                                                    |
141                                                    |
142                                                    |
143                                                    |
144                                                    |
145                                                    |
146                                                    |
147                                                    ▼
─────────────────────────────────────────────────────────────────────────
148            A7              M5a,M4b              M&A dialogue
149                                                    |
150                                                    |
151                                                    |
152                                                    |
153                                                    |
154                                                    |
155                                                    |
156                                                    |
157                                                    |
158                                                    |
159                                                    |
160                                                    |
161                                                    |
162                                                    ▼
─────────────────────────────────────────────────────────────────────────
163                            M3a,b;M5a            Aron
164                                                    |
165                                                    |
166                                                    |
167                                                    |
168                                                    |
169                                                    |
170                                                    |
171                            M2a´
172                            M1 embedded
                               in M3b chords
173                            M3
174                            M3b;M5a
                                 ▼
175
176                            Haupt.M4d;
                               distorted
                               M5a inv.;M2b
177                            M2b;M4b/d
─────────────────────────────────────────────────────────────────────────
178            P8              Aron quotes          Aron elaborates
```

		M2b with rptd. notes	"unsichtbar, un-vorstellbar"
179			
180			
181	R3		
182		M4d,M4b	Moses "Darfst?
183			Unvorstellbar..."
184			
185			
186			
187	A7	Haupt,Neben.M5a; accomp=M4b,c	
188			
189			
190			
191			
192			
193			
194			
195		Haupt,Neben.M5a; M4b/d	"Du belohnst..."
196			
197			
198			
199			
200		M1´(R);M4d	
201			
202			
203		Haupt.M4c;M4b	
204			
205			
206		+M5	
207			
208	I2	mel=row; accomp=M4d	Moses "Reinige dein
209			Denken...
210			
211			
212			
213			
214			
215			
216		+M4c	
217			
218	A7	strong M3b; Haupt.M5	Aron
219		distorted M2	
220		M3b	
221		M3b,M5	
222		M3b,M5;M2b	
223			
224			

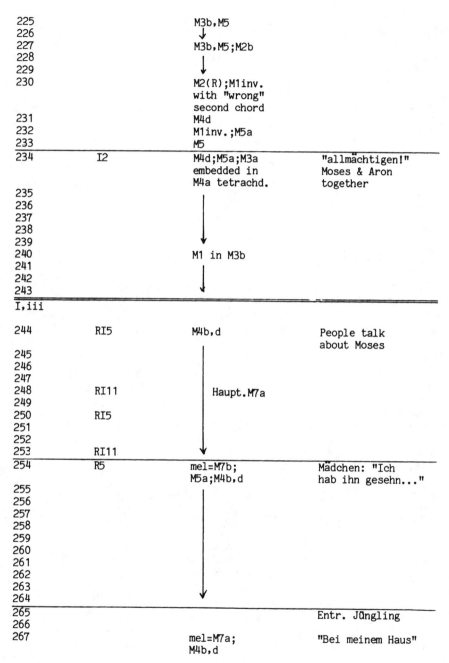

225		M3b,M5	
226		↓	
227		M3b,M5;M2b	
228			
229		↓	
230		M2(R);M1inv. with "wrong" second chord	
231		M4d	
232		M1inv.;M5a	
233		M5	
234	I2	M4d;M5a;M3a embedded in M4a tetrachd.	"allmächtigen!" Moses & Aron together
235			
236			
237			
238			
239		↓	
240		M1 in M3b	
241			
242		↓	
243			

I,iii

244	RI5	M4b,d	People talk about Moses
245			
246			
247			
248	RI11	Haupt.M7a	
249			
250	RI5		
251			
252			
253	RI11	↓	
254	R5	mel=M7b; M5a;M4b,d	Mädchen: "Ich hab ihn gesehn..."
255			
256			
257			
258			
259			
260			
261			
262			
263			
264		↓	
265			Entr. Jüngling
266			
267		mel=M7a; M4b,d	"Bei meinem Haus"

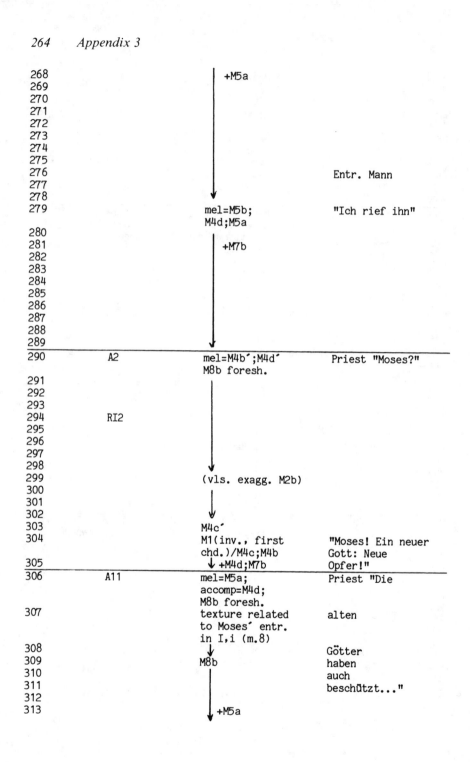

268		+M5a	
269			
270			
271			
272			
273			
274			
275			
276			Entr. Mann
277			
278			
279		mel=M5b; M4d;M5a	"Ich rief ihn"
280			
281		+M7b	
282			
283			
284			
285			
286			
287			
288			
289			
290	A2	mel=M4b´;M4d´ M8b foresh.	Priest "Moses?"
291			
292			
293			
294	RI2		
295			
296			
297			
298			
299		(vls. exagg. M2b)	
300			
301			
302			
303		M4c´	
304		M1(inv., first chd.)/M4c;M4b	"Moses! Ein neuer Gott: Neue
305		+M4d;M7b	Opfer!"

306	A11	mel=M5a;
		accomp=M4d;
		M8b foresh.
			Priest "Die

307		texture related to Moses´ entr. in I,i (m.8)	alten
308			Götter
309		M8b	haben
310			auch
311			beschützt..."
312			
313		+M5a	

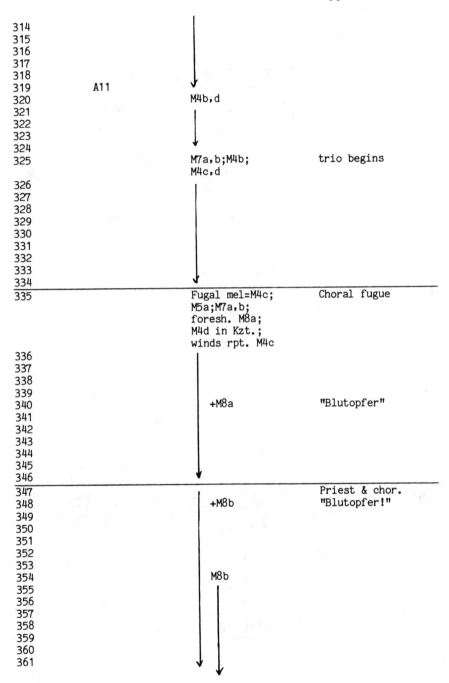

```
314
315
316
317
318
319        A11
320                        M4b,d
321
322
323
324
325                        M7a,b;M4b;          trio begins
                           M4c,d
326
327
328
329
330
331
332
333
334
335                        Fugal mel=M4c;      Choral fugue
                           M5a;M7a,b;
                           foresh. M8a;
                           M4d in Kzt.;
                           winds rpt. M4c
336
337
338
339
340                        +M8a                "Blutopfer"
341
342
343
344
345
346
347                                            Priest & chor.
348                        +M8b                "Blutopfer!"
349
350
351
352
353
354                        M8b
355
356
357
358
359
360
361
```

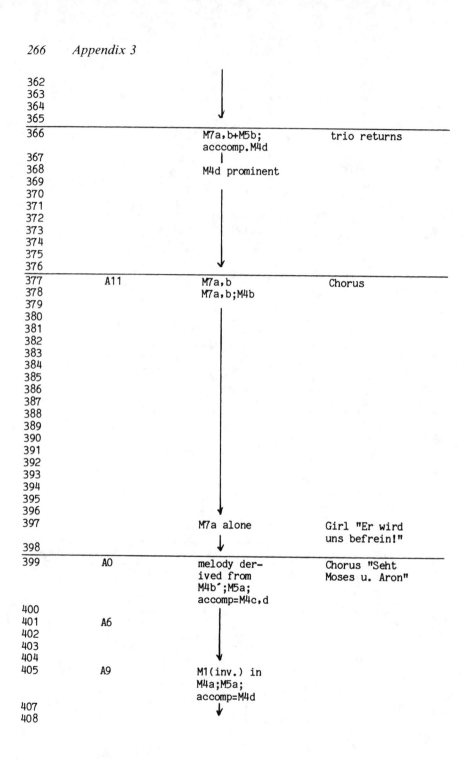

362			
363			
364			
365			
366		M7a,b+M5b; acccomp.M4d	trio returns
367			
368		M4d prominent	
369			
370			
371			
372			
373			
374			
375			
376			
377	A11	M7a,b	Chorus
378		M7a,b;M4b	
379			
380			
381			
382			
383			
384			
385			
386			
387			
388			
389			
390			
391			
392			
393			
394			
395			
396			
397		M7a alone	Girl "Er wird uns befrein!"
398			
399	A0	melody der- ived from M4b´;M5a; accomp=M4c,d	Chorus "Seht Moses u. Aron"
400			
401	A6		
402			
403			
404			
405	A9	M1(inv.) in M4a;M5a; accomp=M4d	
407			
408			

409			
410			
411			
412			
413			
414	RO,R6	M4c,d;M5a	
415	A6		
416			
417			
418			
419	P9	M1inv;M3a;M4d	"Aron, ge-
420		M3b,M5a	wiss nicht mehr
421	R3	M3b/M4d;M5a	jung..."
422			
423	P9		
424			
425	P3		
426			
427	R6	M3b;M4c	
428			
429			
430		+M4d	
431		M5a;M4d	
432			
433	PO,9,3		
434		+3-note motives related to M3a,M8b	"sind ferner, sind näher..."
435			
436	A3		
437			
438			
439			
440		M1 embedded in M3b	"Seht Moses! Seht Aron!"
441		M4b´,M5a	
442		M7a; chords=M1+M3	"Und sind jetzt da!"

I,iv

443	A2	M2b,M1; M3inv. + thirds (M3) in mel=mat´l.	"Bringt ihr Erhörung"
444			
445			
446			
447		+M1	
448		+M1inv.	
449			
450		+M1inv.	
451			

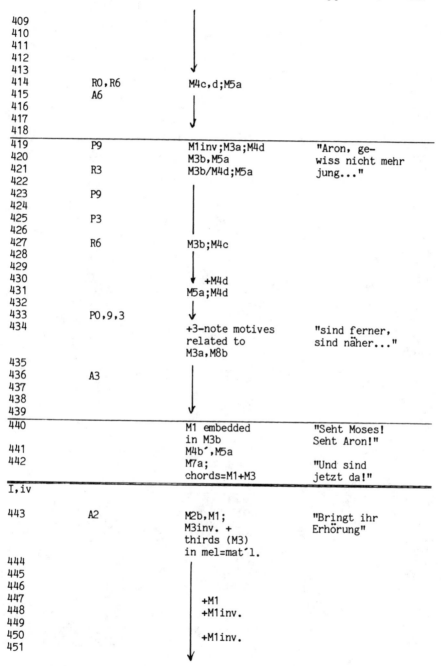

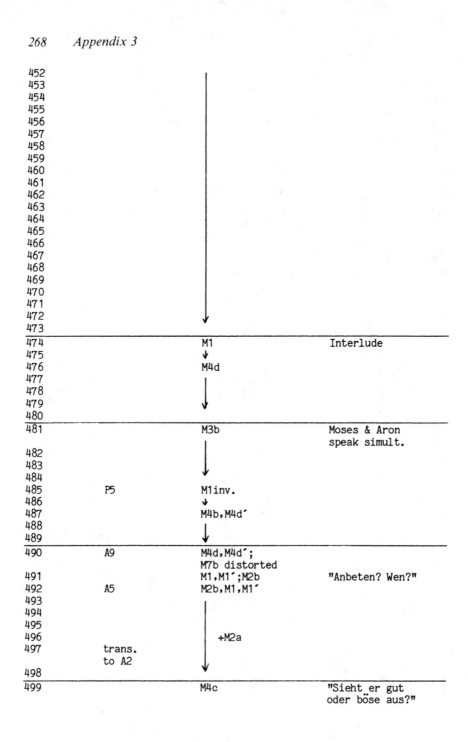

452			
453			
454			
455			
456			
457			
458			
459			
460			
461			
462			
463			
464			
465			
466			
467			
468			
469			
470			
471			
472			
473			
474		M1	Interlude
475		↓	
476		M4d	
477			
478			
479			
480			
481		M3b	Moses & Aron speak simult.
482			
483			
484			
485	P5	M1inv.	
486		↓	
487		M4b,M4d´	
488			
489			
490	A9	M4d,M4d´; M7b distorted	
491		M1,M1´;M2b	"Anbeten? Wen?"
492	A5	M2b,M1,M1´	
493			
494			
495			
496		+M2a	
497	trans. to A2		
498			
499		M4c	"Sieht er gut oder böse aus?"

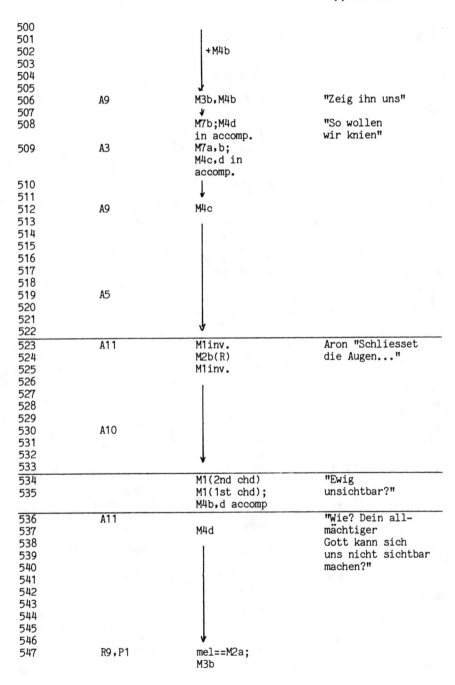

500			
501			
502		+M4b	
503			
504			
505			
506	A9	M3b,M4b	"Zeig ihn uns"
507			
508		M7b;M4d in accomp.	"So wollen wir knien"
509	A3	M7a,b; M4c,d in accomp.	
510			
511			
512	A9	M4c	
513			
514			
515			
516			
517			
518			
519	A5		
520			
521			
522			
523	A11	M1inv.	Aron "Schliesset
524		M2b(R)	die Augen..."
525		M1inv.	
526			
527			
528			
529			
530	A10		
531			
532			
533			
534		M1(2nd chd)	"Ewig
535		M1(1st chd); M4b,d accomp	unsichtbar?"
536	A11		"Wie? Dein all-
537		M4d	mächtiger
538			Gott kann sich
539			uns nicht sichtbar
540			machen?"
541			
542			
543			
544			
545			
546			
547	R9,P1	mel==M2a; M3b	

548		
549		
550	↓	
551	exagg.M5a;M4c	
552	M7a,b exagg.	"Ich sah..."
553	↓	
554	M2b/M4b,d	Priest entr.
555		
556	+M3a	
557		
558	↓	
559	M4b,d	
560	M4d,M3b comb.	
561	M4d,M4c	
562	M6,M3	mocking laughter
563	M4b,c	
564	theme built	"Bleib uns
	on M5a + lin.	fern mit
	triad (M3a)	deinem Gott"
565	theme M5a,M3+	
	M4c,d accomp.	
566		
567		
568		
569		
570		
571		
572		
573		
574		
575		
576		
577		
578		
579		
580		
581		
582	↓	
583	M7a,b;M4b	"Wir wollen
	ref. to mm.	durch ihn
	389-97 and	nicht befreit
	248ff	sein!"
584	↓	
585	M4c,d	"Bleib uns fern"
586	↓	
587	M4c,d;M5a	
	distorted	
588	↓	
589		
590	(M4b?)	"der Allgegen-
		wärtiger..."
591	↓	
592		

593		M6,M3	
594		↓	
595	R11 (out of order)	M7a,b;M4c	
596			
597			
598		M5a,M4c	
599		M5	
600		↓	
601		M3a	
602			
603		↓	
604		M3a	
605		M4d;Haupt.M3a	
606		M3a	
607	P4	+M3b	
608		+M4d	
609	P1	↓	
610		M3a	
611	P10	(ostinato)	
612			
613	P2		
614		↓	
615	R1	Haupt.M5a	
616		+M1	
617			
618		↓	
619		M7a,b	
620		↓	
621		M1	
622	A0	M3a	
623		M1; Haupt.M2a	Moses "Allmäch-tiger, meine
624		M1; Haupt.M2a	Kraft ist zur Ende.
625		M5+M4c	Mein Gedanke ist machtlos
626			in Arons Wort"
627		↓	
628		M3b	Aron menaces
629		M4c,M3	Moses
630		M1+M3b; M4c,M5a	Chorus: "Aron!"
631		M4c,M2b	
632		M1,M3b; mel= M5a; M5a inv.	Aron "Das Wort bin ich und die
633		↓	Tat!"
634		M4c+M5a;mel=M5a	
635		M5a rptd.	"Aron, was
636		M4b;M5a	tust du?"
637		↓	
638		M4c	(no text)

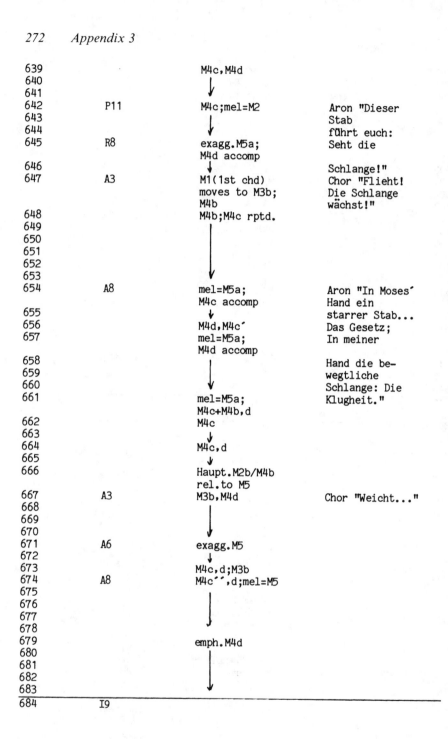

639		M4c,M4d	
640			
641		↓	
642	P11	M4c;mel=M2	Aron "Dieser
643			Stab
644		↓	führt euch:
645	R8	exagg.M5a;	Seht die
		M4d accomp	
646		↓	Schlange!"
647	A3	M1(1st chd)	Chor "Flieht!
		moves to M3b;	Die Schlange
		M4b	wächst!"
648		M4b;M4c rptd.	
649			
650			
651			
652			
653		↓	
654	A8	mel=M5a;	Aron "In Moses'
		M4c accomp	Hand ein
655		↓	starrer Stab...
656		M4d,M4c´	Das Gesetz;
657		mel=M5a;	In meiner
		M4d accomp	
658		↓	Hand die be-
659			wegtliche
660		↓	Schlange: Die
661		mel=M5a;	Klugheit."
		M4c+M4b,d	
662		M4c	
663		↓	
664		M4c,d	
665		↓	
666		Haupt.M2b/M4b	
		rel.to M5	
667	A3	M3b,M4d	Chor "Weicht..."
668			
669			
670		↓	
671	A6	exagg.M5	
672		↓	
673		M4c,d;M3b	
674	A8	M4c´´,d;mel=M5	
675			
676			
677		↓	
678			
679		emph.M4d	
680			
681			
682			
683		↓	
684	I9		

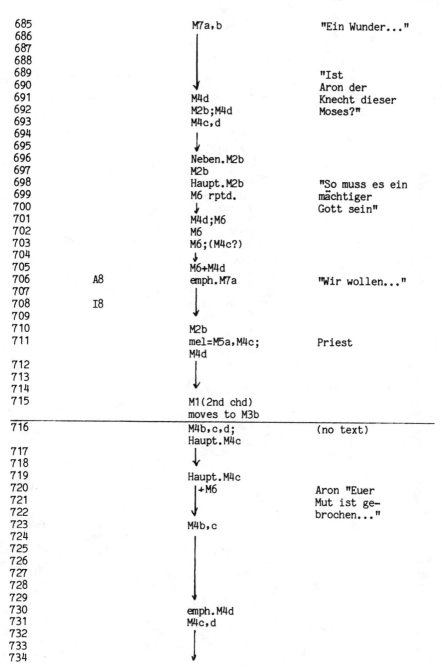

685		M7a,b	"Ein Wunder..."
686			
687			
688			
689			"Ist
690			Aron der
691		M4d	Knecht dieser
692		M2b;M4d	Moses?"
693		M4c,d	
694			
695			
696		Neben.M2b	
697		M2b	
698		Haupt.M2b	"So muss es ein
699		M6 rptd.	mächtiger
700			Gott sein"
701		M4d;M6	
702		M6	
703		M6;(M4c?)	
704			
705		M6+M4d	
706	A8	emph.M7a	"Wir wollen..."
707			
708	I8		
709			
710		M2b	
711		mel=M5a,M4c;	Priest
		M4d	
712			
713			
714			
715		M1(2nd chd)	
		moves to M3b	
716		M4b,c,d;	(no text)
		Haupt.M4c	
717			
718			
719		Haupt.M4c	
720		+M6	Aron "Euer
721			Mut ist ge-
722			brochen..."
723		M4b,c	
724			
725			
726			
727			
728			
729			
730		emph.M4d	
731		M4c,d	
732			
733			
734			

735		M4d;mel=M5a	Chor "Stark ist Pharao!"
736			
737			
738			Aron "Seht Moses'
739			Hand: gesund..."
740	A6	+exagg.M5	
741			
742		M4c	"Aber Moses' Herz..."
743		M5a twice	
744		M4c	
745			
746	(P6)	M3a;M2a,b	
747		Haupt.M2b	
748		M4b,c,d	"Aussatz!"
749			
750	A3	M4d	
751		M4d,M3b	
752		M4b,d	
753			"Flieht!"
754			
755		M5	
756			
757		Haupt.M4d	
758		M4d cont.	
759			"Aussatz!"
760		M3b	
761			
762			
763		M2b;mel=M2c	
764		M2b;M3b	
765		M2b	
766		M4d	
767	A8	M2b;M1inv.	
768		mel=M5+M4c; M4d accomp	Aron "Erkennt euch darin"
769			
770			
771		M3b	
772			
773		M1;Haupt.M5a to M2b	"Jetzt aber wohnt in Moses'
774		M4c,d;M2b	Busen..."
775		emph.M5a;M3a	
776		M5a (violin)	
777			
778		M5a twice	
779		M4d	
780		M1;(M3,M6)	
781	A5	M3b ostinato	
782			
783			

784		M3a	
785			
786		⎪ +M4d+M3a	
787		⎪	
788		⎪	
789		↓	
790		M2b;M4c;M2a	
791		all M4c	
792		↓	
793			
794		M7a,b;	"Ein Wunder
		M4c accomp	führt
795		M4a,c	Aron..."
796		M3b,M6	
797		↓	
798		Haupt.M5a	"Durch Aron"
799		↓	
800		M2b	"lässt Moses"
801		M5	
802		M4d	
803		⎪	
804		⎪	
805		⎪	
806		⎪	
807		Haupt.M2b;M4d;	"So wird
		M6	dieser
808		⎪	Gott..."
809		⎪	
810		↓	
811		(from m.690)	
812			
813		↓	
814		(M3,M6,M4)	
815		M1(1st chd)	"Allmächtiger
816		M1inv.(2nd	Gott!"
		chd);M4c+d	
817		M7a,b	"Alles für
		(rhythm only)	Freiheit!"
818	RI9x	M7a	
819		(M3)	
820		M7 (rhythm)	
821	R10x	orig. M7b	
822	zy	M4b/d	
823	RI9	M4d	
824		M7;M4b,d	
825			
826			
827		⎪ +M4c	
828		⎪	
829		⎪	"Auf! Auf!
830		⎪	
831		↓	Auf in die
			Wüste!"

832			
833		M4b,d	Priest
834		↓	
835	P4	M4d´	Moses
836		↓ +M2b	
837		↓ +M2b	
838	P4+A3	M2b;M5a	Aron
839			
840			
841			
842			
843			
844			
845		M2b	
846		M2b	
847		↓	
848		Haupt.M5a;	(ref. to
		M3;M4d´	wilderness)
849		↓	
850			
851		M1(2nd chd.)	
		moving to M3b	
		(recap.m.163ff)	
852		M3a	
853		↓	
854		M3a,b	
855		Haupt.M5a,M3b	
856		M3b cont.	
857		↓	
858		↓ +M3a	
859		Haupt.M2b	
860		mel=based on	(Aron)
		M4c,M5a,M2b	
861		M4c,d	
862		↓	
863		↓ mel=M2b	
864		M4c,d	
865		M5a;M4c	
866		Haupt.M2a;	
		accompM3b/M4d	
867		↓	
868		M2b/M4b,d	
869		M4c,d	
870		M4d only	
871		↓	
872			
873		M4c;mel=M2b	
874		↓ M4d,c,M5	
875		M4d;M4d,c	
876		M4d;M4c	
877		↓	
878			
879		M3	Aron "Es ist

880		M3b;M5a	euer Blut
881		M5a;M1	das dies
882		M5a;M3b	Land ernährt
883		M3a	wie das
884		M3a,b	Wasser des
885			Nil..."
886			
887			
888			
889			
890			
891			
892		M5a;M3b	(no text)
893	AO		
894		chor.A5; Aron M2b	"Auserwählt"
895			
896		M5a;Haupt.M2a	
897		M4d;M2b	
895			
896		M5a;Haupt.M2a	
897		M4d;M1;M2a,b	
898		M4c,d;M2a´´	
899			
900			
901			
902			
903			
904		Haupt.M2a/M4b, M4d moving to M5	
905		M4d lin;M3b	
906		Haupt.M2a; M4d,M3b	
907			
908			
909		M4c,d;M2a	
910			
911			
912		Haupt.M2a;M4c	
913			
914		M2b;M4c	
915		M1,M2b	
916		M4c,d	
917		M1 (2nd–1st)	
918			
919		Haupt.M2a´´;	"auserwählt"
920			
921		+M6	
922			
923			
924			
925		M3b	

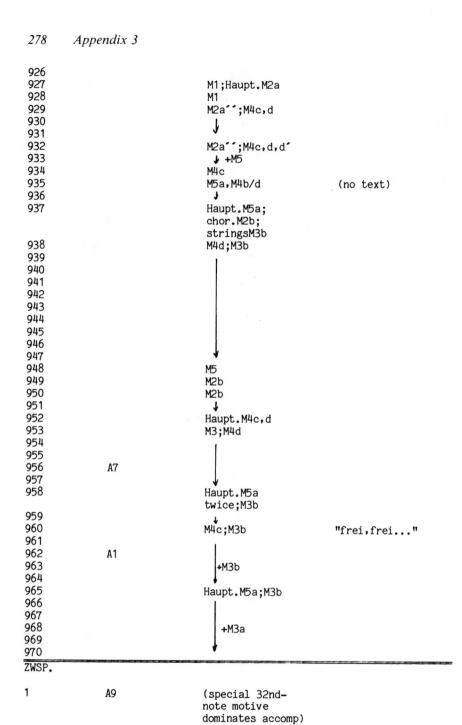

926			
927		M1;Haupt.M2a	
928		M1	
929		M2a´´;M4c,d	
930			
931			
932		M2a´´;M4c,d,d´	
933		+M5	
934		M4c	
935		M5a,M4b/d	(no text)
936			
937		Haupt.M5a; chor.M2b; stringsM3b	
938		M4d;M3b	
939			
940			
941			
942			
943			
944			
945			
946			
947			
948		M5	
949		M2b	
950		M2b	
951			
952		Haupt.M4c,d	
953		M3;M4d	
954			
955			
956	A7		
957			
958		Haupt.M5a twice;M3b	
959			
960		M4c;M3b	"frei,frei..."
961			
962	A1		
963		+M3b	
964			
965		Haupt.M5a;M3b	
966			
967			
968		+M3a	
969			
970			

ZWSP.

1	A9	(special 32nd-note motive dominates accomp)

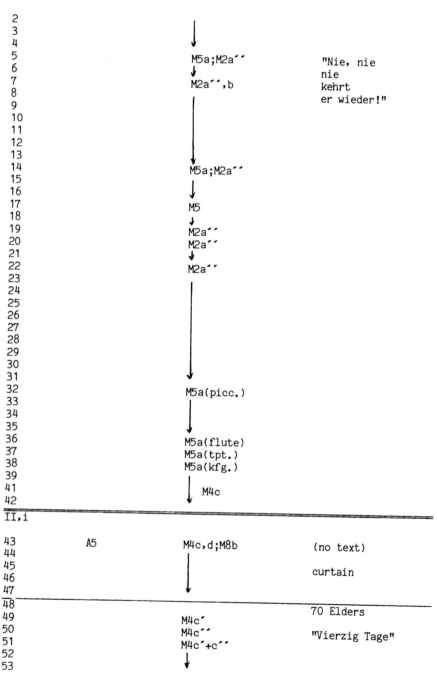

2
3
4
5   M5a;M2a´´   "Nie, nie
6   nie
7   M2a´´,b   kehrt
8   er wieder!"
9
10
11
12
13
14   M5a;M2a´´
15
16
17   M5
18
19   M2a´´
20   M2a´´
21
22   M2a´´
23
24
25
26
27
28
29
30
31
32   M5a(picc.)
33
34
35
36   M5a(flute)
37   M5a(tpt.)
38   M5a(kfg.)
39
41   M4c
42

II,i

43   A5   M4c,d;M8b   (no text)
44
45   curtain
46
47

48   70 Elders
49   M4c´
50   M4c´´   "Vierzig Tage"
51   M4c´+c´´
52
53

54			
55			
56		↓	
57			
58			
59		M1(inv.),M1	
60			
61		↓	
62	A1	Haupt. M4c´(inv.); M4c;mel=M7b	"Immer besetzt..."
63			
64			
65			
66			
67			
68			
69			
70			
71			
72		↓	
73	A5	M4c´´,M4d	
74		↓ +M3	
75		M4c(inv.),d	
76		↓	
77		M4c´´,c´´	
78			
79			
80			
81			
82		↓	
83			
84	RI9	↓	Aron
85			
86		M4c´	
87			
88		↓	
89			
90		M4c;M5a;M6	
91			
92		↓	
93	A4	M6	
94			
95		↓	
96			"Gedanken"
97		M2b (vl.)	
98		mel=M2b	
99		↓	
100			
101		M2b	70 Elders
102	A1	M3;M4c,d	
103		M4d,c	
104		↓	

105			
106		M4d,c′	
107			
108		+M3/M4d	
109		+M4c	
110			
111		↓	
112			
113		REST,FERMATA	
II,ii	– CONT.	FROM	II,i –
114	A3	M4d′	"Wo ist Moses?"
115		M2b;M3b;M4c′	
116		M4c;M3b	
117		↓	
118		M4d;M3b	
119		↓	
120		M3b	
121		⎮ M2b	
122		↓	
123		M4c;M3b	
124		↓	
125		M2b,M3b incl.M1(1st)	
126		M4c	
127		M4d,d′	
128	trans. A3–A5	↓	
129	A5	M4c,d	
130			
131		↓	
132			
133		M2b′twice	
134			
135	A10	↓	Aron "Volk Israels!"
136		M4c	
137			
138		↓	
139		M4c′′,M3	
140		M4f	
141		M4c;M3	
142		M4d	
143		M5a;M3	
144		M4d	
145		M3a,b	
146		↓	
147		M6′	
148		M4c′′,d	"...ihn getötet!"
149		↓	
150	RI10,RI6 RI2,P2	M4c′ 4 x + wh.tone sc.	
151	A9	M4c′′,d;M3b;	

		M2b; M5a	
		distorted	
152		M4b,c´	
153			
154			
155			
156			
157		+M4d	
158			
159			
160			
161			
162			
163		M3b	
164		↓	
165		M4c´	
166	A10	M4c´´,d,d´	
167			
168		↓	
169		M4d´/M3a	
170		M4c´/M3a	
171		M4c´/M3a	
172			
173		M3a	Aron "Volk Isra-
174		M5a rptd.	els! Deine
175		M5a	Götter geb
		↓	ich dir
176		M5a rptd.;M4c´	wieder..."
177		M5a	
178		M5a;M3a	
179		M5a;M3a	
180		M5a;M4d	
181		M5a	
182		M3a,M5a	
183		↓ +M4d	
184			
185		M5	
186		mel=M5	
187		M3a	"...Götter
188		M1(1st);M3a	gegenwärtigen..."
189		M1(1st);M4c	
190			
191		M4c,M3a	Chor "Jubelt,
		↓	freuet euch!"
192		mel=M3a--M5a	Aron
193		M4c;M5a;M6--5	
194		M3a;M5	
195		M3b;M6;	
		M1(1st)inv.	
196		M3b;M5a rptd.	
197		M3a,b;M5	
198		↓	
199			

200	A6	M4c=M8a; M1(2nd)	Aron "Bringt Gold her-
201		M6	bei!"
202		M4b,c;M6→M4d	
203		M4b,c,d	
204			
205		+M3c,M4c	
206			
207			
208			
209			
210		+M4f	
211			
212			
213			
214			
215		+(M6)	
216		+M4b,c,d	
217			
218		M4b,c;M5a; +M4d;M8a	
219		+M4d	
220		M4b,c,d;M6	
221			
222		incr. use	
223		of 3rds(rel.	
224		to M3)	
225			
226			
227			
228			
229			
230		(M3)	
231		M6,emph.M4c	
232		M4d,f	"Gerechtigkeit"
233			
234			
235			
236			
237			
238		M4d	
239		emph.M4c	
240		M4c alone	
241	I9	M8a;M4f (mel=built of 2nds(M4) and 3rds(M3))	"Juble,
242	P5	M4c´´	Israel,
243	I9	M4d;M8a/M4c´	freue dich
244			Isra-
245			el!"
246	A3	M4b	
247			

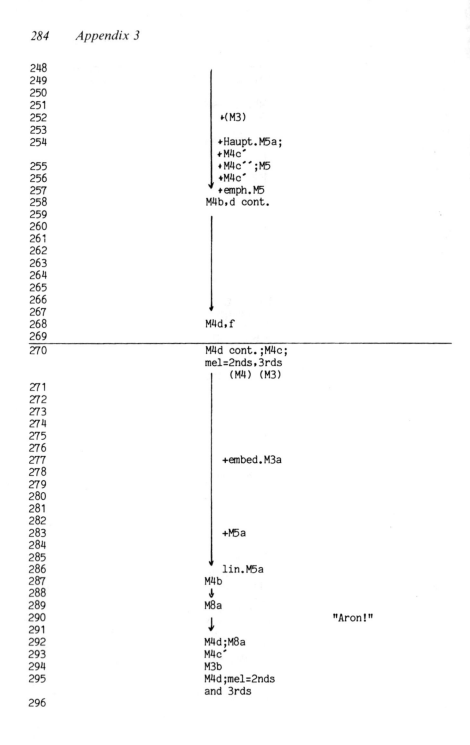

248		
249		
250		
251		
252	+(M3)	
253		
254	+Haupt.M5a; +M4c´	
255	+M4c´´;M5	
256	+M4c´	
257	↓ +emph.M5	
258	M4b,d cont.	
259		
260		
261		
262		
263		
264		
265		
266		
267	↓	
268	M4d,f	
269		
270	M4d cont.;M4c; mel=2nds,3rds (M4) (M3)	
271		
272		
273		
274		
275		
276		
277	+embed.M3a	
278		
279		
280		
281		
282		
283	+M5a	
284		
285		
286	↓ lin.M5a	
287	M4b	
288	↓	
289	M8a	
290		"Aron!"
291	↓	
292	M4d;M8a	
293	M4c´	
294	M3b	
295	M4d;mel=2nds and 3rds	
296		

297			
298		↓	
299			
300	A6		
301		M3b	"Juble,
302		↓	Israel!"
303		M3b,M4d	
304		↓	"Juble,
305			Israel!"
306		M4b/d;emph.M3a	
307		emph.M5a;M4b	"Juble!"

II,iii

308	A4	M5a,M3b	Aron allows
309		M5a	worship of
310		M5a rptd.	golden calf
311		M5a,M3b	
312		M3b,a	
313		M3a,b	
315		M3b;M5	
316		M5a;M4c´´	
317		M3b	
318		↓	
319			

320	A6	emph.M5a; M2b,b´	Offertory procession
321		M3b;M2b,b´	
322		↓	
323		M4c´´;M2b´	
324			
325		↓	
326	A6		
327			
328		M5a;M4b	
329		↓	
330	A2	M3b	Animals
331			
332		↓	
333		M6;M4d gliss	
334		M3b;M4d gliss	
335		M3b;M4d gliss	
336			
337			
338			
339			
340			
341			
342			
343		↓	
344		M4d,(f)	
345		↓	
346			

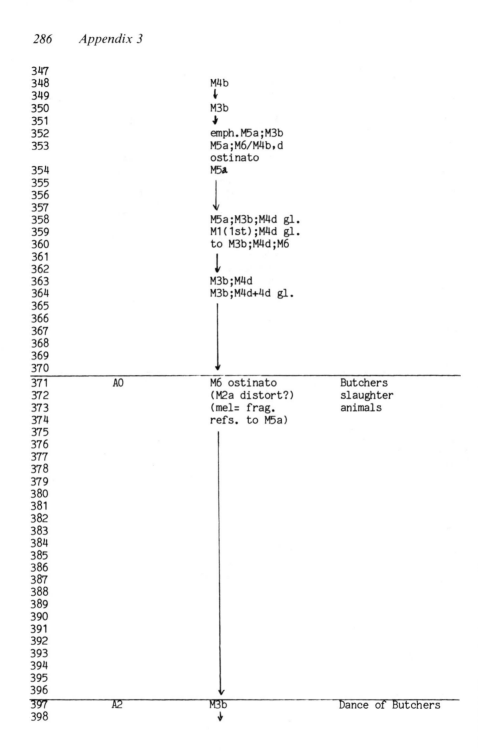

```
347
348              M4b
349               ↓
350              M3b
351               ↓
352              emph.M5a;M3b
353              M5a;M6/M4b,d
                 ostinato
354              M5a
355
356                |
357               ↓
358              M5a;M3b;M4d gl.
359              M1(1st);M4d gl.
360              to M3b;M4d;M6
361
362               ↓
363              M3b;M4d
364              M3b;M4d+4d gl.
365
366
367
368
369
370               ↓
```

371	A0	M6 ostinato	Butchers
372		(M2a distort?)	slaughter
373		(mel= frag.	animals
374		refs. to M5a)	

```
375
376
377
378
379
380
381
382
383
384
385
386
387
388
389
390
391
392
393
394
395
396               ↓
```

397	A2	M3b	Dance of Butchers
398		↓	

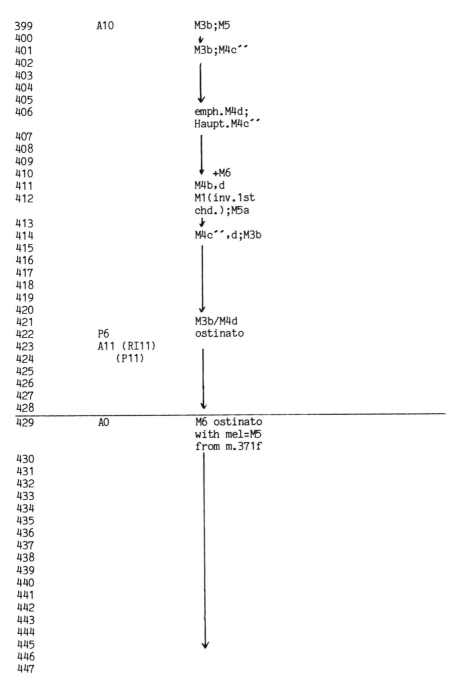

399	A10	M3b;M5
400		↓
401		M3b;M4c‵‵
402		
403		
404		
405		↓
406		emph.M4d;
		Haupt.M4c‵‵
407		
408		
409		
410		↓ +M6
411		M4b,d
412		M1(inv.1st
		chd.);M5a
413		↓
414		M4c‵‵,d;M3b
415		
416		
417		
418		
419		
420		↓
421		M3b/M4d
422	P6	ostinato
423	A11 (RI11)	
424	(P11)	
425		
426		
427		
428		↓
429	A0	M6 ostinato
		with mel=M5
		from m.371f
430		
431		
432		
433		
434		
435		
436		
437		
438		
439		
440		
441		
442		
443		
444		
445		↓
446		
447		

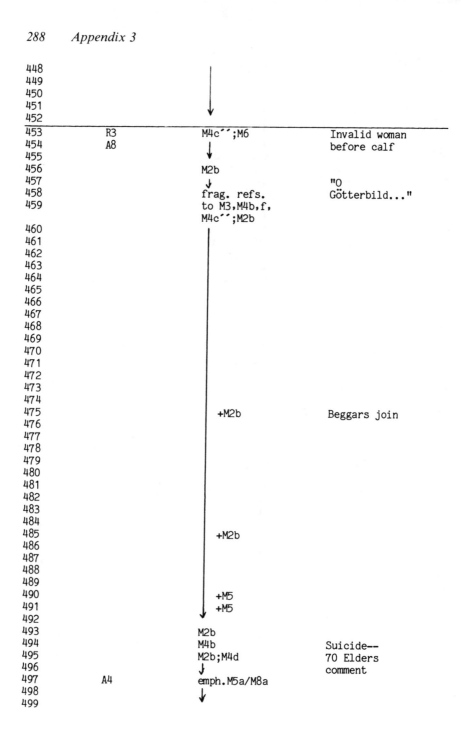

448			
449			
450			
451			
452			
453	R3	M4c´´;M6	Invalid woman
454	A8		before calf
455			
456		M2b	
457			"O
458		frag. refs.	Götterbild..."
459		to M3,M4b,f,	
		M4c´´;M2b	
460			
461			
462			
463			
464			
465			
466			
467			
468			
469			
470			
471			
472			
473			
474			
475		+M2b	Beggars join
476			
477			
478			
479			
480			
481			
482			
483			
484			
485		+M2b	
486			
487			
488			
489			
490		+M5	
491		+M5	
492			
493		M2b	
494		M4b	Suicide--
495		M2b;M4d	70 Elders
496			comment
497	A4	emph.M5a/M8a	
498			
499			

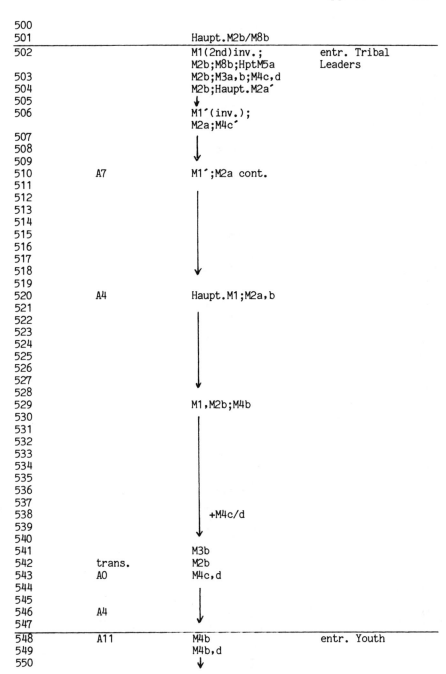

500			
501		Haupt.M2b/M8b	
502		M1(2nd)inv.; M2b;M8b;HptM5a	entr. Tribal Leaders
503		M2b;M3a,b;M4c,d	
504		M2b;Haupt.M2a´	
505			
506		M1´(inv.); M2a;M4c´	
507			
508			
509			
510	A7	M1´;M2a cont.	
511			
512			
513			
514			
515			
516			
517			
518			
519			
520	A4	Haupt.M1;M2a,b	
521			
522			
523			
524			
525			
526			
527			
528			
529		M1,M2b;M4b	
530			
531			
532			
533			
534			
535			
536			
537			
538		+M4c/d	
539			
540			
541		M3b	
542	trans.	M2b	
543	A0	M4c,d	
544			
545			
546	A4		
547			
548	A11	M4b	entr. Youth
549		M4b,d	
550			

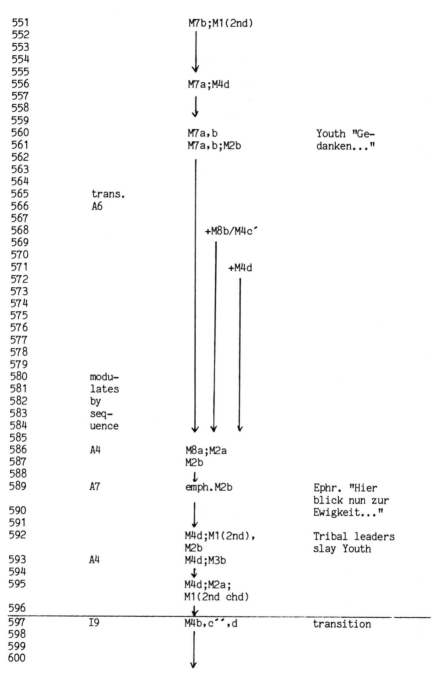

551		M7b;M1(2nd)	
552			
553			
554			
555			
556		M7a;M4d	
557			
558			
559			
560		M7a,b	Youth "Ge-
561		M7a,b;M2b	danken..."
562			
563			
564			
565	trans.		
566	A6		
567			
568		+M8b/M4c´	
569			
570			
571		+M4d	
572			
573			
574			
575			
576			
577			
578			
579			
580	modu-		
581	lates		
582	by		
583	seq-		
584	uence		
585			
586	A4	M8a;M2a	
587		M2b	
588			
589	A7	emph.M2b	Ephr. "Hier
			blick nun zur
590			Ewigkeit..."
591			
592		M4d;M1(2nd),	Tribal leaders
		M2b	slay Youth
593	A4	M4d;M3b	
594			
595		M4d;M2a;	
		M1(2nd chd)	
596			
597	I9	M4b,c´´,d	transition
598			
599			
600			

Line	Col A	Col M	Notes
601			
602			
603			
604			
605	A11	M1,M2b	Drunkenness,
606			fighting
607			
608		M2b	
609		M1,M2b	
610			
611			
612			
613			
614			
615		Haupt.M2b	
616			
617			
618		+M3a	
619			
620			
621			
622		Haupt.M2b	
623			
624			
625		M3a;M4c	
626			
627			
628			
629	A8	Haupt.M2b; M3a cont.	
630		Haupt.M7b;M3a	
631		M2b/M4c´´;M3a	
632			
633			
634			
635			
636			
637		Haupt.M8a; M2b/M4c´	
638		M6;M2b/M4c´	
639	A8 in trans.	Haupt.M8a; M6;M4c´	
640			
641			
642	A1		
643		M4c,d; M2b/M4c´	
644			
645			
646			
647			
648			

649		Haupt.M8a/	
		M4c´´;M4d	
650		M4c´´,d	
651			
652			
653			
654			
655			
656			
657	A7	Haupt.M7a;	
		M8;M3a	
658		↓	
659		M2b	
660		↓	
661		M2b,M4d	
662		M7b	
663			
664			
665			
666			
667			
668		↓	
669		Haupt.M7b	
670			
671	A4	M4c,c´´,d	
672			
673		↓	
674			
675		Recap.m.606f	70 Elders:
		M1;M4c´´,d	"Selig ist
676		↓	das Volk..."
677			
678		emph.M2b;M6	
679		mel=M2b/M4c´	
680			
681		+M4d	
682			
683			
684			
685		M6	
686	A11	↓ M3a	
687		refs. to Aron´s	
		aria, I,m.178f	
688		↓	
689			
690		M1;M3a;M2b	
691		+Haupt.M2b	
692			
693		M2b/M4c´	
694			
695		↓	
696	trans.	M3b	
697		M4c´´;M4d	
698	R10	↓	

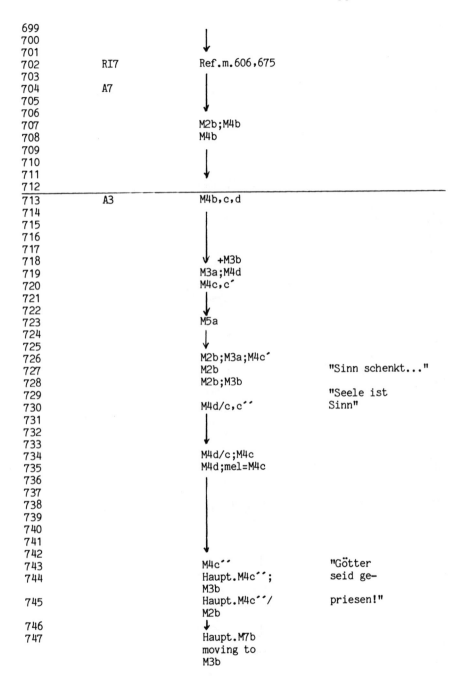

699			
700		↓	
701			
702	RI7	Ref.m.606,675	
703			
704	A7	↓	
705			
706		↓	
707		M2b;M4b	
708		M4b	
709			
710			
711		↓	
712			
713	A3	M4b,c,d	
714			
715		↓	
716			
717			
718		↓ +M3b	
719		M3a;M4d	
720		M4c,c´	
721			
722		↓	
723		M5a	
724			
725		↓	
726		M2b;M3a;M4c´	
727		M2b	"Sinn schenkt..."
728		M2b;M3b	
729			"Seele ist
730		M4d/c,c´´	Sinn"
731			
732		↓	
733			
734		M4d/c;M4c	
735		M4d;mel=M4c	
736			
737			
738			
739			
740			
741			
742		↓	
743		M4c´´	"Götter
744		Haupt.M4c´´; M3b	seid ge-
745		Haupt.M4c´´/ M2b	priesen!"
746		↓	
747		Haupt.M7b moving to M3b	

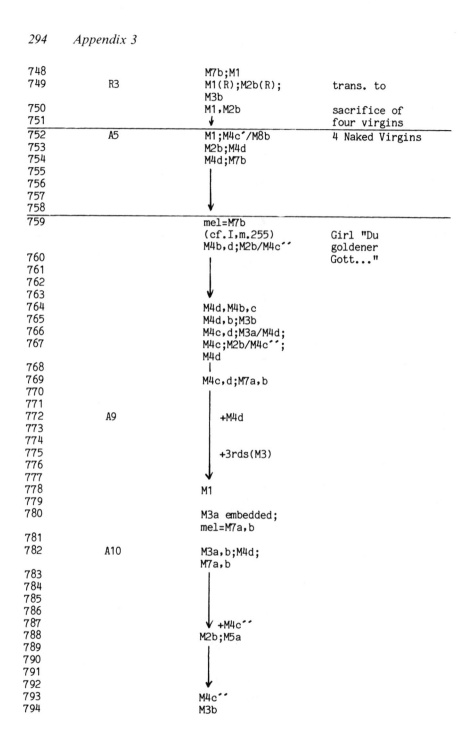

748   M7b;M1
749   R3   M1(R);M2b(R);   trans. to
                       M3b
750   M1,M2b   sacrifice of
751   ↓   four virgins
752   A5   M1;M4c´/M8b   4 Naked Virgins
753   M2b;M4d
754   M4d;M7b
755
756
757
758
759   mel=M7b
                       (cf.I,m.255)   Girl "Du
                       M4b,d;M2b/M4c´´   goldener
760   ↓   Gott..."
761
762
763
764   M4d,M4b,c
765   M4d,b;M3b
766   M4c,d;M3a/M4d;
767   M4c;M2b/M4c´´;
                       M4d
768 |
769   M4c,d;M7a,b
770
771
772   A9   +M4d
773
774
775   +3rds(M3)
776
777
778   M1
779
780   M3a embedded;
                       mel=M7a,b
781
782   A10   M3a,b;M4d;
                       M7a,b
783
784
785
786
787   ↓ +M4c´´
788   M2b;M5a
789
790
791
792
793   M4c´´
794   M3b

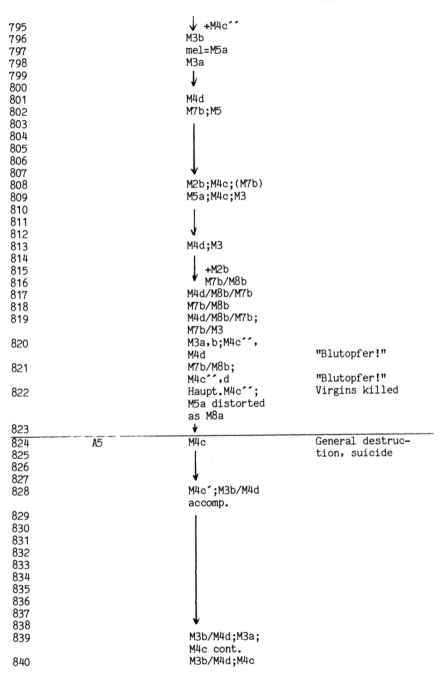

795		↓ +M4c˝	
796		M3b	
797		mel=M5a	
798		M3a	
799		↓	
800			
801		M4d	
802		M7b;M5	
803			
804			
805			
806			
807			
808		M2b;M4c;(M7b)	
809		M5a;M4c;M3	
810			
811			
812			
813		M4d;M3	
814			
815		+M2b	
816		M7b/M8b	
817		M4d/M8b/M7b	
818		M7b/M8b	
819		M4d/M8b/M7b;	
		M7b/M3	
820		M3a,b;M4c˝,	
		M4d	"Blutopfer!"
821		M7b/M8b;	
		M4c˝,d	"Blutopfer!"
822		Haupt.M4c˝;	Virgins killed
		M5a distorted	
		as M8a	
823		↓	
824	A5	M4c	General destruc-
825			tion, suicide
826			
827			
828		M4c´;M3b/M4d	
		accomp.	
829			
830			
831			
832			
833			
834			
835			
836			
837			
838			
839		M3b/M4d;M3a;	
		M4c cont.	
840		M3b/M4d;M4c	

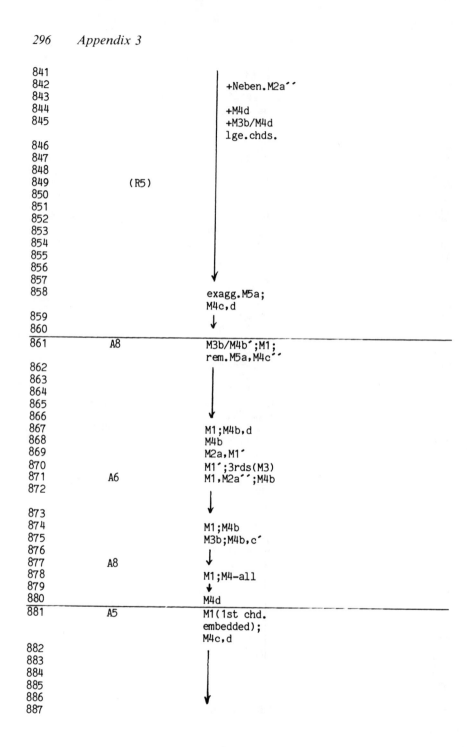

```
841
842                              +Neben.M2a´´
843
844                              +M4d
845                              +M3b/M4d
                                 lge.chds.
846
847
848
849         (R5)
850
851
852
853
854
855
856
857
858                              exagg.M5a;
                                 M4c,d
859
860
```

```
861         A8                   M3b/M4b´;M1;
                                 rem.M5a,M4c´´
862
863
864
865
866
867                              M1;M4b,d
868                              M4b
869                              M2a,M1´
870                              M1´;3rds(M3)
871         A6                   M1,M2a´´;M4b
872

873
874                              M1;M4b
875                              M3b;M4b,c´
876
877         A8
878                              M1;M4-all
879
880                              M4d
```

```
881         A5                   M1(1st chd.
                                 embedded);
                                 M4c,d
882
883
884
885
886
887
```

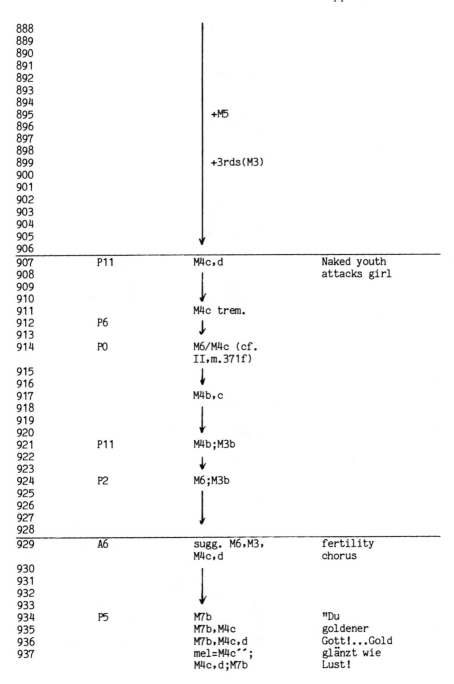

888			
889			
890			
891			
892			
893			
894			
895		+M5	
896			
897			
898			
899		+3rds(M3)	
900			
901			
902			
903			
904			
905			
906			
907	P11	M4c,d	Naked youth
908			attacks girl
909			
910			
911		M4c trem.	
912	P6		
913			
914	P0	M6/M4c (cf. II,m.371f)	
915			
916			
917		M4b,c	
918			
919			
920			
921	P11	M4b;M3b	
922			
923			
924	P2	M6;M3b	
925			
926			
927			
928			
929	A6	sugg. M6,M3, M4c,d	fertility chorus
930			
931			
932			
933			
934	P5	M7b	"Du
935		M7b,M4c	goldener
936		M7b,M4c,d	Gott!...Gold
937		mel=M4c´´; M4c,d;M7b	glänzt wie Lust!

938	P10	M7b;M4c,d	"Du goldener
939	P4	M4d;M6	Gott!"
940		↓	
941		M4c,d	
942	A6	M4c/d;(M6)	
943		↓	
945		M2b	
946		M2b/M4c´´	
947		M1(1st);	
		M2b/M8b	
948		↓	
949	A5	M4c;M1	
950		↓	
951		M3b	
952		Haupt.M4c´´;	
		M4d;M2b;M6	
953		↓ M3	
954		NebenM5a;M4c	
955		↓	
956		M4d	trans. to
957		↓	Moses´ return;
958		M1,M2b;	fire
		M1 embedded	dying out
959			
960			
961		↓	
962		M2b rptd.	
963	+A6	M1;Haupt.M2b	
964			
965			
966		↓	

I,iv

967	A5	M5a;Haupt.M2b	A man peers
968		Haupt.M2b/M4d	toward Mount
969	A6	M2b;M1,M1´	of Revelation
970	A5		
971			
972		↓ +M4c	
973	A9		
974		– G.P. –	"Moses steigt
			vom Berg herab!"
975	A3	M4c,d	Sleepers awake
976		↓	
977		M4c,c´´,d	
978		↓	
979			
980		M4d	Moses "Vergeh,
		↓	du Abbild..."
981	A0	M1(1st chd.)	
982		M1(1st) emb.	People cry out
983		M1(1st);	
		M4c´´,d	

II,v			
984	A0	(M4c´´)	Moses "Aron, was
		↓	hast du getan?"
985		M3b;M4c	Aron "Nicht
		↓	neues..."
986		M4c;M1(1st)	
987		exagg.M5a;M3a,	
		M3b;M4c,d	
988		Moses M4c,d;	
		Aron M5	
989		M5	
990	A8	M5a;M2b;M1	
	A5	M1;M2b	
991		M2b alone	M: "Schweig!"
		M5c;M4c´´/M2b	A: "...Mund..."
992		M1	
993		M1 embedded	M: "Bei meinem
		in M3b	Gedanken..."
994	A8	↓	
995		3rds(M3) as	
		M4 dyads	
996		↓	
997	A6	mel=M5a;ac.M5	
998		exagg.M5	
999	A9	mel=M5a;M4c;M6	
1000		↓	
1001	A0	M3b;M6	Moses
1002		M6;M4c	
1003		orig.M1;M2a	"Das ist das
		↓	Gesetz!"
1004		M4d;M2´a	
1005		↓	
1006		Haupt.M4c´´;M2b	
1007		M3a;Haupt.M5a	Aron
1008	A5	M1;exagg.M5	
1009		M4c,d;M1´;M5	
1010		M4d;M3b	Moses
1011	A0	↓	
1012		M5a;M3b	Aron
1013	A7	↓	
1014			
1015		Haupt.M5	
1016		+M6	
1017			
1018		+M4d	
1019		↓	
1020		M4b;(HptM6?)	
1021		M1(1st)emb.;	Moses "Ich liebe
		M4b	meinem Gedanken"
1022		M4d	
1023	trans.P2	M4c,d	Aron
1024	A6	↓	

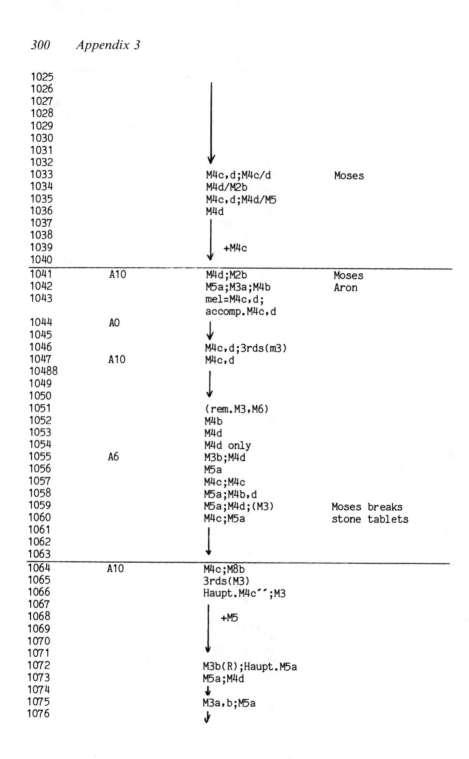

1025			
1026			
1027			
1028			
1029			
1030			
1031			
1032			
1033		M4c,d;M4c/d	Moses
1034		M4d/M2b	
1035		M4c,d;M4d/M5	
1036		M4d	
1037			
1038			
1039		+M4c	
1040			
1041	A10	M4d;M2b	Moses
1042		M5a;M3a;M4b	Aron
1043		mel=M4c,d; accomp.M4c,d	
1044	A0		
1045			
1046		M4c,d;3rds(m3)	
1047	A10	M4c,d	
10488			
1049			
1050			
1051		(rem.M3,M6)	
1052		M4b	
1053		M4d	
1054		M4d only	
1055	A6	M3b;M4d	
1056		M5a	
1057		M4c;M4c	
1058		M5a;M4b,d	
1059		M5a;M4d;(M3)	Moses breaks
1060		M4c;M5a	stone tablets
1061			
1062			
1063			
1064	A10	M4c;M8b	
1065		3rds(M3)	
1066		Haupt.M4c´´;M3	
1067			
1068		+M5	
1069			
1070			
1071			
1072		M3b(R);Haupt.M5a	
1073		M5a;M4d	
1074			
1075		M3a,b;M5a	
1076			

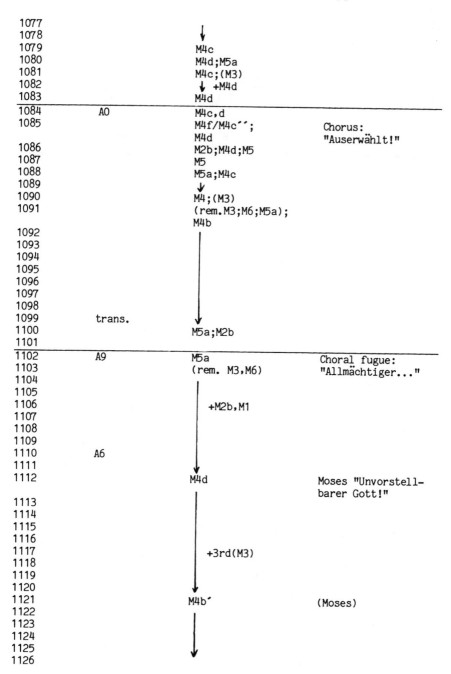

```
1077
1078                              ↓
1079                         M4c
1080                         M4d;M5a
1081                         M4c;(M3)
1082                              ↓ +M4d
1083                         M4d
1084          A0            M4c,d
1085                         M4f/M4c´´;              Chorus:
                             M4d                     "Auserwählt!"
1086                         M2b;M4d;M5
1087                         M5
1088                         M5a;M4c
1089                              ↓
1090                         M4;(M3)
1091                         (rem.M3;M6;M5a);
                             M4b
1092
1093
1094
1095
1096
1097
1098
1099          trans.
1100                         M5a;M2b
1101
1102          A9            M5a                      Choral fugue:
1103                         (rem. M3,M6)             "Allmächtiger..."
1104
1105
1106                              +M2b,M1
1107
1108
1109
1110          A6
1111
1112                         M4d                      Moses "Unvorstell-
                                                      barer Gott!"
1113
1114
1115
1116
1117                              +3rd(M3)
1118
1119
1120
1121                         M4b´                     (Moses)
1122
1123
1124
1125
1126
```

1127	M4c``	
1128	(M5a?)	
1129		
1130	↓	
1131		
1132	M4b`	
1133		Moses "O
1134	↓	Wort, du
1135		Wort das mir
1136	M4 single	fehlt!"
	dyad alone	

END II

Appendix 4

Translation of "Arons Tod," III,
DICH[tung] 20

1. Scene

    M: Aron, your time has come: you must die!

    A: I have hoped to set foot in the Promised Land.

    M: We two cannot go there.
          Can you not surmise why?
          Did not the Eternal command us then:
          Speak to the Rock, the water will pour out!
          Haven't we, however, struck the Rock?

    A: But the Almighty placed me with you to make you clearly intelligible.
          I was to speak in images (*Bildern*) where you spoke in concepts (*Begriffen*);
          To the heart when you spoke to the brain.
          To the eyes, however, I was to turn, when both were not enough to lead the people;
          Visible wonders to do when the spoken did not persuade.

    M: Then you also know why you will not see the Promised Land:
          Because you did not really need to see it—
          You had beheld it as you took on God's voice through me and grasped God's way.
          You spoke then as the people understood it and struck on the Rock—
          So you lost the Land, but you had been in it.
          You were to lead the God-Idea (*Gottesgedanken*) into your idea (*Vorstellung*).
          But you had only too often allowed your Idea to invade your God-concept.
          And therefore you must now surrender.
          Lie down low, die! I will reconcile you with God.

2. Scene

    M: The Eternal, who took you to Himself as He still was yours,
          Gives you now the earth again.
          The Land, into which I lead you, will not touch his body.
          His grave will be where no one will find it;
          It will also not thereby call to mind that he no more lives who feels as you do.
          I wander no further with you—hear what I say to you!
          Forget me now, because you are nearing the Land that you should have enjoyed so
             long, until the Lord spread you out in other lands.

    Chor: Eleazar, son of Aron, will you now be intercessor between us and God?
          Will you understand our need, feelings, what we must, know how to say what we
             want to hear, and lead (us) before our eyes to what is far from us?

    M: Chosen People of God:
          You blessed/happy people! You proud, elevated people!
          Alone in the world has the Lord called you to the honor of His name:
          The Eternal (*Ewigen*).
          I now no longer go with you,
          And I will leave you, as my brother Aron,
          But the Eternal who chose you to your duty,
          That you would be filled with sorrow and joy,
          As long as there are people on this earth,
          And as long as enemies are found to Him and you:

The Almighty has graced you.

When Aron and Moses are past, when Eleazar and Joshua are dead:

Always will one be with you, to keep the God-Idea of your chosen-ness clean/pure, as I received it from the Eternal.

And always even if all believe, you will be in doubt and know the Right by which to believe your mission:

The ungratifying, pure teachings of God.

So shall scorn attend you, persecution consecrate you;

So shall sorrow sanctify you!

Chor: Consecrate us, Moses in the name of the Eternal, the Almighty,

Who led us out of the Land of Horror

And will bring us into the Land of Desirelessness,

Where milk and honey flow

And the pure Idea of the one God will be thought and felt by all.

Amen!

Notes

Introduction

1. Letter to Henri Hinrichsen, March 20, 1914, in *Contemporary Music Catalogue (with 1976–77 Supplement)*, (New York: C.F. Peters, 1977), p. 86.

2. Willi Reich, *Schoenberg: A Critical Biography*, trans. L. Black (London: Longman, 1971; 1st ed. 1968).

3. H.H. Stuckenschmidt, *Arnold Schoenberg: His Life, World and Work*, trans. H. Searle (New York: G. Schirmer, 1977; 1st German ed. 1974). Hereafter to be cited as Stuckenschmidt, *Schoenberg*.

4. Hans Keller wrote numerous articles (see Bibliography) including "Moses, Freud and Schoenberg," *MMR* 88 (1958), 12, 63; and "Schoenberg and the First Sacred Opera," *Essays on Music: An Anthology from 'The Listener,'* ed. F. Aprahamian, (London: Cassell, 1967).

5. Karl H. Wörner wrote many articles (see Bibliography), and especially the monograph *Schoenberg's 'Moses and Aaron'*, trans. P. Hamburger (London: Faber and Faber, 1963; 1st German ed. *Gotteswort und Magie: die Oper 'Moses und Aron,'* Heidelberg, 1959).

6. Oliver W. Neighbour, "Schoenberg, Arnold," *New Grove* XVI, 719–23.

7. Arnold Schoenberg, "Composition with Twelve Tones," (1941), in *Style and Idea*, ed. L. Stein, trans. L. Black (New York: St. Martin's Press, 1975).

8. An earlier version of this research appears in Pamela White, "The Genesis of 'Moses und Aron,'" *JASI* 6/1 (1982), 8–55.

9. Stuckenschmidt, *Arnold Schoenberg*, p. 34.

10. Alexander Ringer, "Schoenberg and the Prophetic Image in Music," *JASI* 1 (1976), 30.

11. Clara Steuermann, "From the Archives: Schoenberg's Library Catalogue," *JASI* 3/2 (1979), 203–18; H.H. Stuckenschmidt, *Arnold Schoenberg*, throughout; Jan Maegaard, *Studien zur Entwicklung des Dodekaphonischen Satzes bei Arnold Schönberg*, 3 vols. (Copenhagen: Wilhelm Hansen, 1972), I, pp. 17–19.

12. For example, Albrecht Dümling, *Die fremden Klänge der Hängenden Gärten* (Munich: Kindler Verlag, 1981); Alan Philip Lessem, *Music and Text in the Works of Arnold Schoenberg: the Critical Years, 1908–1922* (Ann Arbor: UMI Research Press, 1979); Jean Marie Christensen, "Arnold Schoenberg's Oratorio 'Die Jakobsleiter'," 2 vols. (Ph.D.

dissertation, UCLA, 1979); John Crawford, "Die Glückliche Hand: Schoenberg's Gesamtkunstwerk," *Musical Quarterly* 40 (1974), 583–601.

13. For example, Allan Janik and Stephen Toulmin, *Wittgenstein's Vienna* (New York: Simon & Schuster, 1973); William Johnston, *The Austrian Mind: An Intellectual and Social History,* 1848–1938 (Berkeley: University of California Press, 1972); Frederick Morton, *A Nervous Splendor: Vienna 1888/1889* (New York: Penguin, 1979); Richard Samuel and R. Hinton Thomas, *Expressionism in German Life, Literature and Theater* (1910–1924) (Cambridge: W. Heffner & Sons, 1939); Carl Schorske, *Fin-de-siècle Vienna: Politics and Culture* (New York: Knopf, 1980); Walter Sokel, *The Writer in Extremis: Expressionism in Twentieth-Century German Literature* (Stanford: Stanford University Press, 1959). For a complete list of resources on this subject, see Bibliography.

14. For example, see Carl Dahlhaus, "Musikalische Prosa," *Schönberg und Andere: Gesammelte Aufsätze zur Neuen Musik,* (Mainz: Schott, 1978), pp. 134–45; and Janik and Toulmin, "Language, Ethics and Representation," *Wittgenstein's Vienna,* pp. 120–66.

15. For example, see Joan Allen Smith, "Sprechstimmen-Geschichte: An Oral History of the Genesis of the Twelve-Tone Idea," Ph.D. dissertation, Princeton University, 1977, pp. 43ff.

16. For example, Peter Gay, *Freud, Jews and Other Germans: Masters and Victims in Modernist Culture* (New York: Oxford University Press, 1978); and Alfred D. Low, *Jews in the Eyes of the Germans* (Philadelphia: Institute for the Study of Human Issues, 1979).

17. See especially Alexander Ringer "Arnold Schoenberg and the Politics of Jewish Survival," *JASI* 3/1 (1979), 11–48; and the other essays included in Bibliography, "Books and Articles on Arnold Schoenberg." See also his more general study "Dance in a Volcano," *Comparative Literature Studies* 12/3 (1975), 248–59.

18. Dika Newlin, "Self-Revelation and the Law: Arnold Schoenberg in His Religious Works," *Yuval* 1 (1968), 204–20.

19. Leonard Stein, "Schoenberg's Jewish Identity," *JASI* 3/1 (1979), 3–10.

20. Milton Babbitt, "Moses and Aaron," in *Perspectives on Schoenberg and Stravinsky,* B. Boretz and E.T. Cone, eds. rev. ed. (New York: W.W. Norton, 1972), pp. 53–60.

21. David Lewin, "'Moses und Aron': Some General Remarks, and Analytic Notes for Act I, Scene 1," in B. Boretz and E.T. Cone, eds., *Perspectives,* pp. 61–77; and "Inversional Balance as an Organizing Force in Schoenberg's Music and Thought," *PNM* 6/2 (1968), 1–21 (especially analysis of *Moses und Aron* Act I, Scene 3, pp. 15–20).

22. For example, Rudolf Stephan, "Arnold Schönbergs Oper Moses und Aron," *Moses und Aron: Zur Oper Arnold Schönbergs,* Bernsberger Protokolle 28, (Bernsberg: Thomas-Morus Akademie, 1979), p. 75–98.

23. Karl H. Wörner, *Schoenberg's 'Moses and Aaron,'* pp. 92–95.

24. (Ann Arbor: UMI Research Press, 1979).

25. John Crawford, "The Relationship of Text and Music in the Vocal Works of Schoenberg, 1908–1924," Ph.D. dissertation, Harvard University, 1963.

26. Christensen, *Arnold Schoenberg's Oratorio Die Jakobsleiter* (Ph.D. dissertation, UCLA, 1979).

27. For example, Reinhold Brinkmann, "Schönberg und das expressionistische Ausdruckskonzept," *Bericht über den 1. Kongress der Internationalen Schönberg-*

Gesellschaft Wien, 4. bis 9. Juni 1974, ed. R. Stephan, (Vienna: Verlag Elisabeth Lafite, 1978), pp. 15–19; and "Schönberg und George: Interpretation eines Liedes," *AMw*, 26 (1969), 1–28; Thomas Clifton, "On Listening to Herzgewächse," *PNM* 11/2 (1973), 87–103; Carl Dahlhaus, "Schönbergs Musikalische Poetik," *AMw*, 33/2 (1976), 81–88; Robert Falck, "Schoenberg's (and Rilke's) "Alle, welche dich suchen," *PNM* 12/1 (1973–74), 87–98; and David Lewin, "Toward the Analysis of a Schoenberg Song (Op. 15, No. XI)," *PNM* 12/1 (1973–74), pp. 43–86.

28.   Robert Jay Fleisher, "Schoenberg, Dualism and *Moses und Aron,*" DMA dissertation, University of Illinois of Urbana-Champaign, 1980.

29.   Wörner, *Schoenberg's 'Moses and Aaron'.*

30.   Odil Hannes Steck, *Moses und Aron, Die Oper von Arnold Schönberg und ihr biblischer Stoff* (Munich: Kaiser, 1981).

31.   For example, Hans Redlich, "Schoenberg's Religious Testament," *Opera* 16/6 (1965), pp. 401–7, in anticipation of the first production at Covent Garden.

32.   Hans Keller, "Schoenberg's 'Moses and Aron,'" *The Score*, 21 (1957), 30–45; followed by several more articles on the opera. See Bibliography, "Books and Articles about 'Moses und Aron'."

33.   Hans-Joachim Kraus et al., *Moses und Aron: Zur Oper Arnold Schönbergs*, Bernsberger Protokolle Nr. 8 (Bernsberg: Thomas-Morus Akademie, 1979).

34.   Hans-Joachim Kraus, "Moses und der Unvorstellbarer Gott," ibid., pp. 7–24.

35.   Eugen Biser, "Der Unvorstellbare Gott das Geheimnis ins Bild Gebracht," ibid., pp. 25–49.

36.   H.G. Adler, "Arnold Schönberg, eine Botschaft an die Nachwelt," ibid., pp. 50–74.

37.   Several West German radio broadcasts in connection with recent productions, cited in Eugen Biser "Der Unvorstellbare Gott das Geheimnis ins Bild Gebracht," and H.G. Adler, "Arnold Schönberg, eine Botschaft an die Nachwelt."

38.   Michael Cherlin, "Formal and Dramatic Organization in Schoenberg's 'Moses und Aron,'" Ph.D. dissertation, Yale University, 1983.

Chapter 1

1.   Arnold Schoenberg, *Fundamentals of Musical Composition,* ed. G. Strang with L. Stein (London: Faber and Faber, 1967), p. 117.

2.   Josef Rufer, *The Works of Arnold Schoenberg: A Catalogue of Compositions, Writings and Paintings,* trans. D. Newlin (London: Faber & Faber, 1962; 1st German ed. 1959), pp. 82–88.

3.   Jan Maegaard, *Studien zur Entwicklung des dodekaphonischen Satzes bei Arnold Schönberg,* 3 vols. (Copenhagen: Wilhelm Hansen, 1972), pp. 127–30, 134–36 (all Maegaard citations are in Volume I).

4.   Christian M. Schmidt, ed., *Moses und Aron,* Arnold Schönberg Sämtliche Werke (Mainz & Vienna: B. Schott's Söhne & UE, 1980), III/B/8; *Kritischer Bericht,* III/B/8,1. Hereafter to be cited as Schmidt/KB).

5.   Ernst Hilmar, ed., *Arnold Schönberg Gedenkausstellung* 1974 (Vienna, UE, 1974), p. 46. The present discussion of this source represents a revision of "The Genesis of Schoenberg's 'Moses und Aron,' *JASI* 6/1 (1982), 8–55.

6. At the Arnold Schoenberg Institute Archive, Los Angeles, California, reference "DICH 17."

7. At the Schoenberg Institute Archive, reference "DICH 29." The earliest dated source is "DICH 24" ("17.18.Juni 1926"), also at the Archive.

8. At the Schoenberg Institute Archive, reference "DICH 33." See note 26 for description.

9. Erwin Stein, ed., *Arnold Schoenberg Letters,* trans. E. Wilkins and E. Kaiser (London: Faber and Faber, 1964), p. 184.

10. Rufer cites a three-page text source for *Moses und Aron* which he dates 1926 (Rufer, *The Works of Arnold Schoenberg,* p. 158, Rufer's ref. no. 65). No such source can be found currently in the *Nachlass* with a 1926 dating. It is possible that fragmentary texts for *Der Biblische Weg* were confused with *Moses und Aron* sources due to the frequent appearance of the name "Aruns," the main character in the play, which is easily mistaken for "Aron." Also, Jan Maegaard describes a text source which corresponds in every detail with DICH[tung] 17, but also has noted "Datum oben: 21/VI.1926" (Maegaard, *Studien,* vol. 1, p. 128). This cannot actually be found on the manuscript.

   The date 21/VI.1926 is, in fact, found at the top of the fourth page of another of Schoenberg's "DICH" sources, DICH[tung] 33, a loose collection of seven small sheets of notebook and scrap paper of various sizes containing jottings clearly identifiable as notes for the play *Der Biblische Weg.* The confusion of this source with a source for *Moses und Aron* stems from Schoenberg himself—the envelope containing the seven pages is labeled in Schoenberg's heavy black crayon "DICH 33/NOTES TO MOSES UND ARON." On the back of the envelope, however, Gertrud Schoenberg added, correctly, "Ist irrtumlich von A.S. so beseichnet! Es sind vorarbeiten für den biblischen Weg!/GS." In addition, on the third page of this source, among jottings for characters appearing in Act I of the play, Schoenberg wrote the phrase "Moses am brenn. Dornbusch," as noted above. This notation is not inconsistent with references to Moses made within the play itself, and does not necessarily constitute an early source for the opera specifically. Nevertheless, it certainly confirms the interconnectedness of the two works in early concept.

11. At the Schoenberg Institute Archive, reference "Text Manuscript."

12. Datings of sources are summarized in Maegaard, *Studien,* pp. 130–34.

13. Stein, ed., *Arnold Schoenberg Letters,* pp. 138–39. (Also cited in Maegaard, *Studien,* p. 128).

14. For convenience, the labels of musical sources will conform to those used in Schmidt/KB. Source Ab is at the Schoenberg Institute Archive; folio 6 = #2981–2, 2984–5.

15. At the Pierpont Morgan Library, New York, the Mary Flagler Cary Music Collection.

16. The sources to *Moses und Aron* are sorted by paper type in Schmidt/KB, pp. 1–32.

17. Described in Schmidt/KB, pp. 30–32; original at the Schoenberg Institute Archive, reference #2771–2996 (listed erroneously in Schmidt as "2771–2866").

18. At the Schoenberg Institute Archive, reference "Moses und Aron, Act III Text."

19. Berlin, *Staatsbibliothek Preussischer Kulturbesitz,* Musikabteilung, reference "N.Mus.Nachl. 15,1"; formerly owned by Josef Rufer.

20. At the Schoenberg Institute Archive, reference "Text to Moses und Aron."

21. Stein, ed., *Arnold Schoenberg Letters,* pp. 157–58.

22. Maegaard suggests dating the *Kompositionsvorlage* as early as "1930, kurz vor Anfang der Komposition," *Studien,* p. 128.

23. Stein, ed., *Arnold Schoenberg Letters,* p. 158.

24. At the Schoenberg Institute Archive, reference "Text to Moses und Aron," "DICH 21," and "DICH 22."

25. Arnold Schoenberg, *Moses und Aron,* Schott Studien-Partitur.

26. At the Schoenberg Institute Archive, reference "Instructions, Moses und Aron."

27. At the Schoenberg Institute Archive, reference "Schema Sheets, Moses und Aron."

28. At the Schoenberg Institute Archive, reference "Ein Notizenbuch..."

29. For example, many text sources for *Die Jakobsleiter* and *Der Biblische Weg* at the Schoenberg Institute Archive are very similar in appearance.

30. At the Schoenberg Institute Archive, reference "Text Fragments, Acts II, III."

31. At the Schoenberg Institute Archive, reference "Box A," "Box B," and "Text Fragments." Not listed in Rufer, *The Works of Arnold Schoenberg* or in Maegaard, *Studien.*

32. At the Schoenberg Institute Archive, reference "Moses und Aron," pp. 30–34.

33. Cited in Rufer, *The Works of Arnold Schoenberg,* p. 87.

34. At the Schoenberg Institute Archive, reference "Vorarbeit," reference #3063–3073.

35. This is consistent with Schmidt's findings in Schmidt/KB, pp. 20–21, where he indicates what he believes to be the first writing down in earlier sources ("*Erstniederschrift*") of each measure of the final version.

36. No discrepancy is presented by the presence in Source Ab of additional sheets of the same paper type (sheets 8–11). These could have been left over from earlier composing, even found alongside the early folio from Source Aa. Sheets 8–11 plainly contain sketches made alongside Act II in the complete score, since they contain measure numbers from Act II in the final version, and therefore do not represent an earlier layer of sketching.

37. At the Schoenberg Institute Archive, reference #3019–3046.

38. In a private collection in Basel; listed in Schmidt/KB, p. 19; photocopy available at the Schoenberg Institute Archive.

39. While "Thema" might seem to be the meaning of Schoenberg's notation "T" for his prime row form, Reinhold Brinkmann suggested to me that "T" actually stands for "Tonika," based on the much earlier use of both "T" and "D" in the sources to the Suite for Piano, op. 25, as described in his *Kritischer Bericht* to *Klavier- und Orgelmusik,* Arnold Schönberg Sämtliche Werke, II/B/4, pp. 77–89. Facsimile is shown in figure 1-7.

40. Maegaard, *Studien,* pp. 124–25.

41. Stein, ed., *Arnold Schoenberg Letters,* pp. 70–71.

42. Ibid., p. 82.

43. Ibid., p. 184.

44. Arnold Schoenberg, *The Biblical Way,* trans. Wesley Blomster (unpublished manuscript), p. 83.

45. Arnold Schoenberg, "Composition with Twelve Tones" (1941), in *Style and Idea*, ed. Leonard Stein, trans. L. Black (New York: St. Martin's Press, 1975), p. 224.

46. Arnold Schoenberg, "Heart and Brain in Music" (1946), in *Style and Idea*, p. 55; and "Constructed Music" (ca. 1931), in *Style and Idea*, p. 107.

47. Sketches from Source Aa, 12r–14r as transcribed in Schmidt/KB, pp. 129–32.

48. "Volk Israels deine "Götter geb ich dir wie der und dich ihnen wie dich verlangt./Lasset dem Ewigen die Ferne/Gemäss sind euch Götter alltags nahen Inhalts/Gegenwärtig in jedem Geschehnis sichtbar in jeder Gestalt/Erzeugnis Wunschens und Hoffens Denkens und Fühlens Liebens und Hasse/Ihr spendet diesen...." (transcribed in Schmidt/KB, p. 201).

49. "Volk Israels!/bitte die ewigen Götter./Die bis jetzt dir geholfen./sie helfen dir weiter./Jawohl der Einzige hat euch verlassen./Der Ewige ist verblichen/Der Allmächtige ist gestürtzt/Und nun wollen wir uns wieder/unseren sichtbaren Götternnanvertrauen, die Gestaltman-/nehmen, wie wir sie begreifen können....," "DICH 20", p. 16.

50. Transcribed in Schmidt/KB, p. 243.

51. Arnold Schoenberg, "Composition with Twelve Tones," in *Style and Idea*, p. 219.

52. All musical examples are taken from Arnold Schoenberg, *Moses und Aron,* 2 vols., ed. C. Schmidt, Arnold Schönberg Sämtliche Werke, III/B/8, (Mainz: B. Schott's Söhne and Vienna: UE, 1980), except where otherwise noted. Used by permission of Belmont Music Publishers, Los Angeles, California 90049.

53. Transcribed in Schmidt/KB, p. 200.

54. Full sheets containing 32 preprinted staves, imprinted "Lausanne-Foetisch Frères S.A.— Vevey—Neuchâtel A32."

55. Terminology for row forms used in the following analysis (in this chapter only) is from Schoenberg's own row charts (see figure 1-6). More lengthy discussion of row terminology is found in chapter 4.

56. Another similar use of material shared by two row forms to modulate is described by David Lewin in "'Moses und Aron': Some General Remarks, and Analytical Notes for Act I, Scene 1," in *Perspectives on Schoenberg and Stravinsky,* rev. ed., ed. B. Boretz & E.T. Cone (New York W.W. Norton, 1972; 1st ed. 1968), pp. 61–77. The combinatorial property which he points out is that the inner two trichords of any prime row form are identical, in order, with the inner two trichords of the retrograde inversion form beginning on a pitch a half step below the initial pitch of the prime. More lengthy discussion of this property is found in chapter 4.

57. Stein, ed., *Arnold Schoenberg Letters,* pp. 164–65.

58. For example, in Arnold Schoenberg, *Style and Idea:* "New Music, Outmoded Music, Style and Idea" (1946), pp. 113–24;; "My Evolution" (1949), pp. 79–80; "Brahms the Progressive" (1947), pp. 398–441; and "Bach" (1950), pp. 393–97.

59. This is consistent with Martha McLean Hyde's findings in various Schoenberg sketches, confirming Schoenberg's assertion in "Composition with Twelve Tones" that the row does serve as the basis for both the harmonic and the formal structure, and that a composition need have only one set. See "The Telltale Sketches: Harmonic Structure in Schoenberg's Twelve-Tone Method," *MQ* 66 (1980), 560–80; "The Roots of Form in Schoenberg's

Sketches, *JMT* 24 (1980), 1–36; "Schoenberg's Sketches and His Compositional Methods," paper presented at the AMS/SMT Annual Meeting, Denver, Colorado, November 7, 1980; and *Schoenberg's Twelve-Tone Harmony: The Suite Op. 29 and the Compositional Sketches* (Ann Arbor: UMI Research Press, 1982).

Chapter 2

1. *Die Bibel/oder die ganze/Heilige Schrift/des/Alten und Neuen Testaments,/nach der deutschen Übersetzung / D. Martin Luthers*, (Berlin: britische under ausländische Bibelgesellschaft, 1907). At the Arnold Schoenberg Institute, Los Angeles.

2. Clara Steuermann, "From the Archives: Schoenberg's Library Catalogue," *JASI*, 3/2 (1979), 203–18.

3. An annotated list of the collection will be given in Pamela White and Juli Carson, "From the Archives: Schoenberg's Library, *JASI*, in progress.

4. Joan Allen Smith, "*Sprechstimmen-Geschichte*: An Oral History of the Genesis of the Twelve-Tone Idea" (Ph.D. dissertation, Princeton, 1977.)

5. H.H. Stuckenschmidt, *Arnold Schoenberg: His Life, World and Work*, trans. H. Searle (New York: Schirmer, 1977).

6. Ibid., p. 18.

7. Ibid.

8. Ibid., p. 31.

9. Ibid., p. 26. Stuckenschmidt mentions an ensuing "discussion about God and nature."

10. Important works include: Ilsa Barea, *Vienna: Legend and Reality* (London: Secker & Warburg, 1966); Frank Field, *The Last Days of Mankind: Karl Kraus and His Vienna* (London: MacMillan, 1967); Allan Janik and Stephen Toulmin, *Wittgenstein's Vienna* (New York: Simon & Schuster, 1973); William Johnston, *The Austrian Mind: An Intellectual and Social History, 1848–1938* (Berkeley: University of California Press, 1972); Frederick Morton, *A Nervous Splendor: Vienna 1888/1889* (New York: Penguin, 1979); Carl Schorske, *Fin-de-siècle Vienna: Politics and Culture* (New York: Knopf, 1980).

11. For a particularly good discussion of this death preoccupation, see F. Morton, *A Nervous Splendor*, and W. Johnston, *The Austrian Mind*.

12. See Erik Erikson, *Childhood and Society*, second edition (New York: W.W. Norton, 1963); Robert Kegan, *The Evolving Self: Problem and Process in Human Development* (Cambridge, Mass.: Harvard University Press, 1982); and James Fowler, *Stages of Faith: The Psychology of Human Development and the Quest for Meaning* (San Francisco: Harper and Row, 1981).

13. Fowler, *Stages of Faith*. See especially pp. 69–77 and 151–73. See also Lawrence Kohlberg, *Collected Papers on Moral Development* (San Francisco: Harper and Row, 1981).

14. Stuckenschmidt, *Schoenberg*, p. 34.

15. The record of the baptism is recorded in Stuckenschmidt, *Schoenberg*. The present author was able to confirm this documentation and to read the additional details in the church's archives, (Dorotheergasse 19, Vienna), in June 1982.

16. Archives of the Evangelische Dorotheerkirche.

17. Alexander Ringer, "Arnold Schoenberg and the Prophetic Image in Music," *JASI* 1/1 (1976), p. 30.

18. Archives of the Evangelische Dorotheerkirche. Incorrectly noted by Stuckenschmidt as 7 October.

19. Arnold Schoenberg, Modern Psalm No. 9, 28 Jan. 1950, *Moderne Psalmen*, ed. Gertrud Schoenberg and Rudolf Kolisch, (Mainz: B. Schott's Söhne, 1956).

20. At the Arnold Schoenberg Institute Archive; described in Jan Maegaard, *Studien zur Entwicklung des dodekaphonischen Satzes bei Arnold Schönberg* (Copenhagen: Wilhelm Hansen, 1972), p. 22.

21. For a discussion of Schoenberg's early musical training and influences, see Ena Steiner, "Schoenberg's Quest: Newly Discovered Works from His Early Years," *MQ* 60 (1974), pp. 401-20.

22. Arnold Schoenberg, "Composition with Twelve Tones" (1941), in *Style and Idea*, pp. 216-17.

23. Arnold Schoenberg, "My Evolution" (1949), ibid., p. 86.

24. Albrecht Dümling, *Die fremden Klänge der Hängenden Gärten* (Munich: Kindler Verlag, 1981).

25. Based on extant correspondence, published in Jelena Hahl-Koch, ed., *Arnold Schönberg/Wassily Kandinsky: Briefe, Bilder und Dokumente einer aussergewöhnlichen Begegnung*, (Salzburg: Residenz Verlag, 1980).

26. Maegaard, *Studien*, pp. 66-67.

27. The influence of Kandinsky on *Die Glückliche Hand* is described in detail in John Crawford, "Die Glückliche Hand: Schoenberg's Gesamtkunstwerk," *MQ* 60 (1974), 583-601.

28. Ibid., p. 583. John Crawford, citing Josef Rufer, *The Works of Arnold Schoenberg* gives 11 October 1908. Maegaard considers this early sketch not to belong to Op. 18. See *Studien*, I, p. 67.

29. Details of extant sketches and drafts are included in Maegaard, *Studien*, pp. 66-68; and Rufer, *The Works of Arnold Schoenberg*, pp. 36-38.

30. Walter Sokel, *The Writer in Extremis, Expressionism in Twentieth-Century German Literature* (Stanford: Stanford University Press, 1959), p. 30.

31. Crawford, "Die Glückliche Hand," pp. 583-601.

32. Stein, ed., *Arnold Schoenberg Letters*, p. 44.

33. Crawford, "Die Glückliche Hand," p. 585.

34. Sokel, *The Writer in Extremis*, p. 36.

35. Cited in Crawford, "Die Glückliche Hand," p. 583.

36. Alan Philip Lessem, *Music and Text in the Works of Arnold Schoenberg: The Critical Years 1908-1922* (Ann Arbor: UMI Research Press, 1979), p. 101.

37. Crawford, "Die Glückliche Hand," p. 586.

38. Wassily Kandinsky, *Concerning the Spiritual in Art*, trans. M.T.H. Sadler, (New York: Dover, 1977; 1st German edition, Vienna, 1911).

39. Hahl-Koch, *Arnold Schönberg/ Wassily Kandinsky*, p. 36.

40. Kandinsky, *Concerning the Spiritual in Art*, p. 55; also cited in Crawford, "Die Glückliche Hand," p. 586.

41. Schoenberg, *Style and Idea*, pp. 365–9.

42. Arnold Schoenberg, *Theory of Harmony*, trans. R. Carter (Berkeley: University of California Press, 1978), p. 416. The role of subjectivity, the internal "must," or "innerer Weg," is also discussed by Reinhold Brinkmann in "Schönberg und das expressionistische Ausdruckskonzept," in R. Stephan, ed., *Bericht über den 1. Kongress der Internationalen Schönberg-Gesellschaft Wien, 4. bis 9. Juni 1974* (Vienna: Verlag Elisabeth Lafite, 1978), pp. 15–19.

43. A good reproduction may be found in Jelena Hahl-Koch, *Arnold Schoenberg/ Wassily Kandinsky*, p. 164.

44. Rufer, *The Works of Arnold Schoenberg*, Color Plate III.

45. Hahl-Koch, *Arnold Schoenberg/ Wassily Kandinsky*, p. 272.

46. Schoenberg's sketches for stage sets for *Die Glückliche Hand* are reproduced in ibid., pp. 105–19.

47. Crawford, "Die Glückliche Hand," p. 589.

48. Kandinsky, *Concerning the Spiritual in Art*, pp. 14–15, 55.

49. Stuckenschmidt, *Arnold Schoenberg*, p. 233.

50. Ibid., p. 234.

51. At the Arnold Schoenberg Institute Archive.

52. Honoré de Balzac, *Seraphita* (Paris: Flammarion, [n.d.],), pp. 126–27). At the Arnold Schoenberg Institute Archive.

53. Ibid., p. 237.

54. *Philosophische Erzählungen* (Leipzig: Insel Verlag, 1910), p. 89. At the Arnold Schoenberg Institute Archive.

55. Emanuel Swedenborg, *Theologische Schriften*, trans. L. Briegen-Wasservogel (Jena: Diederichs, 1904). At the Arnold Schoenberg Institute Archive.

56. Both Schoenberg's and Kandinsky's interest in theosophy is discussed further by Jelena Hahl-Koch in her introduction to the Schoenberg-Kandinsky correspondence. See "Kandinsky und Schönberg: zu den Dokumenten einer Künstlerfreundschaft," in Hahl-Koch, *Arnold Schoenberg/ Wassily Kandinsky*, especially p. 186.

57. Stuckenschmidt describes this period in detail in *Arnold Schoenberg*, pp. 233–48.

58. Maegaard, *Studien*, pp. 74–5.

59. Walter Klein, "Das Theosophische Element in Schönbergs Weltanschauung," *Arnold Schönberg zum fünfzigsten Geburstag, 13. Sept. 1924*, (Vienna: Sonderheft der Musikblätter des Anbruch, 1924), pp. 273–74.

60. Arnold Schoenberg, *Style and Idea*, p. 154, p. 223, pp. 53 and 75, and p. 126.

61. Arnold Schoenberg, "Art and the Moving Pictures," Ibid., p. 154.

62. Conversation between Arnold Schoenberg and Leonard Stein, late 1940s, as reported by Stein, Los Angeles, CA, January 1981.

63. Further discussion of the influence of Balzac and the *Seraphita* vision on the genesis of *Die Jakobsleiter* is given in Jean Marie Christensen, "Arnold Schoenberg's Oratorio 'Die Jakobsleiter,' 2 vols. (Ph.D. dissertation, UCLA, 1979).

64. Stein, ed., *Arnold Schoenberg Letters*, pp. 35–36.

65. Letter to Henri Hinrichsen, C.F. Peters Musikverlag, Leipzig, 20 March 1914, in *Edition Peters: Contemporary Music Catalogue (with 1976–77 Supplement)* (New York: C.F. Peters, 1977), p. 86.

66. Cf. Stage 4, "Individuative-Reflective Faith," in James Fowler, *Stages of Faith*, pp. 78–85, 174–83.

67. Stein, ed., *Arnold Schoenberg Letters*, p. 280, a letter to Herman Scherchen.

68. Schoenberg, *Style and Idea*, p. 369.

69. Reclam pl. #'s 2761–5, 1781–5, 2801–5, 2821–5, 2841–5, 2861–5, date identified in Arthur Hübscher, *Schopenhauer-Bibliographie*, (Stuttgart: F. Frommann-G. Holzboog, 1981), pp. 35–36.

70. Arnold Schoenberg, *Theory of Harmony*, trans. R. Carter (Berkeley: University of California Press, 1978; trans. of 3rd German ed., 1922), p. 414.

71. Schoenberg, *Style and Idea*, pp. 457–58, pp. 141–42.

72. Ibid., pp. 79–80.

73. Quoted from a personal interview in Joan Allen Smith, "Sprechstimmen-Geschichte," p. 43.

74. This topic is discussed in detail later in this chapter.

75. Allan Janik and Stephen Toulmin, *Wittgenstein's Vienna* (New York: Simon & Schuster, 1973), p. 74. The same authors also liken Kraus to Kierkegaard, pp. 79 and 179ff. Schopenhauer, Kant and Nietzsche are all mentioned many times in Kraus' literary journal, *Die Fackel.*

76. Nietzsche wrote of *The World as Will and Idea* that it was "a mirror in which I espied the world, life, and my own nature depicted with a frightful grandeur," and "It seemed as if Schopenhauer were addressing me personally. I felt his enthusiasm, and seemed to see him before me. Every line cried aloud for renunciation, denial, resignation." Trans. Will Durant, *The Story of Philosophy*, 2nd ed. (New York: Simon & Schuster, 1961), p. 303.

77. Arnold Schoenberg, "Problems in Teaching Art," *Style and Idea*, pp. 365–68.

78. Arnold Schoenberg, "About Ornaments, Primitive Rhythms, etc. and Bird Song," *Style and Idea*, pp. 298–302.

79. Arnold Schoenberg, "Brahms the Progressive," *Style and Idea*, pp. 398, 414.

80. See especially pp. 18–19, 92–119.

81. For example, see Schopenhauer's uses of the terms *Vorstellung*, in *Die Welt als Wille und Vorstellung*, ed. L. Berndl, Bibliothek der Philosophen III; Schopenhauers Werke III (Munich: Georg Müller, 1912), pp. 3ff; and *Vorstellung* as Platonic *Idee*, pp. 203ff.

82. Ibid., see especially *Darstellung* as expression in art, pp. 257ff.

83. For further discussion of this philosophical debate see Janik and Toulmin, *Wittgenstein's Vienna*, pp. 31, 120–66.

84. See for example, E. Cassirer, *Philosophie der symbolischen Formen, Teil I: Die Sprache* (Berlin: Bruno Cassirer, 1923).

85. Trans. D.H. Parker in Schopenhauer, *Selections* (New York: Charles Scribner's Sons, 1928), p. 154.

86. Ibid., pp. 176–77.

87. Schoenberg, *Style and Idea*, pp. 113–24.

88. Ibid., p. 55.

89. Detailed descriptions of this material are given in Alexander Goehr, "Schoenberg's *'Gedanke'* Manuscript," *JASI* 2 (1977), pp. 4–25; also described in Rufer, *The Works of Arnold Schoenberg*, pp. 137–38.

90. Schoenberg, *Style and Idea*, p. 136.

91. Ibid., pp. 141–42.

92. Ibid., p. 457.

93. Thanks go to David Schwarzkopf, Eda Kuhn Loeb Music Library, Harvard University, for assistance in transcribing and translating these unpublished essays.

94. Stein, ed., *Arnold Schoenberg Letters*, p. 44.

95. Ibid., p. 186.

96. A further brief discussion of the Idea (*Gedanke*) as central to Schoenberg's thought especially in relation to *Moses und Aron*, is given in Odil Hannes Steck, *Moses und Aron. Die Oper von Arnold Schönberg und ihr biblischer Stoff* (Munich: Kaiser, 1981), pp. 42–44.

97. This fundamental fact has been remarked upon by authors as diverse as Theodor Wiesengrund Adorno in "Sakrales Fragment: Über Schönbergs 'Moses und Aron'," *Gesammelte Schriften* 16, Musikalische Schriften 3 (Frankfurt am Main: Suhrkamp, 1971); pp. 454–75; Karl Wörner in *Schoenberg's 'Moses and Aaron,'* trans. P. Hamburger (London: Faber & Faber, 1963); Hans Keller in "Schoenberg's 'Moses und Aron'," *The Score* 21 (1957), pp. 30–45; and David Lewin in " 'Moses und Aron': Some General Remarks, and Analytic Notes for Act I, Scene 1," in B. Boretz and E.T. Cone, eds., *Perspectives on Schoenberg and Stravinsky* (New York: W.W. Norton, 1972), pp. 61–77.

98. Arnold Schoenberg, *The Biblical Way*, trans. Wesley Blomster from the original manuscript, Berlin, 18 July 1927, at the Schoenberg Institute, (unpublished manuscript, available by courtesy of the translator.)

99. Ibid., pp. 103–4.

100. Arnold Schoenberg, "Karl Kraus" (1913) *Schöpferische Konfessionen*, ed. Willi Reich, (Zurich: Verlag der Arche, 1964), p. 21.

101. Schoenberg, *Theory of Harmony*, p. 415.

102. In Karl Kraus, *Die Fackel*, XI Jahr, No. 300, Ende März 1910; Erscheinen am 9 Avril, p. 9.

103. Willi Reich, *Arnold Schoenberg: A Critical Biography*, trans. L. Black (New York: Da Capo, 1981), pp. 36–38; and Stuckenschmidt, *Schoenberg*, p. 99.

104. Schoenberg, *Style and Idea*, pp. 141–2, 144; 477, 479; 502, 504.

105. H.H. Stuckenschmidt, *Schoenberg*, p. 183.

106. Clara Steuermann, "From the Archives: Schoenberg's Library Catalogue," *JASI*, 3/2 (1979), p. 216. Other authors represented in this list include Altenberg (seven volumes in 1913, one in 1914), Balzac (twelve in 1913, one in 1914, and two in 1918), Maeterlinck (eighteen in 1913, one in 1914), Rilke (nine in 1913 and three in 1914), Wedekind (five in 1913 and one in 1914), and Strindberg with thirty in all by 1914.

107. Oskar Kokoschka, *My Life*, trans. D. Brett (London: Thames & Hudson, 1974), p. 39, quoted in Joan Allen Smith, "Sprechstimmen-Geschichte," p. 11.

108. Interview in Smith, ibid., pp. 17–19.

109. Karl Kraus, *Werke*, Vol. III, p. 34, quoted in Janik and Toulmin, *Wittgenstein's Vienna*, p. 89.

110. Schoenberg's friendship with the Bahrs is mentioned by H.H. Stuckenschmidt in *Schoenberg*, pp. 98–99.

111. Smith, "Sprechstimmen-Geschichte," p. 31.

112. Schoenberg, *Style and Idea*, p. 369.

113. Ibid., p. 144.

114. Kraus, *No Compromise*, pp. 231–32.

115. Willi Reich, *Schoenberg*, p. 36.

116. Harry Zohn, Introduction to Karl Kraus, *Half-Truths and One-and-a-Half Truths*, (Montreal: Engendra Press, 1976), p. 7.

117. Frederick Ungar, Introduction to *No Compromise: Selected Writings of Karl Kraus* (New York: Frederick Ungar Publishing Co., 1977), pp. 8–9.

118. Arnold Schoenberg, *The Biblical Way*, trans. Blomster, p. 8.

119. Stein, ed., *Arnold Schoenberg Letters*, p. 172.

120. Alexander Ringer, "Arnold Schoenberg and the Politics of Jewish Survival," *JASI* 3/1 (1979), 13–19.

121. Stein, ed., *Arnold Schoenberg Letters*, p. 89, footnote.

122. Ibid., p. 89.

123. Ibid., p. 88.

124. Ibid., p. 92–93.

125. See James Fowler's category of "Individuative-Reflective Faith," *Stages of Faith*, pp. 78–85, 174–83.

126. Many theorists from the 1940s onward have written extensively about the "rules" and techniques of dodecaphonic composition, for example René Leibowitz, *Schoenberg and His School*, trans. D. Newlin (New York: Da Capo, 1975; 1st French ed. 1947); and Josef Rufer, *Composition with Twelve Notes Related Only One to Another*, trans. H. Searle (London: Rockliff, 1954). Early proponents of twelve-tone theory included Richard S.

Hill, "Schoenberg's Tone Rows and the Tonal System of the Future," *MQ* 22 (1936), 14ff; and even earlier, Erwin Stein, "New Formal Principles," originally printed in *Anbruch*, 1924, reprinted in *Orpheus in New Guises*, ed. Erwin Stein, (London: Rockliff, 1953).

127. Stein, ed., *Arnold Schoenberg Letters*, pp. 70–71.

128. Ibid., p. 82.

129. Arnold Schoenberg, *Vier Stücke fur gemischten Chor*, Op. 27, (Vienna: UE, 1926), p. 3.

130. Rufer, *The Works of Arnold Schoenberg*, pp. 46–47; confirmed in Jan Maegaard, *Studien* I, 121. Draft for No. 1 bears date of completion: "30.9.1925." Draft for No. 2 bears date of beginning: "16./X.1925," and date of completion: "17./X.1925."

131. Maegaard, *Studien*, pp. 124–25.

132. For further discussion of Schoenberg and the Zionist movement, see Alexander Ringer, "Arnold Schoenberg and the Politics of Jewish Survival," 11–48.

133. Reprinted in *JASI* 3/1 (1979), 46–68.

134. Trans. Wesley Blomster, unpublished manuscript.

135. Stein, ed., *Arnold Schoenberg Letters*, pp. 35–36.

136. Cited above in "Schoenberg and Schopenhauer."

137. Stein, ed., *Arnold Schoenberg Letters*, p. 93.

138. Schoenberg, *Style and Idea*, p. 429.

139. Ibid., p. 222.

140. New York: Association Music Publishers, 1930; reprint of edition Berlin: Bote und Bock, 1930.

141. Exodus 20:3–4a, 7a, *The New Oxford Annotated Bible*, Revised Standard Version, ed. H.G. May and B.M. Metzger (New York: Oxford University Press, 1971; Old Testament section 1952).

142. Alexander Ringer, "Schoenberg and the Concept of Law," *Bericht über den 1. Kongress der Internationalen Schönberg-Gesellschaft Wien, 4. bis 9. Juni 1974*, ed. R. Stephan, (Vienna: Verlag Elisabeth Lafite, 1978), pp. 165–72.

143. Schoenberg, *Style and Idea*, p. 86.

144. Dika Newlin, "Self Revelation and the Law: Arnold Schoenberg in His Religious Works," in *Yuval, Studies of the Jewish Music Resource Center* (Jerusalem: Hebrew University, 1968), p. 209, and *Bruckner, Mahler, Schoenberg*, rev. ed. (New York: W.W. Norton, 1978), p. 259.

145. Arnold Schoenberg, *Moderne Psalmen von Arnold Schoenberg*, ed. Rudolf Kolisch and Gertrud Schoenberg, (Mainz: B. Schott's Söhne, 1956).

146. For an excellent discussion of the social and cultural context of German Jews see Peter Gay, "Encounter with Modernism: German Jews in Wilhelminian Culture," and "The Berlin-Jewish Spirit," *Freud, Jews and Other Germans: Masters and Victims in Modernist Culture*, (New York: Oxford University Press, 1978), pp. 93–188.

Chapter 3

1. Schoenberg acknowledged the gift in a letter of 15 March 1933 (see Erwin Stein, ed. *Arnold Schoenberg Letters*, trans. E. Wilkins and E. Kaiser (London: Faber and Faber, 1964), p. 172). In this letter he compared his concept of Moses' story with Eidlitz's and discussed a problematic biblical contradiction between Ex. 17:6 and Num. 20:8. Erwin Stein identifies one of the gift books as *Der Berg in der Wüste*, which is included in the Schoenberg library collection. The second book of the letter must be *Kampf im Zwielicht* (1928), which also appears in the library with a dedication from the author.

2. Cf. letter to Walter Eidlitz, 15 March 1933, in Stein, ed., *Arnold Schoenberg Letters*, p. 172.

3. Outlined in Karl H. Wörner, *Schoenberg's 'Moses und Aron'*, trans. P. Hamburger (London: Faber and Faber, 1963), p. 39.

4. Further brief interpretation of the biblical content and aspects of biblical theology in the text of *Moses und Aron* has been written by Odil Hannes Steck in *Moses und Aron. Die Oper von Arnold Schönberg und ihr biblischer Stoff* (Munich: Kaiser, 1981). Discussion of the free adaptation of biblical material is discussed on pp. 49ff.

5. Stein, ed., *Arnold Schoenberg Letters*, p. 143.

6. Ernst Hilmar, ed. *Arnold Schönberg Gedenkausstellung 1974* (Vienna: UE, 1974), p. 46.

7. Paul Bekker, *Das Musikdrama der Gegenwart: Studien und Charakteristiken*, Kunst und Kultur, 3 (Stuttgart: Strecker and Schröder, 1909).

8. A summary of Brecht's thought is given in Martin Esslin, *Brecht: The Man and His Work* (Garden City, N.Y.: Doubleday, 1961).

9. Richard Samuel and R. Hinton Thomas, *Expressionism in German Life, Literature and Theater (1910-1924)* (Cambridge: W. Heffner & Sons, 1939), pp. 151-62.

10. In DICH[tung] 20 the wording differs only slightly: "Du wirst vor ihren Ohren Wunder tun... Sie werden hören von Deinem Stab, und Deine Klugheit bewundern...."

11. In DICH[tung] 20, "Ich sollte in Bildern reden, wo du in Begriffen, zum Herzen, wenn du zum Hirn sprichst."

Chapter 4

1. Terminology suggested by Reinhold Brinkmann—see note 55 in chapter 1. Milton Babbitt has proposed as P0 the row form which is stated at Aron's entrance in Act I, Scene 2. (See Milton Babbitt, "Three Essays on Schoenberg: (3) 'Moses and Aaron,'" *Perspectives on Schoenberg and Stravinsky*, ed. B. Boretz and E.T. Cone (New York: W.W. Norton, 1972), pp. 55 ff.) It is far less logical to reserve the association of a "prime original" for Aron, or musically to wait for its appearance until the second scene if it is to function as a "prime" at all. Babbitt's conclusion is drawn on the basis of his idea that the first complete linear statement of the row does not occur until that point. It is true that nowhere else in the opera is there so clear a linear succession of prime, retrograde, retrograde inversion, and inversion forms belonging to one aggregate. However, the complete linear statement of a prime form in measure 7 of Act I, Scene 1, clearly serves the purpose of presenting the row.

   Earlier writers on the opera have correctly identified the prime row form as beginning on the pitch A, including Hans Keller in "Schoenberg's 'Moses und Aron',"*The Score* 21

(1957), pp. 30–45, and Karl Wörner in *Schoenberg's 'Moses and Aaron,'* trans. by P. Hamburger (London: Faber and Faber, 1963); and more recent writers, including David Lewin in "Moses und Aron: Some General Remarks, and Analytic Notes for Act I, Scene 1," *Perspectives on Schoenberg and Stravinsky,* ed. B. Boretz and E.T. Cone (New York: W.W. Norton, 1972); and "Inversional Balance as an Organizing Force in Schoenberg's Music and Thought," *PNM* 6/2 (Spring-Summer 1968) pp. 1–21; and Rudolf Stefan, "Arnold Schönbergs Oper 'Moses und Aron'," *Moses und Aron: Zur Oper Arnold Schönbergs,* ed. Hans-Joachim Kraus, Bernsberger Protokolle 8 (Bernsberg: Thomas-Morus-Akademie, 1979), pp. 94ff. Stefan also reproduces Schoenberg's own row chart on p. 95.

2. These symmetrical mirror relationships within the row were first noted by Hans Keller, "Schoenberg's 'Moses und Aaron'," 43; and Karl Wörner, *Schoenberg's 'Moses and Aaron,'* p. 56.

3. David Lewin, "Inversional Balance as an Organizing Force in Schoenberg's Music and Thought," p. 15.

4. David Lewin, "Moses und Aron: Some General Remarks, and Analytic Notes for Act I, Scene 1," pp. 61–77.

5. Ibid., p. 66.

6. Arnold Schoenberg, "Brahms the Progressive" (1947), in *Style and Idea,* ed. Leonard Stein (New York: St. Martin's Press, 1975), p. 399.

7. Ibid., p. 409.

8. Ibid., pp. 398–441. For further critical discussions of the concept of "musical prose," see Carl Dahlhaus, "Musikalische Prosa," *Schönberg und Andere: Gesammelte Aufsätze zur Neuen Musik* (Mainz: Schott, 1978), in which he provides a retrospective historical expansion of Schoenberg's application of the principle of musical prose, and discusses it further in the context of harmonic rhythm and metrical aspects of composition; and Hermann Danuser, "Aphorismus und musikalische Prosa (Der Begriff der musikalischen Prosa bei Arnold Schönberg)," *Musikalische Prosa* (Regensburg: Gustav Bosse Verlag, 1975), pp. 125–44, which includes an analysis of musical prose structures in *Erwartung.*

9. Schoenberg, *Style and Idea,* pp. 173–74.

10. The likeness of Schoenberg's melodies to Wagnerian *endlöse Melodie* has been briefly noted by David Frank Ostwald, in "The Integrated Opera: A Study of the Influence of Richard Wagner's Theories of Theatrical Production on Schoenberg, Berg, and Stravinsky as Opera Composers," Ph.D. dissertation, Carnegie-Mellon University, 1973, p. 103.

11. Schoenberg, "Brahms the Progressive," *Style and Idea,* p. 413.

12. See for example, Schoenberg, "Brahms the Progressive," and "Composition with Twelve Tones (I)" (1941), *Style and Idea,* p. 216.

13. Schoenberg, *Style and Idea,* pp. 287–88.

14. As an example of these methods of articulation of form, a closer structural analysis of Act I, Scene I is given in Pamela White, "Idea and Representation: Source-Critical and Analytical Studies of Music, Text and Religious Thought in Schoenberg's 'Moses and Aron,'" Ph.D. dissertation, Harvard University, 1983, pp. 256–69.

15. Schoenberg, *Arnold Schoenberg Letters,* ed. Erwin Stein, trans. E. Wilkins and E. Kaiser (London: Faber and Faber, 1964), p. 237.

16. Letter dated 4 July 1947, ibid., p. 248.

17. Schoenberg, *Style and Idea*, p. 224.

18. Schmidt/KB, p. 94.

19. Ibid., p. 115.

Chapter 5

1. See, for example, these two works on text expression in Schoenberg's music through the early 1920s: John Crawford, "The Relationship of Text and Music in the Vocal Works of Schoenberg, 1908-1924," Ph.D. dissertation, Harvard University, 1963; and Alan Philip Lessem, *Music and Text in the Works of Arnold Schoenberg: The Critical Years, 1908-1922* (Ann Arbor: UMI Research Press, 1979).

2. Arnold Schoenberg, "Analysis of the Four Orchestral Songs, Op. 22," lecture for Radio Frankfurt, read by Hans Rosbaud 21 February 1932, trans. Claudio Spies, in B. Boretz and E. T. Cone, *Perspectives on Schoenberg and Stravinsky* (New York: Norton, 1972), pp. 31-32.

3. Arnold Schoenberg, "The Relationship to the Text" (1912), *Style and Idea*, p. 141.

4. Schoenberg, "Analysis of the Four Orchestral Songs, Op. 22," p. 41.

5. Ibid., pp. 43-44

6. Schoenberg, "This is My Fault" (1949), *Style and Idea*, p. 146.

7. Karl H. Wörner, *Schoenberg's 'Moses and Aaron'*, trans. P. Hamburger (London: Faber and Faber, 1963) pp. 71-82.

8. Wörner, *Schoenberg's 'Moses and Aaron'*, p. 87.

9. No exhaustive analysis of *Leitmotiv* structure in *Moses und Aron* has been done previously, but Rudolf Stephan in "Schönbergs Oper 'Moses und Aron', *Moses und Aron*, Bernsberger Protokolle 8 (Bernsberg: Thomas-Morus Akademie, 1982), p. 76, mentions the Wagnerian aspect of the opera including *Leitmotive*; and David Frank Ostwald also briefly suggests a use of *Leitmotive* in the opera in "The Integrated Opera: A Study of the Influence of Richard Wagner's Theories of Theatrical Production on Schoenberg, Berg, and Stravinsky as Opera Composers," Ph.D. dissertation, Carnegie-Mellon University, 1973, p. 85.

10. Schoenberg, *Style and Idea*, p. 55.

11. Schoenberg, *Style and Idea*, p. 405.

12. David Lewin has made note of this association, pointing out that the people "will constitute the same sort of vocal mass.... The effect is to bind God and the Volk together in a special way which, so to speak, includes both Aron (singing) and Moses (speaking)." See "Moses und Aron: Some General Remarks, and Analytic Notes for Act I, Scene 1," in *Perspectives on Schoenberg and Stravinsky*, B. Boretz and E. T. Cone, eds. (New York: W.W. Norton, 1972), pp. 62-63.

13. Wörner, *Schoenberg's 'Moses and Aaron'*, p. 71-82; 96-100.

14. Ibid., pp. 55-56.

15. Trichords, as they embody the number 3, may be intended as numerological symbols of perfection. Schoenberg's superstitious interest in numerology is well known and supports this interpretation.

16. This idea is developed in several sources: Karl Wörner, *Schoenberg's 'Moses and Aaron',* p. 56. Hans Keller, "Schoenberg's 'Moses and Aaron,' " *The Score* 21 (1957), p. 43; Dika Newlin, "Self Revelation and the Law: Arnold Schoenberg in His Religious Works," *Yuval, Studies of the Jewish Music Research Center* (Jerusalem: Hebrew University, 1968) pp. 204–20; and most recently, Alexander Ringer, "Schoenberg and the Concept of Law," *Bericht über den 1. Kongress der Internationalen Schönberg—Gesellschaft Wien 4. bis 9. Juni 1974,* ed. Rudolf Stephan (Vienna: Verlag Elisabeth Lafite, 1978), pp. 165–72.

17. Wörner, *Schoenberg's 'Moses and Aaron',* p. 83–84.

18. From Arnold Schoenberg, *Moses und Aron, Oper in drei Akten,* Studien-Partitur (Mainz: B. Schott's Söhne, 1958), Edition Schott 4590, p. 163, used by permission of Belmont Music Publishers, Los Angeles, CA 90049.

Conclusion

1. Arnold Schoenberg, *Style and Idea,* ed. Leonard Stein (New York: St. Martin's Press, 1975) p. 113–24.

2. Arnold Schoenberg, *Theory of Harmony,* trans. Roy Carter (Berkeley: University of California Press, 1978), (trans. of 3rd German ed., 1922), pp. 400–401.

3. Schoenberg, *Style and Idea,* p. 137.

4. Ibid., pp. 173–74.

5. Ibid. p. 353.

6. Ibid., p. 76.

7. Performance in Charlottenburg, Berlin at the Städtische Oper, 4 October 1959, produced by Gustav Rudolf Sellner.

8. Schoenberg, *Style and Idea,* pp. 470–71.

9. Schoenberg, "Criteria for the Evaluation of Music" (1946), *Style and Idea,* p. 126.

10. Ernest Becker, *The Denial of Death* (New York: Free Press, 1973), pp. 171–72.

Bibliography

Works by Arnold Schoenberg: Literary Writings

"Analysis of the Four Orchestral Songs Op. 22." Lectures for Radio Frankfurt read by Hans Rosbaud 21 February 1932. Trans. Claudio Spies, *Perspectives on Schoenberg and Stravinsky*. Ed. B. Boretz and E.T. Cone. New York: Norton, 1972, pp. 25–45.

Arnold Schoenberg Letters. Ed. Erwin Stein. Trans. E. Wilkins and E. Kaiser. London: Faber and Faber, 1964. (1st ed. *Arnold Schönberg: Ausgewählte Briefe*. Mainz: B.Schott's Söhne, 1958.)

Arnold Schönberg/ Wassily Kandinsky: Briefe, Bilder und Dokumente einer aussergewöhnlichen Begegnung. Ed. Jelena Hahl-Koch. Salzburg: Residenz Verlag, 1980.

Berliner Tagebuch. Ed. Josef Rufer. Frankfurt am Main: Propyläen-Verlag, 1974.

Die Glückliche Hand; Totentanz der Prizipien; Requiem; Die Jakobsleiter. Vienna: UE, 1926.

Fundamentals of Musical Composition. Ed. Gerald Strang, with Leonard Stein. London: Faber and Faber, 1967

Letter to Henri Hinrichsen, C.F. Peters Musikverlag, Leipzig, 20 March 1914, in *Edition Peters: Contemporary Music Catalogue (with 1976–77 Supplement)*. New York: C.F. Peters, 1977, p. 86.

Moderne Psalmen. 3 vols., (2 facsim.) Mainz: B. Schott's Söhne, 1956.

Schöpferische Konfessionen. Ed. Willi Reich. Zurich: Verlag der Arche, 1964.

Structural Functions of Harmony. 2nd ed. Ed. Leonard Stein. New York: Norton, 1969.

Style and Idea. Ed. Dika Newlin. New York: Philosophical Library, 1950.

Style and Idea. Ed. Leonard Stein. New York: St. Martin's Press, 1975.

The Biblical Way. Trans. Wesley Blomster, from the German, *Der Biblische Weg* (unpubl. MS, 18 July 1927 at the Schoenberg Institute). Unpublished manuscript.

Theory of Harmony. Trans. Roy Carter. Berkeley: University of California Press, 1978. (Trans. of 3rd German ed., *Harmonielehre*. Vienna, 1922; 1st German ed. Vienna, 1911.)

"The Relationship to the Text." *The Blaue Reiter Almanac*. Ed. Klaus Lankheit. Trans. H. Falkenstein. New York: Viking, 1974, pp. 90–102.

Works by Arnold Schoenberg: Musical Compositions

Arnold Schönberg Sämtliche Werke. Gen. ed. Josef Rufer with Richard Hoffmann. Mainz: B. Schott's Söhne and Vienna: UE, 1961– .

Das Buch der hängenden Gärten, Op. 15. Vienna: UE, 1914.

De Profundis; Psalm CXXX, Op. 50B. Tel Aviv: Israeli Music Publications and New York: Leeds Music Corp., 1953.

Die Glückliche Hand, Op. 18. Vienna: UE, 1916.

Die Jakobsleiter, Oratorium. Vienna: UE and Los Angeles: Belmont, 1980.

Dreimal Tausend Jahre, Op. 50A. Mainz: Schott, 1955.

Erwartung, Monodram, Op. 17. Vienna: UE, 1916.

Fünf Orchesterstücke, Op. 16. Vienna: UE, 1912.

Gurrelieder. Los Angeles: Belmont, 1948. (Rpt. of Vienna: Universal Edition, 1912).

Herzgewächse, Op. 20. Vienna: UE, 1920.

Klavierstücke, Op. 11. Vienna: UE, 1910.

Kol Nidre, Op. 39. Los Angeles: Belmont, 1976.

Moderne Psalmen. 3 vols., (2 facsim.) Mainz: B. Schott's Söhne, 1956.

Moses und Aron. Ed. Christian Schmidt. Arnold Schönberg Sämtliche Werke, III/B/8; Kritischer Bericht, III/B/8,l. Mainz: B. Schott's Söhne and Vienna: UE, 1980.

Moses und Aron, Oper in drei Akten. English translation Allen Forte. Mainz: B. Schott's Söhne, 1958 (ed. #4590).

Moses und Aron, Piano-Vocal Score. Piano Reduction by Winfried Zillig, English translation Allen Forte. Mainz: B. Schott's Söhne, 1957 (ed. #4935).

Ode to Napoleon Buonaparte, Op. 41. New York: G. Schirmer, 1945.

Pierrot Lunaire, Op. 21. Vienna: UE, 1914.

Sechs Stücke für Männerchor, Op. 35. New York: Association Music Publishers, 1930. (Rpt. ed. Berlin: Bote and Bock, 1930.)

Survivor from Warsaw, Op. 46. Los Angeles: Belmont, 1977.

Verklärte Nacht, Sextet, Op. 4. Berlin: Dreililien Verlag, 1905.

Vier Stücke für gemischten Chor, Op. 27. Vienna: UE, 1926.

Von Heute auf Morgen. English translation E. Smith. Mainz: B. Schott's Söhne, 1961.

Writings on Schoenberg: General Books and Articles

Abraham, Gerald. "Schoenberg, Arnold." *Grove's Dictionary of Music and Musicians*, 4th ed. Ed. H.C. Colles. London: MacMillan, 1940. Suppl. Vol., pp. 573–74.

Armitage, Merle. *Schönberg*. New York: G. Schirmer, 1937.

"Arnold Schoenberg." *Edition Peters: Contemporary Music Catalogue (with 1976–77 Supplement)*. New York: C.F. Peters Corporation, 1977.

Arnold Schönberg zum fünfzigsten Geburtstag, 13. Sept. 1924. Vienna: Sonderheft der Musikblatter des Anbruch, 1924.

Arnold Schönberg zum 60. Geburtstag, 13. Sept. 1934. Vienna: UE, 1934.

Babbitt, Milton. "Three Essays on Schoenberg." B. Boretz and E.T. Cone, eds. *Perspectives on Schoenberg and Stravinsky*, rev. ed. New York: W.W. Norton, 1972, pp. 51–52.

––––––. "Twelve-Tone Invariants as Compositional Determinants." *MQ* 46 (1960), pp. 246–59.

Bach, David Josef. "Du Sollst Nicht, Du Musst." *Arnold Schönberg zum 60. Geburtstag*. Vienna: UE, 1934, pp. 62–65.

Bekker, Paul. "Schönberg." *Melos* 2 (1921), pp. 123–29.

Berg, Alban, et al. *Arnold Schönberg*. Munich: R. Piper Verlag, 1912.

Boulez, Pierre. "Schoenberg is Dead." *The Score* 6 (1952), pp. 18–22.

Brinkmann, Reinhold, "Schönberg und das expressionistische Ausdruckskonzept," *Bericht über den 1. Kongress der Internationalen Schönberg-Gesellschaft Wien, 4. bis 9. Juni 1974*, Vienna: Verlag Elisabeth Lafite, 1978, pp. 15–19.

––––––. Schönberg und George: Interpretation eines Liedes." *AMw* 26/1 (1969), pp. 1–28.

Buchanan, Herbert. "A Key to Schoenberg's 'Erwartung.'" *JAMS* 20 (1967), pp. 434–49.

Christensen, Jean Marie. "Arnold Schoenberg's Oratorio 'Die Jakobsleiter'." 2 vols. Ph.D. dissertation, UCLA, 1979.

––––––. "Schoenberg's Sketches for 'Die Jakobsleiter': A Study of a Special Case." *JASI* 2/2 (1978), pp. 112–21.

Clifton, Thomas. "On Listening to 'Herzgewächse'." *PNM* 11/2 (1973), pp. 87–103.

Crawford, John. "'Die Glückliche Hand: Schoenberg's Gesamtkunstwerk." *MQ* 60 (1974), pp. 583–601.

_____. "The Relationship of Text and Music in the Vocal Works of Schoenberg, 1908–1924." Ph.D. dissertation, Harvard University, 1963. Isham Memorial Library, Eda Kuhn Loeb Music Library, Harvard University.

Dahlhaus, Carl. "Musikalische Prosa," *NZM* 125 (1964), pp. 176–82.

_____. *Schönberg und Andere: Gesammelte Aufsätze zur Neuen Musik.* Mainz: Schott, 1978.

_____. "Schönberg und die Programmusik." *Arnold Schönberg Internationale Musikwissenschaftlichen Kongress in der Technischen Universität, Berlin 23. bis 27. Sept. 1974,* Ed. J. Rufer, Berlin: Berliner Festspiele GmbH, 1974, pp. 21–25.

_____. "Schönbergs Musikalische Poetik." *AMw* 33/2 (1976), pp. 81–88.

Danuser, Hermann. *Musikalische Prosa.* Regensburg: Gustav Bosse Verlag, 1975.

Dibelius, Ulrich, ed. *Herausforderung Schönberg: Was die Musik des Jahrhunderts Veränderte.* Munich: Hanser, 1974.

Dümling, Albrecht. *Die fremden Klänge der Hängenden Gärten.* Munich: Kindler Verlag, 1981.

Evans, Edwin. "Schoenberg, Arnold." *Grove's Dictionary of Music and Musicians,* 4th ed, Ed. H. C. Colles. London: Macmillan, 1940. IV, pp. 571–74.

Falck, Robert. "Schoenberg's (& Rilke's) 'Alle welche dich suchen'." *PNM* 12/1 (1973–74), pp. 87–98.

Goehr, Alexander. "Schoenberg's '*Gedanke*' Manuscript." *JASI* 2 (1977), pp. 4–25.

Gradenwitz, Peter. "Religious Works of Arnold Schoenberg." *MR* 21/2 (1960), pp. 19–29.

Griffiths, Paul. "Serialism." *New Grove.* XVII, pp. 162–69.

Henderson, Robert. "Schoenberg and Expressionism." *MR* 19/2 (1958), pp. 125–29.

Hermann, G. and B. Prorini D'Agata, eds. *Arnold Schönberg: 1874–1951; Noten, Schallplatten, Schriften aus der Bestanden der Musikabteilung.* Stuttgart: Stadtbucherei, 1974.

Hill, Richard S. "Schoenberg's Tone Rows and the Tonal System of the Future," *MQ* 22 (1936), p. 14ff.

Hilmar, Ernst, ed. *Arnold Schönberg: Gedenkausstellung 1974.* Vienna: UE, 1974.

Hofmann, Werner, ed. *Schönberg, Webern, Berg: Bilder, Partituren, Dokumente 17. Mai bis 20, Juli 1969.* Vienna: Museum des 20. Jahrhunderts, 1969.

Hyde, Martha MacLean. "The Roots of Form in Schoenberg's Sketches." *JMT* 24 (1980), pp. 1–36.

_____. "Schoenberg's Sketches and His Compositional Methods." Paper presented at the AMS/SMT Annual Meeting, Denver, Colorado, November 7, 1980.

_____. *Schoenberg's Twelve-Tone Harmony: The Suite Op. 29 and the Compositional Sketches.* Ann Arbor: UMI Research Press, 1982.

_____. "The Telltale Sketches: Harmonic Structure in Schoenberg's Twelve-Tone Method." *MQ* 66 (1980), pp. 560–80.

Kandinsky, Wassily. "The Paintings of Schoenberg." *JASI* 2 (1978), pp. 181–84.

Kimmey, John A., Jr., comp. *The Arnold Schoenberg-Hans Nachod Collection.* Detroit: Information Coordinators, 1979.

Leibowitz, René. *Schoenberg and His School.* Trans. D. Newlin. New York: Da Capo, 1975. (Rpt. of New York: Philosophical Library 1949; 1st French ed. *Schoenberg et son école,* Paris, 1947.)

Lessem, Alan Philip. *Music and Text in the Works of Arnold Schoenberg: The Critical Years 1908–1922.* Ann Arbor: UMI Research Press, 1979.

_____. "Schoenberg, Stravinsky, and Neo-Classicism: The Issues Reexamined." *MQ* 68/4 (1982), pp. 527–42.

Lewin, David. "Inversional Balance as an Organizing Force in Schoenberg's Music and Thought." *PNM* 6/2 (Spring-Summer 1968), pp. 1–21.

————. "Toward the Analysis of a Schoenberg Song." *PNM* 12/1 (1973–74), pp. 43–86.

MacDonald, Malcolm. *Schoenberg.* Master Musician Series. London: J. M. Dent & Sons, 1976.

Maegaard, Jan, "Some Formal Devices in Expressionistic Works." *Dansk Aarbog for Musik Forskning,* II (1962), p. 93.

————. *Studien zur Entwicklung des dodekaphonischen Satzes bei Arnold Schönberg.* 3 Vols. Copenhagen: Wilhelm Hansen, 1972.

Neighbour, Oliver W. "Schoenberg, Arnold." *New Grove.* XVI, pp. 701–24.

Newlin, Dika. "Arnold Schoenberg's Debt to Mahler." *Chord and Discord* 2/5 (1948), pp. 21–26.

————. *Bruckner, Mahler, Schoenberg,* rev. ed. New York: W.W. Norton, 1978.

————. *Schoenberg Remembered: Diaries and Recollections.* New York: Pendragon Press, 1980.

————. "Self-Revelation and the Law: Arnold Schoenberg in His Religious Works." *Yuval, Studies of the Jewish Music Research Center.* Jerusalem: Hebrew University, 1968. 1 (1968), pp. 204–20.

————. "Why is Schoenberg's Biography so Difficult to Write?" *PNM* 12/1 (1973–74), pp. 40–42.

Notowicz, Nathan. "Eisler und Schönberg." *Deutsche Jahrbuch der Musik* 8 (1963), pp. 7–25.

Ostwald, David Frank. "The Integrated Opera: A Study of the Influence of Richard Wagner's Theories of Theatrical Production on Schoenberg, Berg, and Stravinsky as Opera Composers." Ph.D. dissertation, Carnegie-Mellon University, 1973.

Perle, George. *Serial Composition and Atonality: An Introduction to the Music of Schoenberg, Berg and Webern.* 4th ed. Berkeley: University of California Press, 1977.

————. "Twelve-Note Composition." *New Grove.* XIX, pp. 286ff.

————. *Twelve-Tone Tonality.* Berkeley: University of California Press, 1978.

———— and Paul Lansky. "Atonality." *New Grove.* I, pp. 669–73.

Reich, Willi. *Arnold Schoenberg: A Critical Biography.* Trans. L. Black, New York: Da Capo, 1981. (1st ed. London: Longman, 1971; 1st German ed. *Arnold Schönberg, oder Der Konservative Revolutionär.* Vienna, 1968.)

————. "Der 'Blaue Reiter' und die Musik." *SMZ* 85 (1945), pp. 341–45.

————. "Schönbergs neue Männerchor." *Modern Music* 9 (1932), pp. 62–66.

Ringer, Alexander. "Arnold Schoenberg and the Politics of Jewish Survival." *JASI* 3/1 (1979), pp. 11–40.

————. "Arnold Schoenberg and the Prophetic Image in Music." *JASI* 1/1 (1976), pp. 26–38.

————. "Faith and Symbol: On Arnold Schoenberg's Last Musical Utterance." *JASI* 6/1 (1982), pp. 80–95.

————. "Schoenberg and the Concept of Law." *Bericht über den 1. Kongress der Internationalen Schönberg-Gesellschaft Wien, 4. bis 9. Juni 1974.* Ed. Rudolf Stephan. Vienna: Verlag Elisabeth Lafite, 1978.

————. "Schoenbergiana in Jerusalem." *MQ* 59 (1973), pp. 1–14.

Rognoni, Luigi. *The Second Vienna School: Expressionism and Dodecaphony.* Trans. R. Mann. London: Calder, 1977. (1st Ital. ed. *Espressionismo e dodecafonia.* Turin, 1954.)

Rosen, Charles. *Arnold Schoenberg.* Modern Master Series Nr. 29. New York: Viking Press, 1975.

Rufer, Josef. *Composition with Twelve Notes Related Only One to Another.* Trans. H, Searle. London: Rockliff, 1954. (1st German ed. *Komposition mit zwölf Töne.* Zurich, 1953.)

————. "Schoenberg—Yesterday, Today and Tomorrow." *PNM* 16 (1977), pp. 125–38.

————. "Schönberg in Berlin." *Internationaler Musikwissenschaftlicher Kongress in der Technischen Universität, Berlin 23. bis 27. Sept. 1974.* Ed. J. Rufer. Berlin: Berliner Festspiele GmbH, 1974, pp. 9–14.

————. *The Works of Arnold Schoenberg: A Catalogue of Compositions, Writings and Paintings.* Trans. D. Newlin. London: Faber and Faber, 1962. (1st ed. *Das Werk Arnold Schönbergs.* Kassel: Barenreiter, 1959.)

Schoenberg, Lawrence and Ellen Kravitz. "A Catalogue of Schoenberg's Paintings, Drawings and Sketches." *JASI* 2 (1978), pp. 185–232.

Searle, Humphrey. "Schoenberg, Arnold." *Grove's Dictionary of Music and Musicians.* 5th ed, Ed. Eric Blom. London: MacMillan, 1954. VII, pp. 513–23.

Simms, Bryan R. "A Major Addition to the Schoenberg Collection at the Library of Congress." Paper delivered at the 46th Annual Meeting of the AMS, Denver, 8 November 1980.

_____. "New Documents in the Schoenberg-Schenker Polemic." *PNM* 16 (1977), pp. 110–24.

Smith, Joan Allen. "Sprechstimmen-Geschichte: An Oral History of the Genesis of the Twelve-Tone Idea." Ph. D. dissertation, Princeton, 1977. Ann Arbor: University Microfilms, 1981.

Stefan, Paul. "Schoenberg's Operas." *League of Composers' Review* 2 (1925), pp. 12–15.

_____. "Schoenberg's Operas." *Modern Music* 7 (1929–30), pp. 24–28.

Stein, Erwin. *Orpheus in New Guises.* London: Rockliff, 1953.

Stein, Leonard. "Schoenberg's Jewish Identity (A Chronology of Source Material)." *JASI* 3 (1979), pp. 3–10.

Steiner, Ena. "Schoenberg's Quest: Newly Discoverd Works from His Early Years." *MQ* 60 (1974), pp. 401–20.

Stephan, Rudolf, ed. *Bericht über den 1. Kongress der Internationalen Schönberg-Gesellschaft Wien, 4. bis 9. Juni 1974.* Vienna: Verlag Elisabeth Lafite, 1978.

_____. "Zwölftonmusik und serielle Musik." *MGG* XIV, cols. 1522–1539.

Steuermann, Clara. "From the Archives: Diaries." *JASI* 2/2 (1978), pp. 143–66.

_____. "From the Archives: Schoenberg's Library Catalogue." *JASI* 3/2 (1979), pp. 203–18.

Stuckenschmidt, H. H. *Arnold Schoenberg: His Life, World and Work.* Trans. H. Searle. New York: G. Schirmer, 1977. (1st German ed. *Arnold Schönberg: Leben, Umwelt, Werk.* Zurich, 1974.)

_____. "'Moderne Psalmen' von Arnold Schönberg: Dichtung und Musik aus der Meisters Nachlass." *OeMZ* 12/2 (1957), pp. 47–50.

_____. "Schönberg." *MGG* XII, cols. 18–26.

_____. "Schönbergs religiose Werke." *SMZ* 97/6 (1957), pp. 256–58.

Viertel, Berthold, "Schönbergs 'Die Jakobsleiter.'" In *Schönberg.* Ed. Merle Armitage. 2nd ed. New York: Schirmer, 1957, pp. 165–81.

Vise, Stephen Solomon. "Wassily Kandinsky and Arnold Schoenberg: Parallelism in Form and Meaning." Ph. D. dissertation, Washington University, 1969.

Vlad, Roman. "'Moderne Psalmen' von Arnold Schönberg." *Melos* 24/9 (1957), pp. 252–55.

Walker, Alan. "Schoenberg's Classical Background." *MR* 19 (1958), p. 283.

Weber, Victor Blaire. "Atonality and Expressionism." Ph. D. dissertation, Yale, 1971.

Wellesz, Egon. *Arnold Schoenberg.* Trans. W. H. Kerridge. London: Dent, 1925. (lst German ed. *Arnold Schönberg.* Leipzig, 1921.)

White, Pamela. "Schoenberg and Schopenhauer." *JASI* 8/1 (1984), 39–57.

Wörner, Karl H. "Arnold Schoenberg and the Theatre." Trans. Willis Wager. *MQ* 48 (1962), pp. 444–60.

_____. "'Die Glückliche Hand': Arnold Schönbergs Drama mit Musik." *SMZ* 104/5 (1964), pp. 274–83.

_____. "Musik zwischen Theologie und Weltanschauung: Das Oratorium 'Die Jakobsleiter.'" *Die Musik in der Geistesgeschichte: Studien zur Situation des Jahres um 1910.* Abhandlung zur Kunst- und Musik- und Literaturgeschichte 92. Bonn: Bouvier, 1970. pp. 171–200.

_____. "Notes on Arnold Schoenberg's Unfinished Oratorio 'Die Jakobsleiter'." *The Score* 25 (1959), pp. 7–16.

_____. "Schönbergs Oratorium 'Die Jakobsleiter'." *SMZ* 105/5 (1965), pp. 250–57.

_____. "'Und trotzdem, bete ich': Arnold Schönbergs letztes Werk." *NZM* 118/3 (1957), pp. 147–51.

Books and Articles on *Moses und Aron*

Adorno, Theodor Wiesengrund. "Sakrales Fragment: Über Schönbergs 'Moses und Aron'." *Gesammelte Schriften* 16. Musikalische Schriften 3. Frankfurt am Main: Suhrkamp, 1971, pp. 454–75.

Babbitt, Milton, "Three Essays on Schoenberg: (3) 'Moses and Aaron,' B. Boretz and E.T. Cone, eds. *Perspectives on Schoenberg and Stravinsky,* rev. ed. New York: W.W. Norton, 1972, pp. 53–60.

Cherlin, Michael. "Formal and Dramatic Organization in Schoenberg's 'Moses und Aron'." Ph.D. dissertation, Yale University, 1983.

Fleisher, Robert Jay. "Schoenberg, Dualism and 'Moses und Aron'." DMA dissertation, University of Illinois, Urbana-Champaign, 1980.

Hommel, Friedrich et al. "Gottsuche, Sex and Crime: Schönbergs 'Moses und Aron' in Frankfurt und Nürnberg." *Opernwelt* 12/2 (1971), pp. 14–16.

Joachim, Heinz. "Arnold Schönberg: 'Moses und Aron' Uraufführung in NWDR Hamburg." *Melos* 21/4 (1954), pp. 115–17.

_____. "Die Stimme aus dem Dornbush: zu szenischen Uraufführung von Arnold Schönbergs 'Moses und Aron.'" *NZM* 118/5 (1957), pp. 275–78.

Keller, Hans. "The New in Review: Schoenberg—III: Moses and Aron." *MR* 19 (1958), p. 52.

_____. "Moses, Freud and Schoenberg." *MMR* 88 (1958), pp. 12, 63.

_____. "Schoenberg and the First Sacred Opera." *Essays on Music: An Anthology from 'The Listener.'* Ed. F. Aprahamian, London: Cassell, 1967. pp. 213–17.

_____. "Schoenberg's 'Moses and Aron'." *The Score* 21 (1957), pp. 30–45.

Kerman, Joseph. "Wagner: Thoughts in Season." *The Hudson Review* 13/3 (1960), 329–49.

Klein, L. "Twentieth-Century Analysis: Essays in Miniature." *Music Educator's Journal,* 53 (1967), pp. 51–52.

Kraus, Hans-Joachim, et al. *Moses und Aron: Zur Oper Arnold Schönbergs.* Bernsberger Protokolle Nr. 8. Gen. ed. Hermann Boventer. Thomas-Morus Akademie, Katholische Akademie im Erzbistum Koln. Bernsberg; Thomas-Morus Akademie, 1979.

Leibowitz, René. "Das unmögliche Meisterwerk." *OeMZ* 28 (1973), pp. 215–19.

Lewin, David. "'Moses und Aron': Some General Remarks, and Analytic Notes for Act I, Scene 1." B. Boretz and E.T. Cone, eds. *Perspectives on Schoenberg and Stravinsky.* Revised edition. New York: W.W. Norton, 1972. pp. 61–77. (Rpt. of *PNM* 6 (1967), pp. 1–17.)

Luttwitz, Heinrich, "'Moses und Aron' von Scho³nberg in der Rheinoper." *NZM* 129/5 (1968), pp. 193–95.

Mengelberg, Karl. "Schönbergs Opera 'Moses en Aaron.'" *Mens en Melodie* 23 (1968), pp. 138–41.

Neighbour, Oliver. "Moses." *MT* 106 (1965), pp. 422–25.

Newlin, Dika. "Role of the Chorus in 'Moses und Aron.'" *American Choral Review* 9/1 (1966), pp. 1–4, 18.

Rebling, Eberhard. "Arnold Schönbergs Lebensbekenntnis: Gedanken zu seiner Oper 'Moses und Aron.'" *Musik und Gesellschaft* 7 (1957), pp. 14–19.

Redlich, Hans Ferdinand. "Schoenberg's Religious Testament." *Opera* 16/6 (1965), pp. 401–7.

Reich, Willi. "Ein Briefwechsel über 'Moses und Aron.'" *SMZ* 97/6 (1957), pp. 259–60.

Skelton, Geoffrey. "Schoenberg's 'Moses und Aron.'" *MT* 95/1336 (1954), pp. 304–5.

Steck, Odil Hannes. *Moses und Aron. Die Oper von Arnold Schönberg und ihr biblischer Stoff.* Munich: Kaiser, 1981.

Stuckenschmidt, Hans Heinz. "Introduction to 'Moses und Aron.'" *Paul Pisk: Essays in his Honor.* Austin, Texas: University of Texas Press, 1966.

Wellesz, Egon. "Schoenberg's Magnum Opus." *OeMZ,* 28 (1973), pp. 209–19.

White, Pamela. "The Genesis of 'Moses und Aron.'" *JASI* 6/1 (1982), pp. 8–55.

_____. "Idea and Representation: Source-Critical and Analytical Studies of Music, Text and Religious Thought in Schoenberg's 'Moses und Aron.'" Ph.D. dissertation, Harvard University, 1983.

Wörner, Karl H. "Polyphonie der Symbole: die 39 Schlusstakte von Schönbergs 'Moses und Aron.'" *Melos* 24/12 (1957), pp. 350–52.

_____. "Der Prophet und der Gaukler." *Opernwelt* 12/2 (1971), pp. 18–21.

_____. "Schoenberg's Biblical Opera *Moses und Aron.*" *MQ* 40 (1954), pp. 403–12.

_____. *Schoenberg's Moses and Aaron.* Trans. P. Hamburger. London: Faber and Faber, 1963. (1st German ed. *Gotteswort und Magie: die Oper 'Moses und Aron,'* Heidelberg: Schneider, 1959.)

Zillig, Winfried. "Schönbergs 'Moses und Aron.'" *Melos* 24/3 (1957), pp. 69–71.

Recordings of *Moses und Aron*

1957. Cond. Hans Rosbaud, Chorus and Orchestra of the Norddeutscher Rundfunk. Moses: Hans Herbert Fiedler; Aron: Helmut Krebs. Liner notes by Allen Forte. Columbia, K3L 241.

1974. Cond. Michael Gielen, Chorus and Symphony Orchestra of the Österreichischen Rundfunk. Moses: Günter Reich; Aron: Louis Devos. Liner notes by C. Schumacher. Philips, 6700 084.

1975. Cond. Pierre Boulez, BBC Symphony Orchestra. Moses: Günter Reich; Aron: Richard Cassilly. Liner notes by Harry Helbreich. Columbia, M2 33594, 1975.

Cultural/Historical Context

Andrews, Wayne. *Siegfried's Curse: The German Journey from Nietzsche to Hesse.* New York: Atheneum, 1972.

Balzac, Honoré de. *Seraphita.* Trans. Clara Bell. Works of Honoré de Balzac, IV. Ed. George Saintsbury. New York: Henry W. Knight, 1901.

Barea, Ilsa. *Vienna: Legend and Reality.* London: Secker and Warburg, 1966.

Becker, Ernest. *The Denial of Death.* New York: Free Press, 1973.

Bekker, Paul. *Das Deutsche Musikleben.* Berlin: Schuster und Loeffler, 1916.

_____. *Klang und Eros.* Gesammelte Schriften, 2. Stuttgart: Deutsche-Verlags-Anstalt, 1922.

_____. *The Changing Opera.* Trans. A. Mendel. New York: Norton, 1935.

_____. *Das Musikdrama der Gegenwart: Studien und Charakteristiken.* Kunst und Kultur, 3. Stuttgart: Strecker und Schröder, 1909.

Cassirer, Ernst. *Philosophie der symbolischen Formen, Teil I: Die Sprache.* Berlin: Bruno Cassirer, 1923.

_____. *Philosophy of Symbolic Forms.* Trans. R. Manheim, New Haven: Yale University Press, 1953. (1st German ed. *Philosophie der symbolischen Formen. I: Die Sprache.* Berlin, 1923.)

Comini, Alessandra. *Gustav Klimt.* New York: Braziller, 1975.

Dube, Wolf-Dieter. *Expressionism.* Trans. M. Whittall. New York: Praeger, 1972.

Durant, Will. *The Story of Philosophy.* 2nd ed. New York: Simon and Schuster, 1961.

Erikson, Erik. *Childhood and Society.* 2nd. edition. New York: W.W. Norton, 1963.

Esslin, Martin. *Brecht: The Man and His Work.* Garden City, N. Y.: Doubleday, 1961.

Field, Frank. *The Last Days of Mankind: Karl Kraus and His Vienna.* London: MacMillan, 1967.

Fischer, Heinrich. "The Other Austria and Karl Kraus." *Tyrannos.* Ed. Hans J. Rehfisch. London: Lindsay Drummond, 1944.

Fowler, James. *Stages of Faith: The Psychology of Human Development and the Quest for Meaning.* San Francisco: Harper & Row, 1981.

Freud, Sigmund. *Moses and Monotheism.* Trans. K. Jones. New York: Vintage, 1967. (1st German ed. 1939.)

Gay, Peter, *Freud, Jews and Other Germans: Masters and Victims in Modernist Culture.* New York: Oxford University Press, 1978.

———. *Weimar Culture: The Outsider as Insider.* London: Secker and Warburg, 1968.

Gruber, Clemens M. *Opern Uraufführungen,* 3. Komponisten aus Deutschland, Osterreich und der Schweiz 1900–1977. Vienna: Gesellschaft für Musiktheater, 1978.

Heller, Erich. *The Disinherited Mind: Essays in Modern German Literature and Thought.* New York: Harcourt, Brace, Jovanovich, 1975.

———. "Dark Laughter." *New York Review of Books,* May 3, 1973.

Hübscher, Arthur. *Schopenhauer-Bibliographie.* Stuttgart: F. Frommann-G. Holzboog, 1981.

Iggers, Wilma Abeles. *Karl Kraus: A Viennese Critic of the Twentieth Century.* The Hague: Martians Nijhoff, 1967.

Janik, Allan and Stephen Toulmin. *Wittgenstein's Vienna.* New York: Simon and Schuster, 1973.

Johnston William. *The Austrian Mind: An Intellectual and Social History, 1848–1938.* Berkeley: University of California Press, 1972.

Kandinsky, Wassily. *Concerning the Spiritual in Art.* Trans. M. T. H. Sadler. New York: Dover, 1977. (1st German ed. *Über das Geistige in der Kunst.* Vienna, 1911.)

Kegan, Robert. *The Evolving Self: Problem and Process in Human Development.* Cambridge, Mass.: Harvard University Press, 1982.

Kohlberg, Lawrence. *Collected Papers on Moral Development.* San Francisco: Harper and Row: 1981.

Kokoschka, Oskar. *My Life.* Trans. D. Brett. London: Thames & Hudson, 1974.

Kraus, Karl. *Die Fackel,* 12 vols. (Nos. 1–922, 'Die letzten Tage der Menschheit (1918–19), and Personenregister). Ed. H. Fischer. Personenregister comp. F. Ogg. Munich: Kösel-Verlag GmbH, 1968–76. (1st German ed., 37 Jg., Nr. 1–917/922. Vienna: Kraus, 1899–1936.)

Loewenberg, Alfred. *Annals of Opera 1597–1940.* 3rd. ed. Totowa, N.J.; Rowman and Littlefield, 1978.

Low, Alfred D. *Jews in the Eyes of the Germans.* Philadelphia: Institute for the Study of Human Issues, 1979.

Lyon, James K. *Bertolt Brecht in America.* Princeton: Princeton University Press, 1980.

Maur, Karin, ed. *Oskar Schlemmer: Ausstellung der Staatsgalerie Stuttgart Aug.-Sept. 1977.* Stuttgart: Staatsgalerie Stuttgart, 1977.

Mendelssohn-Bartholdy, Felix. *Elijah: An Oratorio,* Op. 70. English translation W. Bartholomew. London: Novello, [19––].

Mies, Georg Achim. "*Die Kurzoper: Materialen zur Geschichte und Ästhetik der experimentellen musikdramatischen Kleinform im ersten drittel des 20. Jahrhunderts.*" Ph.D. dissertation, Freie Universität Berlin, 1971.

Mordden, Ethan. *Opera in the Twentieth Century: Sacred, Profane, Godot.* New York: Oxford, 1978.

Morton, Frederick, *A Nervous Splendor: Vienna 1888/1889.* New York: Penguin, 1979.

New Oxford Annotated Bible. Revised Standard Version. Ed. H.G. May and B.M. Metzger. New York: Oxford University Press, 1971. (Old Testament section, 1952.)

Rank, Otto. *Art and Artist.* Trans. C. F. Atkinson. New York: Agathon Press, 1968.

———. *The Myth of the Birth of the Hero.* Ed. P. Freund. New York: Vintage, 1964.

Ringer, Alexander. "Dance in a Volcano." *Comparative Literature Studies.* (Special Issue: "Media and Society: Montage, Satire and Cultism between the Wars." Ed. H. Knust.) 12/3 (1975), pp. 248–59.

Samuel, Richard and R. Hinton Thomas. *Expressionism in German Life, Literature and Theater (1910-1924)*. Cambridge: W. Heffner and Sons, 1939.

Schopenhauer, Arthur. *Die Welt als Wille und Vorstellung*. Ed. L. Berndl. Bibliothek der Philosophen III; Schopenhauers Werke III. Munich: Georg Muller, 1912.

_____. *Parerga und Paralipomena: Kleine philosophische Schriften*. 2 vols. Leipzig: Reclam, [n.d., 189–].

_____. *Selections*. Ed. and trans. D. H. Parker. New York: Scribner's Sons, 1928.

Schorske, Carl. *Fin-de-siècle Vienna: Politics and Culture*. New York: Knopf, 1980.

Sokel, Walter. *The Writer in Extremis: Expressionism in Twentieth-Century German Literature*. Stanford: Stanford University Press, 1959.

Smith, Marjorie H. "Expressionism in Twentieth-Century Stage Design." Ph. D. dissertation, University of Michigan, 1957.

Stieger, Frank. *Opernlexikon*. 4 Vols. Tutzing: Hans Schneider, 1975–1981.

Thompson, James R. "Twentieth-Century Scene Design: Its History and Stylistic Origins." Ph.D. dissertation, University of Minnesota, 1957.

Ungar, Frederick, ed. *No Compromise: Selected Writings of Karl Kraus*. New York: Frederick Ungar Publications, 1977.

Zohn, Harry. *Karl Kraus*. New York: T. Wayne, 1971.

_____, ed. and trans. *Half-Truths and One-and-a-Half-Truths*. Montreal: Engendra Press, 1976.

_____. *In These Great Times*. Montreal. Engendra Press, 1976.

Index